Praise for Jack Miles's

GOD IN THE QUR'AN

"Keenly interesting, incisive. . . . [An] illuminating critique."
—*Booklist* (starred review)

"Literary, and astute. . . . Good reading and an excellent tool for interfaith dialogue." —*Kirkus Reviews* (starred review)

"[Miles's] newest book represents the crowning achievement of his
life's work." —Jonathan Kirsch, *Jewish Journal*

"Miles's unique talent for writing about religion won him a Pulitzer
Prize for *God: A Biography*, and now the scholar has written a study of
Allah. . . . Miles's book is a road map toward interfaith understanding."
—*The National Book Review*

"[A] highly engaging and resourceful book."
—Patrick Ryan, *Commonweal*

"A valuable and insightful perspective on Islam and the Qur'an."
—*Library Journal*

"In its stunning scope, its forensic analysis, and its lofty message, *God
in the Qur'an* has no predecessor and no competitor among books
that scan the horizon of Abrahamic scriptures. At once accessible
and challenging, the biblical/Qur'anic narratives are recounted here
with clarity and conviction. The reader—whether religious or non-
religious, Jewish, Christian, Muslim, or atheist—is offered a new
vista into divine-human encounters evoked by one of their most
skilled interpreters, Jack Miles. A milestone of literary and theological scholarship." —Bruce Bennett Lawrence, author of
The Koran in English: A Biography

"The culmination of an extraordinary three-part biography—or theograpy, as he has termed it—of the central character in the sacred scriptures of Jews, the Christians, and now the Muslims. In this book, as in the previous books in the trilogy, Miles draws upon rich theological learning that he manages to lightly and gracefully. Above all, he draws upon unfailing moral intelligence, sympathetic imagination, and human decency." —Stephen Greenblatt, author of *The Rise and Fall of Adam and Eve*

"Extraordinary, beautifully written.... This is one of the finest books I have ever read on the Qur'an, and everyone who truly wants to understand Islam and Muslims should read it." —Amir Hussain, author of *Muslims and the Making of America*

"A careful, critical, loving, and deeply perceptive examination of how God really appears in this sacred scripture. This is a remarkable contribution to a remarkable topic and a book not to be missed." —Reuven Firestone, author of *An Introduction to Islam for Jews*

"Jack Miles has done it again! In a fascinating and creative way, his latest book helps Jews and Christians understand the Qur'an, not by paraphrasing or summarizing its teachings, but by having Allah speak directly.... Brilliant." —Father James L. Heft, author of *Passing on the Faith*

"With *God in the Qur'an*, Jack Miles completes the literary pilgrimage that gave us *God: A Biography* and *Christ: A Crisis in the Life of God*. This time Allah is the central character, and drawing on the Qur'an, but also the Hebrew Bible and the New Testament ... Miles mines all three texts to strikingly original effect, generating new insights about the Qur'an but also about its sibling scriptures." —Jane McAuliffe, editor of *Encyclopaedia of the Qur'ān*

"Takes readers on a journey through those elements of qur'anic sacred history that have parallels in the Bible. Miles's commentary is penetrating." —Gabriel Said Reynolds, *First Things*

Jack Miles

GOD IN THE QUR'AN

Jack Miles pursued religious studies at Pontifical Gregorian University, Rome, and the Hebrew University of Jerusalem, and holds a doctorate in Near Eastern languages from Harvard University. In 2002 he was named a MacArthur Fellow, and he currently serves as Distinguished Professor Emeritus of English and Religious Studies at the University of California, Irvine, and Senior Fellow for Religion and International Affairs with the Pacific Council on International Policy. In the 2018–2019 academic year, he served as Corcoran Visiting Chair in Christian-Jewish Relations at Boston College. His book *God: A Biography* won a Pulitzer Prize. He served as editor for the *Los Angeles Times Book Review* and was a member of that newspaper's editorial board. His writing has appeared in *The Atlantic, The New York Times, The Washington Post*, and *The Boston Globe*, among many other publications. He lives in Southern California and Boston.

www.jackmiles.com

Also by Jack Miles

God: A Biography
Christ: A Crisis in the Life of God

AS EDITOR

The Norton Anthology of World Religions

GOD IN THE QUR'AN

GOD
IN THE QUR'AN

Jack Miles

VINTAGE BOOKS
A Division of Penguin Random House LLC
New York

Grateful acknowledgment is made to the following for permission
to reprint previously published material:
DE GRUYTER MOUTON: Excerpt from *On Understanding Islam* by Wilfred C. Smith,
copyright © 1981 by Mouton Publishers. Reprinted by permission of De Gruyter
Mouton. DAN O'BRIEN: Excerpt of "God's Brother" by Dan O'Brien, originally
published in *Scarsdale* by Measure Press Inc., Evansville, Indiana, in 2015. Reprinted
by permission of Dan O'Brien. ONEWORLD PUBLICATIONS, c/o PLSCLEAR:
Excerpt from *Sufism: A Beginner's Guide* by William C. Chittick, copyright © 2000 by
William C. Chittick. Reprinted by permission of Oneworld Publications, c/o PLSClear.
W. W. NORTON & COMPANY, INC.: Excerpt of "It Is Enough to Enter"
from *Pitch: Poems* by Todd Boss. Copyright © 2012 by Todd Boss.
Reprinted by permission of W. W. Norton & Company, Inc.

The Library of Congress has cataloged the Knopf edition as follows:
Name: Miles, Jack, 1942– author.
Title: God in the Qur'an / Jack Miles.
Description: New York : Alfred A. Knopf, 2018. |
Includes bibliographical references and index.
Identifiers: LCCN 2018005105
Subjects: LCSH: Qur'an—Criticism, interpretation, etc. | God (Islam).
Classification: LCC BP134.G6 M55 2019 | DDC 297.2/11—dc23
LC record available at https://lccn.loc.gov/2018005105

Vintage Books Trade Paperback ISBN: 978-0-307-38994-7
eBook ISBN: 978-0-525-52161-7

Author photograph © Louis Pescevic
Book design by M. Kristen Bearse

www.vintagebooks.com

Printed in the United States of America
10 9 8 7 6 5 4 3 2 1

For Catherine

One who has lived many years in a city, as soon as he
    goes to sleep,
Beholds another city full of good and evil, and his own
    city vanishes from his mind.
He does not say to himself, "This is a new city: I am
    a stranger here."
Nay, he thinks he has always lived in this city and was
    born and bred in it.

—Rumi

Contents

GOD IN THE QUR'AN

Foreword

Of God, Religion, and the Violence of Sacred Scripture

Among all the books that have been written about God, I myself have written two: one about God in Jewish scripture and another about God in Christian scripture. The book before you—about God in Muslim scripture, the Qur'an—is the third in the series. I am a Christian, a practicing Episcopalian, but I approach God in all three of these books not directly but only through the respective scriptures of the three traditions. I write, moreover, not as a religious believer but only as a literary critic writing quite consciously for an audience crowded with unbelievers.

What this means is that I approach the scriptures not through belief but through a suspension of disbelief. Suspension of disbelief is a notion introduced into English literary criticism by the nineteenth-century poet and critic Samuel Taylor Coleridge. It is by the temporary suspension of disbelief that any of us is able to "let go" and enjoy a novel, a film, or a television series like *Game of Thrones* on its own terms. When we go to the movies on a summer night and see a romantic comedy, we do not object as the film goes along that the lovers on screen are not real lovers but only two actors pretending to be in love. We disbelieve in their ultimate reality, of course, but for the duration of the film, we "allow" them to be real. We play along.

You can play along in the same way even when a literary character is divine. Not long ago, for a course I taught, I had occasion to re-read

Homer's *Iliad*, this time in the wonderful Robert Fagles translation. The Greek god Zeus is a major character in that epic—the greatest of the Olympian gods. I do not believe that Zeus exists, but for the duration of my reading, I willingly played along with Homer, allowing Zeus to shape the course of *The Iliad* as powerfully as he does.

As a Christian, by a kind of reversal, I can temporarily suspend my belief that the God of the Bible is indeed much more than a literary character and take him as no more than that for the duration of an exercise in literary appreciation. Just as I can go to St. Peter's Basilica in Rome on a Sunday to worship and then go back on a Monday to study its art and architecture, so I can hear Christ's Sermon on the Mount on Sunday as a part of my worship and then study it on Monday as relevant data about Christ as a literary character. The two exercises are different, deeply so, but they are not mutually exclusive and can be mutually stimulating.

Literary criticism, beginning in this way with the aesthetic experience of a work of literature, is different from literary history or historical criticism. Historical criticism is concerned with such questions as Who wrote this work? When did he write it? Why did he write it? For what audience did he write it? Or did she write it? Or they? Was it originally in the language in which we now read it? What sources did they draw on, if any, as they wrote it, or is it truly an original creation? Has it been revised over time? Is it in circulation in more than one form? If so, which form is best? Is it perhaps the redacted combination of more than one version of itself? What has been its reception over time? Has it been translated? Has it ever been suppressed?

And so forth. Such questions—legitimate as they are, fascinating as they can be, and endless as they also are—are not the subject matter of this book. A scholar may have answered dozens of such questions about a given work of literature, indeed spent a lifetime answering them, without ever quite engaging the work in itself, as an aesthetic creation separable to some extent, as all great works are, from the time and place and circumstances in which it arose. Historical criticism need not interfere with literary appreciation, and the two can often be symbiotic, but the two are even then distinguishable.

In what follows, we will consider a cast of iconic characters who appear both in the Bible and in the Qur'an through an ongoing comparison whose focus at every point will be on God as the understood

central character. Our modest goal will be a certain aesthetic appropri-
ation not of the entire Bible or the entire Qur'an but just of these related
passages within the two. My hope is that you will join me by whatever
suspension of belief or disbelief works for you as I give primary consideration to Allah, God, as the overwhelmingly dominant central figure
in the passages from the Qur'an.

Over the centuries, the view most often taken of the Qur'an by Jews
and Christians alike has been the view classically taken by Jews of the
New Testament—namely, "What's true is not new, and what's new is
not true." Non-Muslims have disbelieved and dismissed what Muslims
believe of the Qur'an—namely, that it is God's last word to mankind, the
crown of revelation, restoring what Jews and Christians had lost from or
suppressed in their scriptures by oblivion or corruption. My invitation
here to Jews and Christians and the many others who disbelieve that
bold Muslim claim is that, as a modest exercise in literary appreciation,
they temporarily suspend their disbelief while together we attempt an
engagement with God as the central character of the Qur'an, and with
the Qur'an as an elusively powerful work of literature. My invitation to
Muslims is that just as they might pray in a mosque on Friday but study
its dome as students of architecture on a Tuesday, so they too might
play along with this "Tuesday exercise," this literary engagement with
just a few selections from the Qur'an, read in conjunction with matching passages from the Bible. Honoring the Holy Qur'an in this way, as
literature, is a way to open it, with sympathy, to new readers.

In the first of my books on God, *God: A Biography,* I wrote about God as
he instructed Israel to remember him:

> In times to come, when your child asks you, "What is the
> meaning of these instructions, laws and customs which Yah-
> weh our God has laid down for you?" you are to tell your child,
> "Once we were Pharaoh's slaves in Egypt, and Yahweh brought
> us out of Egypt by his mighty hand. Before our eyes Yahweh
> worked great and terrible signs and wonders against Egypt,
> against Pharaoh and his entire household. And he brought us
> out of there to lead us into the country which he had sworn

to our ancestors that he would give us. And Yahweh has commanded us to observe all these laws and to fear Yahweh our God, so as to be happy for ever and to survive, as we do to this day." (Deuteronomy 6:20–24)

This was the Yahweh who—as "the LORD" in most translations—is the initially invincible protagonist of the Tanakh or Jewish Bible, which became, as included in the Christian Bible, the Old Testament.[1] Yet in the Tanakh, after Yahweh's encounter with Job, he falls strangely silent: he never speaks again, and it seems that Israel comes to count decreasingly on His "mighty hand." He is remembered with gratitude and devotion, to be sure, but his power becomes a distant future hope rather than a compelling present reality.

In my second God book, *Christ: A Crisis in the Life of God*, I wrote about God as Yahweh the Jew—the God of the Jews returning to action as a Jew himself:

> In the beginning was the Word:
> the Word was with God
> and the Word was God. (John 1:1)

And then the stunning claim:

> The Word became flesh,
> he lived among us,
> and we saw his glory,
> the glory that he has from the Father as only Son of the
>   Father,
> full of grace and truth. (John 1:14)

This claim was stunning less for any arcane metaphysical reason, I argued, than for the fact that this divine Jew, confronted with Caesar as the new Pharaoh, does not, as of old, crush the brutal Roman oppressor with mighty hand and outstretched arm but instead goes meekly to His own Roman crucifixion. Yes, Jesus rises from the tomb, and his followers take his resurrection as the promise of eternal life, and yet Caesar is still Caesar, and in a few decades will destroy the Jerusalem Temple and send God's people into exile and mass enslavement. If this is victory, the terms have changed so radically as to signal a crisis in the life of God.

But as this book is to be about God in the Qur'an, why am I not talking about Allah—God in the Qur'an—from the first sentence? Why trouble to say even this much about God in those earlier scriptures?

I do so because I undertook this book in early 2017 in the aftermath of an American presidential election heavily impacted by continuing "jihadi" attacks all over the world. Throughout that electoral campaign, fear of further such attacks had been intensely on American minds. During the Republican National Convention in 2016, one prime-time speaker evoked that fear as follows:

> On Monday, an Afghan refugee in Germany used an ax and knives to slash and wound train passengers while shouting *"Allahu akbar."* Last week, ISIS claimed responsibility after a Tunisian man drove a cargo truck into a crowd in Nice, France. He murdered 84 people including 10 children, three Americans, and injured over 300 others. Two days before that, radical Islamists in Bangladesh killed 20 hostages, including three American college students. Two weeks ago, almost 300 people were killed and more than 200 were wounded in bombing attacks in Baghdad.
>
> Last month, a radical Islamist in Paris stalked a French police officer to his home where he murdered the officer, tortured his wife to death in front of their three-year-old son, while streaming it all on social media. He was pondering out loud whether to kill the three-year-old when he was killed by police.
>
> Two days before that, an attacker pledging allegiance to ISIS killed 49 people in an Orlando nightclub, and wounded dozens more.
>
> All this in just the past 37 days. We cannot let ourselves grow numb to these accumulating atrocities. One analysis estimated that since January 2015 some 30,000 people have been killed at the hands of terrorists.

Newt Gingrich, who spoke these words, was sadly mistaken in believing that electing Donald J. Trump, the Republican nominee, to the American presidency could bring such violence under peaceful control. Trump was elected, but more than a year later, on November 24, 2017, gunmen carrying the black flag of the Islamic State killed more than 300 worshippers at the Bir al-Abed Sufi mosque in Egypt. Gingrich was not inventing the atrocities that he recited, nor was he mistaken in claiming that the Muslim terrorists who perpetrate atrocities like the Bir al-Abed slaughter (it should be noted that many more Muslims than non-Muslims have died at the hands of such terrorists) do invoke Islam as justification and motivation, however repugnant their doing so may be to other Muslims.[2] An American writing about the Qur'an, which is the foundation of Islam, could scarcely ignore the fact that all this was in the air or that there are passages in the Qur'an that lend themselves to such terrifying use.

Before this book comes to its conclusion, we may have visited a couple of those passages, but we have some important preliminary work to do. While I would not care to defend the claim that Islam is a "religion of peace," neither would I defend the same claim for Christianity or Judaism. I do not deny that true religious pacifism has existed at times and still exists in a few places, but not one of these three religions deserves that title. Moreover, to clear the air just a little, we need to consider in general terms the relationship between violence as espoused by a religious community, *any* religious community, and violence as expressed in that community's sacred scriptures. In particular, what sort of obligation, if any, does war, strife, or violence in Jewish and Christian scripture impose on either Jews or Christians?

Let me illustrate the complexity of that question for these two traditions by choosing two or three quotations from the scriptures of each, beginning with Christianity. Only then will we be ready to turn again to Islam.

The belief that Jesus is the Word Incarnate—the Word who was with God and who was God before the creation of the world—has been foundational in Christianity for centuries. This is, to be sure, the Christ of faith rather than the Jesus of history, but the faith has its history no less than Jesus does, and, historically, this belief has been central to it. In the Roman Catholicism of my boyhood, every celebration of the Mass ended with the first chapter of the Gospel of John—the very chapter that, quoted above, identifies Jesus as the Word Incarnate. These were the words that the devout Catholic, leaving morning Mass, was to hear last and take with him out into the world.

With that in mind, let us turn to the final appearance of the Incarnate Word of God in the New Testament. This appearance comes at the end of Chapter 19 of Revelation, the last book in the New Testament, where we read:

> And now I saw heaven open, and a white horse appear; its rider was called Trustworthy and True; in uprightness he judges and makes war. His eyes were flames of fire, and his head was crowned with many coronets; the name written on him was known only to himself, *his cloak was soaked in blood.* He is known by the name, The Word of God. Behind him, dressed in linen of dazzling white, rode the armies of heaven on white horses. From his mouth came a sharp sword with which to strike the unbelievers; he is the one *who will rule them with an iron sceptre,* and tread out the wine of Almighty God's fierce retribution. On his cloak and on his thigh a name was written: *King of kings and Lord of lords.*
>
> I saw an angel standing in the sun, and he shouted aloud to all the birds that were flying high overhead in the sky, "Come here. *Gather together at God's great feast.* You will eat the flesh of kings, and the flesh of great generals and heroes, the flesh of horses and their riders and of all kinds of people, citizens and slaves, small and great alike." (19:11–18)

Here, near the end of the New Testament, is a picture of Christ as a warrior mounted on a white horse, His cloak drenched in blood, leading an army similarly mounted, ruling the world with an iron scepter, slaughtering His enemies, "the pagans," with a miraculous sword, and summoning the vultures to feed on the flesh of their corpses. In the *New Jerusalem Bible* translation just quoted, the italicized phrases all come from the Old Testament; their multiplication is designed to make this sanguinary passage seem the final victory of Good over Evil. And there are other allusions that could have been italicized. "The wine of Almighty God's fierce anger," for example, is an allusion to the Book of Isaiah 63:3–6, in which Yahweh answers as follows the rhetorical question "Why are your garments red / your clothes like someone treading the winepress?"

> I have trodden the winepress alone;
> of my people, not one was with me.
> So I trod them down in my anger,
> I trampled on them in my wrath.
> Their blood squirted over my garments
> and all my clothes are stained.
> For I have decided on a day of vengeance,
> my year of retribution has come.
> I looked: there was no one to help me;
> I was appalled but could find no supporter!
> Then my own arm came to my rescue
> and my own fury supported me.
> I crushed the peoples in my anger,
> I shattered them in my fury
> and sent their blood streaming to the ground.

Is this Christianity? One possible answer is, Of course it's Christianity. *It's right there in the Bible!* Moreover, if American Christianity is the Christianity in question, an extremely familiar anthem comes to mind—namely, the "Battle Hymn of the Republic," whose opening stanza alludes to God's trampling his enemies till their blood streams like juice from grapes trampled in a winepress:

> Mine eyes have seen the glory of the coming of the Lord:
> He is trampling out the vintage where the grapes of wrath
>   are stored;
> He hath loosed the fateful lightning of His terrible swift
>   sword:
> His truth is marching on.

The "terrible swift sword" of Julia Ward Howe's Civil War battle song is the "sword to strike the pagans with" that comes out of the mouth of Christ in the passage quoted above from Revelation.

So this sort of rhetoric has a Christian history, and even an American history. And yet if you know a Christian, can you not imagine him or her saying, "I don't care whether all this is in the Bible! This ruthless man-on-a-horse is not the Jesus I believe in! This is not my religion!"

Which answer is correct? In theory, either is correct. A Christian Crusader determined to model himself on the Jesus of Revelation 19:11–21 could do so. Perhaps General William Tecumseh Sherman, marching through Georgia to the sea, felt empowered to do so. A Christian with an absolutist view about Christian scripture might feel himself obligated to do so even now. In practice, however, even if many Christians have thought this way in the past, fewer do so now. Most do not take so absolutist a view of Christian scripture as to regard themselves as remotely obligated to imitate Jesus the mounted mass killer. It would be a grievous mistake to regard Christians as a dangerous population because they honor such scripture as the Word of God. It would be a mistake to fear that any one among their number—*any one of them!*—just might be led on from scripture to mass murder. What matters, in short, is never what any scripture says in the abstract but what those who honor it as scripture take concretely from it.

Here, now, is an example from Jewish scripture.

In the Book of Exodus, the Israelites, just after miraculously escaping the pursuing army of Pharaoh, must trek through the Sinai Desert to the mountain where God will make His covenant with them. En route, they repulse an attack by the Amalekites. But God, we learn, is not satisfied with mere victory over the Amalekites:

> Yahweh then said to Moses, "Write this down in a book to commemorate it, and repeat it over to Joshua, for I shall blot out all memory of Amalek under heaven." (17:14)

What does it mean to "blot out all memory" of a people? In a word, it means to exterminate that people. God is promising that He will perpetrate genocide against Amalek, and God has a long memory. Centuries later, the Israelite armies have the upper hand against Amalek at last and God shares His intentions with King Saul:

> "I intend to punish what Amalek did to Israel—laying a trap for him on the way as he was coming up from Egypt. Now,

go and crush Amalek; put him under the curse of destruction
with all that he possesses. Do not spare him, but kill man and
woman, babe and suckling, ox and sheep, camel and donkey."
(1 Samuel 15:2–3)

Is this Judaism? Again, one possible answer is, Of course, it's Judaism. *It's right there in the Bible!* And, in fact, in the rhetoric of Rabbinic
Judaism over the centuries as well as, more recently, that of the State
of Israel, "Amalek" has been a kind of shorthand for "deadly enemy of
Israel," whoever at any given moment the enemy of the day might be.
Israeli prime minister Benjamin Netanyahu declared Iran a "new Amalek" in a 2010 speech given, of all places, in Auschwitz.[3] The point of
the speech was that Iran constituted an existential threat to Israel, a
threat to its very survival, and yet the allusion inescapably evokes the
memory of Israel as itself an existential threat—indeed as the literal
annihilator—of Amalek, down to the last suckling babe.

The inflammatory charge of genocide, or genocidal intent, is regularly leveled at Israel by its Palestinian antagonist. So this biblical prec-
edent is not so arcane or remote as it might seem. And yet if you know
a Jew, can you not imagine him or her saying, "I don't care whether all
this is in Torah or the Book of Samuel or wherever else. This baby-
killer is not the God I worship! This is not my faith!"

Which answer is correct? Again, a Jew who *wanted* to imitate God by
dealing with his enemies as genocidally as God dealt with Amalek, an
Israeli who *wanted* to exterminate all the Iranians, does have scriptural
warrant for doing so. It would be a grievous mistake, however, to regard
the Jews as a dangerous population because they honor such scripture
as the Word of God, as if to fear that any one among their number—
any one of them!—just might be led on from scripture to genocide. In
practice, the overwhelming majority of Jews, including Jewish Israelis,
belong to a nation so horrendously traumatized by Nazi genocide that
they recoil from the prospect of perpetrating genocide against anybody
simply because God was genocidal in the Tanakh. My point, again, is
that what matters is not what any scripture says in the abstract but what
those who honor it as scripture take concretely from it.

As I have begun in this way, you may well be bracing yourself for
a similar cherry-picked shocker from the Qur'an, about which I could

ask, Is this Islam? and then go on, as above, to ask, But can you imagine a Muslim who ...? and so forth. I could do that, but I am not going to, because my announced subject is not the violence of the Qur'an but God in the Qur'an. God in the Muslim scripture, like God in the Jewish and Christian scriptures, has His violent moments, but there is more to Him than His violence. I did not avoid the topic of violence in my first two books. I will not avoid it here. But I will present it only to the extent that it figures in a larger exposition. It would be a gross distortion—a gross *literary* blunder—to allow one aspect of any character to eclipse every other aspect. I have engaged the general subject of violence in scripture first only because—for you, my readers, and for me as well—terrorism by Muslims invoking the Qur'an and crying *"Allahu akbar"* has moved that unwelcome subject to the front of our minds.

I acknowledge that there are passages in the Qur'an, such as several in Sura 9, that a terrorist could use to justify murder, even mass murder. I acknowledge that there are Muslims who do so use those passages, and we have good reason to fear them and defend against them. The danger they pose is real and is spreading. My hope, however, is that by beginning as I have with comparable passages from the Bible, I have created a structure of plausibility for my claim that it would be a mistake—in our historical context, a horrendous, self-defeating mistake—to regard any and every Muslim as a terrorist-in-waiting simply because he or she honors the Qur'an as sacred scripture. I have begun with violent moments in the Jewish and Christian scriptures not as a prelude to immersion in the same violence as found in the Qur'an, but simply to acknowledge in advance that there is violence in the Qur'an, to demonstrate how fully it can be matched in the Jewish and Christian scripture, and then to set the subject aside for selective reintroduction later only as part of a more nuanced and contextualized encounter with the riveting divine character at the center of this classic Muslim scripture.

We will encounter this character not by setting out on a forced march through the Qur'an from first word to last, but rather by following in the footsteps of several thoughtful writers and visiting a set of key episodes or salient personalities taken from the Jewish and Christian scriptures as they appear in the Qur'an. Jews and Christians are often surprised to discover that iconic figures from their scriptures do indeed appear, even repeatedly, in the Qur'an. This striking fact will be for us, in the discussions that follow, a doorway into the Qur'an. How does the Qur'an expand upon, contract, or revise the Bible's account of a given biblical character or episode? This will be the opening question.

The answer to that question will frame a further question. My Bible-Qur'an comparisons will differ from those that others have attempted (and from which I readily concede that I have learned much)[4] by focusing at every point on what Allah reveals directly or indirectly *about Himself* through the Qur'an's various allusions, expansions, revisions, and so forth. As much as possible, within this series of explorations, I will avoid expressions like, "The "Qur'an says" or "from the qur'anic point of view." Expressions like these have the usually unintended but unfortunate effect of muting the presence of Allah, who—through the Angel Gabriel—*speaks* the Qur'an from its first word to its last. My preference will be to write, whenever possible, "Allah says" or "Allah insists" or the like. In so doing, I will clearly be calling on my non-Muslim readers to engage in a suspension of disbelief and, for the duration of this exercise, to take the Muslim scripture on its own terms. Doing this will be particularly revealing at those points where Allah explicitly corrects what Muhammad may have heard from Jewish or Christian sources. When this is the case, and often even when it is not, I will regularly draw attention to Allah's version as a correction, in conformity with the standard Muslim assumption.

When speaking of God in the Qur'an, I do usually call Him "Allah," though I could as easily call Him "God." Arabic *'ilāh,* "god," becomes *'allāh* by the elision of *'al-'ilāh* ("*the* god"). The cognate Hebrew singular noun *'eloah,* "god," becomes the plural *'elohim* through the honorific "pluralization of majesty." When speaking of *'elohim* in the Old Testament, I call Him "Elohim," paralleling "Allah," though, again, I could as easily call Him "God." *The Qur'an* in the Penguin Classics series, which will be our citation text for that scripture, translates *'allāh,* with good reason, as "God," but usage has varied among Qur'an translations into English. Usage has similarly varied among Bible translations regarding the Hebrew God-name *yhwh. The New Jerusalem Bible,* our citation text for that scripture, translates this name "Yahweh," where other translations commonly substitute "the LORD." I too translate *yhwh* as "Yahweh." *The New Jerusalem Bible* translates *'elohim* as "God," though, as already noted, I will translate this name as "Elohim." When, as often happens, the two

Hebrew god-names alternate in a single context, I will regularly write "Yahweh Elohim," as the Bible itself does early in the Book of Genesis. Confusing as all this now sounds, it will be simple to follow in practice.

As names, *Allah, Yahweh,* and *Elohim* do all refer to the same being; but when their presence in the two different scriptures is under comparative consideration, clarity and simplicity are enhanced by using the different names, rather than saying, laboriously, endlessly, and confusingly, "God in the Bible," "God in the Qur'an," and so forth. By using the several names, I can reserve *God* for occasional instances of more general or common reference and for retrospective use in the afterword to this book. For a different reason, clarity is similarly served in discussions of qur'anic texts when singular pronouns referring to God are capitalized—thus, *He, His,* and *Him,* though such is not ordinarily my practice. The reason is that in the Qur'an, when Allah is in dialogue with one man or another, the pronoun *he* often occurs with ambivalent reference. Capitalizing references to Allah makes such passages more easily readable.

Engaging Allah in the Qur'an only through a selected few passages, and these few engaged only in comparison with their biblical counterparts, will make for an informal and conversational encounter with the Muslim scripture rather than an exhaustive, formal one, yet an encounter with its own distinct fascination. In the Qur'an, when Allah instructs Muhammad about what His Prophet is to say about these biblical subjects, He is clearly speaking to someone who knows this subject matter already in a general way and needs only to have his understanding refreshed, corrected, or completed. Allah is the instructor; Muhammad is the pupil; we, as readers of the Qur'an in English translation, are invited to listen in and learn.

What Allah requires of mankind in the Qur'an is, above all, that they should acknowledge His divinity, submitting to him as the one and only God. The Arabic word *'islam* means "submission"; the Arabic word *muslim* (from the same Arabic root *s-l-m*) names one who has so submitted. Such has been Allah's requirement from the dawn of human history, the Qur'an teaches, and so its message is emphatically not a new message. As the Qur'an understands religious history, Adam was a *muslim* in his time; Abraham was another *muslim*; Joseph a third; and so forth down past the *muslim* Christ to Muhammad. But a key part of the message of the Qur'an is that the never-changing message of *'islam* has been lost or corrupted over the intervening aeons. What Allah, as the author and the speaker of the Qur'an, therefore requires of Jews and Christians is that they should acknowledge that they have lost or adulterated what God revealed to them; and, accordingly, that they should acknowledge their need of Muhammad as the messenger bringing at last Allah's final and definitive message to them as to all of mankind.

I neither defend nor attack this religious claim. My procedure, rather, is first and last to *observe*. In both the Jewish and the Christian Bible, God reveals Himself indirectly not only through words but often also through actions that invite characterization by an observant interpreter. Similarly, then, in the Qur'an: By observing closely how the Qur'an revises subject matter that it has in common with the Bible, an observant interpreter may infer how differently the Qur'an characterizes God.

To say this is not to imply that the comparisons ahead will uncover differences alone and not similarities. Far from it! The similarities, on the whole, greatly outnumber the differences, even if it will inevitably be the differences that most intrigue. By an odd and, in my judgment, regrettable symmetry, some Muslims and some Christians deny that their respective scriptures are speaking of the same God. I believe that they do speak of the same God. While the Jewish and Christian scriptures, which came to completion centuries before Muhammad was born, do not ever speak of the Qur'an, the Qur'an does speak of Torah and Gospel, which are important parts of the Jewish and Christian scriptures, and no attentive literary interpretation of the Qur'an can fail to conclude that its divine speaker certainly does identify Himself as the God whom Jews and Christians worship and as the author of their scriptures. Within this tripartite literary identity, however, there are sharply different emphases, and it can be rewarding to discover these different emphases expressed in easily overlooked textual details. It isn't the devil, in this case, that is in the details but the deity.

The goal is not to put one presentation of God in competition with another, much less to turn Muslims into non-Muslims, or non-Muslims into Muslims. Muslim Americans readily make the Qur'an available in English translation to non-Muslims and welcome them as Qur'an readers, while Christian and Jewish Americans are at least as active in publishing and freely distributing their scriptures. The same can often be said of the publishing arms of other faiths. So then, as we are—all of us—potentially *reading* each other's scriptures already, I invite you to join me in nothing more threatening than a comparative reading of a modest selection of paired passages from the Qur'an, on the one hand, and from the Bible, on the other.

We will typically begin with a substantial quote from the Qur'an and then, in the process of discussing it, read more selectively from related passages in the Bible. Our reading of both scriptures will have what I call a *theographical* focus. Theology typically employs the difficult tools of philosophy. Theography gravitates toward the more user-friendly and descriptive tools of literary appreciation and, to a point, even toward the tools of biography. Rather than attempt to state the significance of the divine character in philosophical terms, theography aspires more modestly to *meet* him in the same simple way that characters can always be met on the pages of a work of literary art. The only entrance requirement is a willingness to be met and occasionally to be surprised. The goal is not a general introduction to the Qur'an: such an undertaking would obviously require, as a bare starting minimum, reading the entire Qur'an. Neither will the result be, to repeat, an essay in *kalam* or Islamic theology, pondering the meaning of the traditional ninety-nine "beautiful names" of God and moving on from there.

The goal and my hope is that the result will be a kind of first visit. As a fourteen-year-old boy and a member of my high school's track team, I was taken by bus to compete at Stagg Field at the University of Chicago. This was my first visit to that university, or any university. When my event was over, and the bus not scheduled to leave for another three hours, I wandered the campus in wonderment: entire buildings devoted to subjects that for me had just been words in the encyclopedia! *Botany, paleontology, philosophy*—what was behind those doors? I could scarcely guess. The Collegiate-Gothic architecture of the gymnasium itself made it look to me like some kind of strange church. Where was I? What kind of dangerous wonderland had I wandered into?

It was under the grandstand at Stagg Field, as I learned only many years later, that the world's first self-sustaining nuclear reaction had occurred, in 1942, the year of my birth, under the direction of the great Enrico Fermi. Danger indeed! Stagg Field (built in 1893) was later torn down, to be replaced by the university's grand Regenstein Library, where I would work as a postdoctoral fellow twenty years later. How little I knew on that first visit of all that surrounded the dilapidated old stadium at the heart of that great university! And yet there was a thrill about that visit. A thrill and a beginning. Think of this visit to the Qur'an as a bit like that one, entirely preliminary but open to the thrill of discovery—even if perhaps you have visited the Qur'an before.

The Bible, almost five times longer than the Qur'an, is a vast anthology, the work of many different authors, who wrote over one thousand years' time between about 900 BCE and about 100 CE. The Qur'an as historians know it[5] came into being during an intense twenty years' time, late in the life of just one man: the prophet Muhammad, who received it in the early seventh century CE as a revelation from Allah. Our sharply limited double engagement with these two scriptures will be by way of the two exceptional translations already mentioned—namely, *The New Jerusalem Bible* (Doubleday, 1990) and Tarif Khalidi's *The Qur'an* (Penguin Classics, 2009).

The New Jerusalem Bible is a late editorial descendant of *La Bible de Jérusalem,* a French Catholic translation of the Bible from the original languages, originally published in 1961. The decision that the French team of translators and commentators then made to employ the generally accepted linguistic reconstruction of the proper name of Israel's God broke with centuries of pious practice, Christian as well as Jewish.

There is no doubt that Ancient Israel did refer to God by his proper name, however it may have been pronounced. After the slaughter of Pharaoh's pursuing army, Moses and the escaped and victorious Israelites sing a song of victory. In the New Revised Standard Version, this song includes the following:

> The LORD is my strength and my might,
>   and he has become my salvation;
> this is my God, and I will praise him,
>   my father's God, and I will exalt him.
> The LORD is a warrior;
>   the LORD is his name. (Exodus 15:2–3)

Biblical English, filled with rarely used words like *exalt*, tends to be heard through an anesthetizing mental filter, but on a moment's reflection, is it not obvious that "the LORD" bespeaks a *title* or a *role* and not a name? The New Jerusalem Bible translates the final couplet:

> Yahweh is a warrior;
> Yahweh is his name.

The warrant for this translation is simply that it better reflects the Hebrew text as originally written, read, and recited.

This modern reintroduction of *Yahweh,* however respectfully employed, has provoked various reactions in various quarters. First, the use of a proper name for the one and only God can make Him seem just one god among many. Second, God by another name can seem at first like a "strange god," even when the stories told of Him conform in every other detail to the familiar biblical outlines. Third, the new usage can seem to scorn centuries of devout practice, Christian as well as Jewish. For the purposes of the comparative reading undertaken in this book, however, I have found it helpful to employ that name, as well as the others mentioned, precisely because doing so allows "Yahweh" to be as "strange" a deity for the average Western reader as "Allah," with the result, ideally, that both may be seen with fresh eyes. The underlying theographical assumption, however, remains that one and the same unique divine being is being referred to.

The New Jerusalem Bible has been from the outset preeminently a study edition. In the abundance and interpretive energy of its notes and the detail of its elaborate cross-indexing, it was in fact a pioneer among the various study editions of the Bible in English that appeared in the latter half of the twentieth century. Some have found the literary verve of its language too free for a Bible translation, but others (and I include myself) have found this freedom a liberating strength.

The New Jerusalem Bible conveniently includes and integrates portions of the original Christian Bible that were excised or demoted as apocryphal or "deuterocanonical" by the sixteenth-century Protestant reformers and that are not always included even as an appendix in modern English Bible translations published from within the broader Protestant tradition. Since the Bible as it was known in Arabia at the time when the Qur'an was revealed included these later-excised books, *The New Jerusalem Bible* seems an appropriate citation text for this study.

The Study Quran takes its place within the same, distinctively American tradition of study editions of classic texts. The work of a team of American Muslim scholars, both Sunni and Shi'a, under the editorship of the eminent S. H. Nasr, it is, like *The New Jerusalem Bible,* meticulously cross-indexed—a great boon to lay Qur'an readers otherwise likely to be bewildered by the work's way of dealing many times with the same personages. Its copious notes draw on no fewer than forty-one commentators, most of them ancient commentators accessible only to trained exegetes, and these too are an education in themselves.

The style of *The Study Quran* is self-consciously formal or stately, occasionally employing an archaic expletive like *fie!* or archaic adverbs like *haply* and *verily* and regularly capitalizing not just every pronoun but every noun or adjective that refers to Allah. The rationale for this stylistic choice is the fact that Arabic speakers who hear Allah speaking in the Qur'an do not hear a colloquial or everyday Arabic. As S. H. Nasr writes in his general introduction,

> The revelation of the Quran in Arabic lifted this language out of time and created a work that stands above and beyond historical change. Arabic as a human language used for daily discourse of course continued and in fact spread far beyond Arabia, thanks to the Quran itself. This daily language had undergone some changes over the centuries, but even those transformations have been influenced by the immutable presence of the Quran. The language of the Quran has been "dead" to the changes of this world, but has remained most alive as the embodiment of the ever living Word of God.[6]

I respect *The Study Quran* editors' decision to attempt to employ a translation style "above and beyond historical change," and I have been endlessly instructed by the notes and commentary in this edition, and yet for the purposes of this book, I find the translation approach of Tarif Khalidi, in the Penguin Classics *Qur'an,* more congenial and—with its sensitivity to poetry and to rhythm within the prose—a better stylistic match for *The New Jerusalem Bible.* Khalidi writes of his translation, a solo effort:

> Where some verses of the Qur'an are *mutashabihat* (uncertain in meaning) or abrupt, I have not tried to force meaning into them, nor have I altered the frequent mixture of singular and plural verbal forms in the same sentence. At the same time, it appeared to me to be highly desirable to preserve the sentence structure and word order of the Arabic, as well as its idioms, so long as this did not obscure the sense. In other words, I attempted a balance between the familiarly modern and the alienating archaic, while preferring at all times as literal a rendering as possible. In his translation of *Beowulf,* Seamus Heaney expresses the translator's dilemma as follows:
>
> > It is one thing to find lexical meanings for the words
> > and to have some feel for how the metre might go, but
> > it is quite another thing to find the tuning fork that
> > will give you the note and pitch for the overall music
> > of the work.
>
> In my search for that "tuning fork" I was painfully aware that the cadence of the Arabic could never be truly reproduced, but nevertheless strove for what Heaney calls a "directness of utterance," in order to convey something of the power of juxtapositions, rhythmic recurrence, sonority, verbal energy and rhymed endings of the original.[7]

On a few occasions in the chapters that follow, I will cite another translation than Khalidi's—notably, once or twice, the older translation and commentary of Muhammad Asad, partly because his translation has been widely distributed in the United States by the Council on American-Islamic Relations. Though Asad's edition has been banned for sectarian reasons in Saudi Arabia, its distribution throughout the English-speaking world in the sumptuous edition of the Book Foundation press has been subsidized, interestingly enough, by a Saudi family, the Alireza.[8] The Asad translation is also available online at www.muhammad-asad.com/Message-of-Quran.pdf.

By employing the literary technique that I employ in the chapters that follow, I do not mean to claim that the Qur'an must be read as "just a book." I take no position in these pages on whether the Qur'an is of divine or human authorship, and I certainly do not claim that Samuel Taylor Coleridge's "suspension of disbelief," as alluded to in the opening paragraphs of this foreword, is the only viable approach to sacred scripture. Allah, as the author of the Qur'an, instructed Muhammad endlessly to *recite*—in effect, to proclaim—the revelation that he was receiving through the Angel Gabriel. Muhammad's first hearers not only understood what they heard but, to historic effect, took it to heart. I know that some Muslim readers may claim, on theological grounds, that to read the Qur'an without the frame of its ancient commentaries is inevitably to misread it. Others may make the further claim that to read it in translation is not to read it at all or that to merely *read* it even in the original, as opposed to *hearing* it chanted in Arabic, is not to encounter it as Muslims encounter it.

I have no quarrel with such views, and let my claim in this book be the more modest, if you wish, for such reasons. With only a smattering of Arabic,[9] I freely admit that my readings of selected qur'anic passages do not have behind them an encounter with the rhythm and rhyme of the original language. But I know that many Muslims must approach their sacred scripture, as I do, through translations. I welcome them as I welcome all readers, but I will be adequately rewarded if this book responds to no grander need than the sympathetic curiosity of Jews, Christians, and other non-Muslims to ponder the character of Allah even through the screen of translation. Relatively familiar with the character of God as they know Him from the Bible or from Western literature and culture, Jews, Christians, and others may be happy to encounter Him afresh through this side entrance into the Qur'an. My further heartfelt hope is that, having once entered the Qur'an in this way, non-Muslims may move a step past the stereotype that has lingered in the English-speaking world at least since Edward Gibbon wrote, in *The Decline and Fall of the Roman Empire,* of "Mahomet, with the sword in one hand and the Koran in the other, erect[ing] his throne on the ruins of Christianity and of Rome."[10] We must all learn, in other words, to read one another's scriptures, be they secular or sacred, with the same understanding and accommodating eye that we turn upon our own.

I

Adam and His Wife

Who is God? When the question is engaged philosophically or theologically, an answer may begin almost anywhere. But when the question is engaged scripturally, answers must always begin with (and largely stay with) what the scripture *tells* us about God. This limitation is something like the border of a tennis court. Arbitrary as it is, we may accept it and even recognize that without it, the game would lose much of its excitement and delight. Of course, tennis players do not live their entire lives on the tennis court, and there will be times in this book when, as it were, we take a "time out" and allow our discussion to wander beyond a strictly limited comparison of the respective texts of the Bible and the Qur'an. The rules of the game require only that we serve notice when we do so.*

The Bible and the Qur'an tell us many things about God, and in many regards they agree, but their agreement does not always leap to the eye because, in literary terms, their respective procedures are so different. The Bible tells an epic story beginning with the creation of the world,

---

* A note about citation format: In all that follows, a citation like "Qur'an 6:20–24" means Qur'an, sura (chapter) 6, verses 20 to 24. "Qur'an 6:20–24, 28" would mean Qur'an, chapter 6, verses 20 to 24 plus verse 28 (thus skipping verses 25–27). "Qur'an 6:20–24, 28–7:1–5" would mean Qur'an, chapter 6, verses 20–24 plus verse 28 and continuing through chapter 7, verses 1–5. "Qur'an 6–7" would mean Qur'an, chapters 6 through 7 in their entirety. The same style is followed for books of the Bible.

including the creation of time, and ending with the end of the world, and the end of time. Allah, speaking in the Qur'an, knows this story well, for He claims it without hesitation as His story, and His manner of speaking implies that Muhammad, to whom He imparts His revelation, also knows at least its main characters and episodes. Where the Qur'an coincides with the Bible, then, it unfolds not as a full retelling of the Bible story, as if that story had never been told before, but rather as a set of selective corrections and expansions of an already received account.

Where more correction is called for, Allah has more to say in the Qur'an. Where less correction is called for, He has less to say. His correction is never merely textual, of course, but always and only substantive. He is not preparing a revised edition of the *text* of the Bible but rather correcting the *content* of the Bible by revising the story that the Bible tells in the course of delivering His new, perfected scripture.

Creation does not contain its Creator. About that, the Bible and the Qur'an are in agreement. There is no greater reality such as might contain both Him and it. Time is not such a reality; it does not contain God. Space does not contain Him either. He is not a part of the space-time world, for He has *made* that world. But God has made His human creature a part of His world, and the human part of God's world began to go wrong almost immediately. About this part of the Bible story, Allah has a good deal to say. Indeed, the subject comes up again and again in the Qur'an, and Allah's corrected versions of the story of what went wrong, though consistent one with another, add different, sometimes complementary, sometimes striking details to the overall revision.

Who is God? To a significant extent, both the Bible and the Qur'an tell us who God is by telling us who or what He is not. Agreeing, as just noted, that God is not the world that He created, the two scriptures nonetheless disagree about the relationship that exists between the Creator and His human creature. This they do, above all, in their respective tellings of the story "Of Man's first disobedience," to quote the immortal first words of John Milton's *Paradise Lost*. In telling that story, Allah effectively reveals Himself in His distinctive relationship to humankind, just as Yahweh does in the biblical Book of Genesis, traditionally understood. Nuances of difference in the narration of humanity's primal act of disobedience thus become nuances of difference in the two scriptures' respective characterizations of God Himself.

An important Qur'anic telling of this primal story comes in Qur'an 7:10–27, which begins as follows:

> We established you firmly upon the earth. We provided you with livelihoods therein—little thanks did you render. We created you, We gave you form, and then We told the angels: "Bow down before Adam." They bowed, all except Satan, who was not among those who bowed. (Qur'an 7:10–11)

The biblical account of the creation of the world and the disobedience of the first humans is told in Genesis 1–3, the Bible's very beginning. Genesis 1, in which Elohim creates the world in six days, climaxing with the creation of the first human couple, corresponds essentially to Allah's "We have indeed established you upon the earth and placed means of livelihood for you therein," but Genesis 1 is not addressed to "you," and it describes a Creator who proceeds without expecting any acknowledgment other than obedience to His one and only command: "Be fruitful, multiply, fill the earth and subdue it" (Genesis 1:28).

And yet as Genesis 2 opens, the earth is strangely devoid of humans, animals, and even plants. It is as if the world of Genesis 1 has been half-uncreated, and God is starting over, this time as Yahweh, beginning at midpoint with the first man rather than ending with him. After fashioning him from dust and puddle water, Yahweh plants a garden, then creates the animals, allowing his still unnamed human creature to name them, and finally issues this command:

> "You are free to eat of all the trees in the garden. But of the tree of knowledge of good and evil, you are not to eat; for, the day you eat of that, you are doomed to die." (Genesis 2:16–17)

Implied in this command is that so long as the man abstains from that one tree, he will *not* die. And indeed, at the end of Genesis 3, we learn that the garden contains a "tree of life," whose fruit confers immortality on those who eat it. This is among the trees whose fruit, as the biblical story of man's first disobedience opens, the man is perfectly free to eat.

What is omitted from Genesis 2 is something that shapes Qur'an 7 from the outset—namely, the presence and involvement of the angels and, above all, of the toweringly important Satan. Their inclusion has the effect, corroborated in other subtle ways, of shifting the scene of the action from earth to heaven, where Allah is attended by His angels. In Qur'an 7, Allah resumes the story, now referring to Himself in the third person:

> He {Allah} said: "What prevented you from bowing down when I commanded you?"
> He said: "I am better than he. You created me of fire but him You created of clay."
> He said: "Descend from it. It is not fit for you to wax proud in it. Depart! You have been disgraced." (Qur'an 7:12–13)

Qur'an 7 contains no reference to the creation of Adam from clay, though this detail is mentioned elsewhere in the Qur'an, as is another crucial detail:

> Remember when your Lord said to the angels: "I am creating a human being from clay. When I give him the right shape and *breathe into him of My spirit*, bow down prostrate before him." (Qur'an 38:71–72, emphasis added)

Adam's body may be made of clay and Satan's of fire, but the first man breathes with the breath of Allah, and perhaps he deserves angelic homage for that reason. (But perhaps not: see Qur'an 2:30–33, as discussed below.)

Grudgingly, Satan concedes Allah's point, but he strikes a stunning bargain with Allah:

> He said: "Defer my judgement until the Day when they are resurrected."
> He said: "You shall be so deferred."
> He said: "Inasmuch as You have led me astray, I shall lie in wait for them along Your straight path. Then I shall assail them from their front and from their backs, from their right and from their left. Nor will You find most of them to be thankful."

He said: "Be gone, accursed and outcast! As for those among
them who follow you, I shall fill hell with you all! And you,
Adam, dwell with your wife in the Garden, and eat wherever
you wish, but do not come near that tree or else you will be
sinners." (Qur'an 7:14–19)

In the Book of Job, Yahweh licenses Satan to torment Job so as to
prove to Yahweh's greater satisfaction that even under torture, Job will
never curse his Creator. Here, Allah licenses Satan to tempt Adam and
his descendants from all sides, luring them off "Your straight path,"
which is Islam, from the moment of human creation until the end of
time.

Just as Allah's garden is a heavenly garden, while Yahweh's garden,
watered by the Tigris and Euphrates, is on earth (Genesis 2:8), so Yahweh's story unfolds in earthly time, while Allah's reckons with eternity
from the very start. The deferral that Satan requests and receives is a
reprieve that runs from the beginning of human history with the creation of Adam to its end on the (capitalized) "Day" when the dead will
all rise and be either rewarded with heaven or punished with hell. Fiery
indeed, Satan is now ultimately destined for hell, the abode of fire and
eternal torment that Allah inflicts on all who do not accept His mercy
and submit to Him, but Allah has granted the rebel angel an extraordinary stay of execution.

The Book of Genesis, narrated by a voice never identified in the
work itself, proceeds step by step as in a novel, a play, or an art film,
building a certain suspense as it goes. Allah, by contrast, delivers what
we might better call an account than a counternarrative. While a con-
ventional narrator would not want to "give the story away" by revealing
the ending prematurely, Allah has no such concern. It is the point of the
story that matters to Him, not the preservation or enhancement of any
mere narrative suspense.

And there are other differences. In Genesis 2, when Yahweh commands the man not to eat the forbidden fruit, He says nothing about a
Serpent who may tempt to disobedience. In Qur'an 7, by contrast, Adam
has *heard* Allah grant Satan his immense historical reprieve, and he has
heard Satan proclaim his diabolical intent to use this very reprieve to
tempt human beings like Adam himself. Adam has thus been more than

amply warned of what lies ahead when Allah issues his prohibition: "And you, Adam, dwell with your wife in the Garden, and eat wherever you wish, but do not come near that tree or else you will be sinners." In Genesis, the comparable prohibition is conveyed to the man alone, and the Serpent, perhaps for that reason, tempts Eve (though she does seem to know of Yahweh's prohibition). In the Qur'an, by contrast, Allah gives the command quite explicitly to both Adam and his wife, even though she is a woman whose name He never speaks.

And now comes the temptation itself:

> And Satan whispered to them to open their eyes to what had been concealed from them of their shame.
>
> He said: "Your Lord forbade you to approach this tree only because you would become angels or turn immortal."
>
> And he swore to them: "I offer you good advice." Thus did he deceive them with florid speech. When they tasted the tree, their shame was visible to them, and they went about sewing leaves of the Garden upon themselves.
>
> Their Lord called out to them: "Did I not forbid you that tree? Did I not tell you that Satan was your undisguised enemy?"
>
> They said: "Our Lord, we wronged ourselves. If You do not forgive us and be merciful towards us. We shall surely be lost."
> (7:20–23)

A deep structural similarity clearly links the Bible and the Qur'an in the telling of this shared story. Allah refers to "what had been concealed from them of their shame." Genesis 2:25 reads: "Now, both of them were naked, the man and his wife, but they felt no shame before each other." In both scriptures, the first couple is deceived by a subtle, confiding, insinuating enemy. In both, they eat from the forbidden tree. In both, a sharp change of attitude toward their own bodies occurs when they do so. Genesis 3:7: "Then the eyes of both of them were opened and they realised that they were naked. So they sewed fig-leaves together to make themselves loin-cloths." These parallels are significant and undeniable.

And yet there are intriguing differences as well. In Qur'an 7 as elsewhere in the Qur'an, though later human reproduction is clearly anticipated, Allah never requires it personally of Adam and his wife. In Genesis 1:28, by contrast, Elohim commands the first couple directly, "Be fruitful, multiply, fill the earth and subdue it." And in Genesis 2:18, when Yahweh Elohim[1] says, "It is not right that the man should be alone," and creates the first woman from a rib of the man, the man welcomes her with what can certainly be read as poetic passion, "This one at last is bone of my bones and flesh of my flesh!" And then he, who has named all the other living creatures, each by its kind, but has no proper name himself, says of her: "She is to be called Woman, because she was taken from Man" (2:23). To this, the anonymous narrator of Genesis adds a telling aside: "This is why a man leaves his father and mother and becomes attached to his wife, and they become one flesh" (2:24).

These passages, especially the reference to "one flesh," suggested to early Christian interpreters, notably to Saint Augustine, that the first couple had been ordered to have—and did have—sexual relations even before eating the forbidden fruit. But in that case, how could they have only "realized that they were naked" *after* eating the fruit?

For Augustine, in *The City of God,* the answer lay in what this realization actually stood for—namely, not sexuality per se but rather sexual passion. It was the brutal intrusion of lust into their reproductive lives that turned their sin of disobedience into "the Fall of Man." Before the Fall, reason had ruled passion. Afterward, passion, uncontrollable passion, ran roughshod over reason. For the Augustine of the *Confessions,* this was all a matter of painful personal experience. Before the Fall, Augustine maintained, Adam's penis would have become reliably erect when and only when Adam was obeying Elohim's command to be fruitful and multiply. No erectile dysfunction would ever complicate his devout obedience. No unwanted erections would complicate his life at other times as Augustine's own had so often done. His life was a kind of Platonic dream come true.

This is the interpretation that stands behind John Milton's evocation of innocent sexual bliss in the Garden of Eden:

> … other Rites
> Observing none, but adoration pure
> Which God likes best, into thir inmost bower
> Handed they went; and eas'd the putting off

These troublesom disguises which wee wear,
Strait side by side were laid, nor turnd I weene
Adam from his fair Spouse, nor *Eve* the Rites
Mysterious of connubial Love refus'd:
Whatever Hypocrites austerely talk
Of puritie and place and innocence,
Defaming as impure what God declares
Pure, and commands to som, leaves free to all.

(*Paradise Lost,* Book Four, lines 736–747)[2]

As Adam and Eve embrace, Satan is spying on them, a scene that William Blake illustrated with pen and watercolor in 1807 and entitled, *Satan Watching the Endearments of Adam and Eve.*[3] The amorous first couple is shown lying nude, "strait side by side" (that is, their bodies pressed close), gorgeous in their physical perfection, and kissing. Satan, with a scaly Serpent coiled around his winged body, hovers above, watching them almost longingly.

There is little or nothing in the Qur'an to invite interpretation along these Augustinian or Miltonian/Blakean lines. Allah's reference to the nakedness of Adam and his wife seems quite strongly to imply that the first couple were celibate until after their sin. What they discovered in the aftermath of their disobedience—to quote *The Study Quran*—was "that which was hidden from them of their nakedness." *The Study Quran* cites an early (eighth-century) commentator, Wahb ibn Munabbih, who proposed that "Adam and Eve were initially cloaked in light, so that their private parts were concealed from them," a concealment that presumably precluded sexual relations. The Book of Genesis leaves us to guess just what the Serpent, whom Jewish and Christian tradition as early as the first century CE identified with Satan, hoped to achieve by his temptation. Allah makes it clear that what Satan consciously sought was precisely the arousal of shame and indecent interest in his target humans.

And yet, in the Qur'an, the seductive malice of Satan is never such as to compromise the final responsibility of each man or woman for him- or herself. For Augustine, mankind's Original Sin left the human race inherently so damaged, so prey to blind passion, that sin was virtually inevitable, thus creating the universal need for the salvation that only Christ could provide. But in Qur'an 15:42-43, Allah puts Satan firmly in his place:

> "Over my servants you shall have no authority except those who follow you, lured away."

> Hell is their appointed place, all of them.

Muhammad Asad translates the same verses to a somewhat sharper interpretive point:

> Verily, thou shalt have no power over My creatures—unless it be such as are [already] lost in grievous error and follow thee [of their own will]: and for all such, behold, hell is the promised goal.

Allah's first two creatures are now aware of their complementary nakedness, and from their coupling, human history will commence, but their nudity does not mean that they are bereft of reason or responsibility. They are not, in the Christian sense of the word, "fallen." They have been displaced but not spiritually deformed.

What is the meaning of nudity? Its meaning varies from culture to culture, from age to age within cultures, and from stage to stage within the life of any individual human being. In all cultures, the nudity of an infant has a meaning different from the nudity of an adult. In Western culture, heir to both the Hellenic artistic tradition, with its celebration of bodily beauty, and the very different Hebraic tradition, a recurrent dream has been of a variously Edenic (biblical) or Arcadian (classical) experience of mutual nudity that could be at once both fully sexual and serenely innocent. John Milton epitomizes this yearning.

And yet nudity can be a terrible humiliation. Enemies are stripped naked in war. (Readers may think of Iraqi prisoners naked, mocked, and abused in America's Abu Ghraib prison.) Even in peacetime, prisoners may be clothed or stripped at the will of the warden. When Allah speaks of human nudity, he sees it surely with reason as a cause more often of sorrow than of joy, implying in the following verses that clothing, after all, is a great blessing, a blessing that, until the moment of their disobedience, the first couple may never have lacked:

> He said: "Descend, enemies one to another! On earth you shall have a dwelling place and livelihood for a while."
> He said: "In it you shall live; in it you shall die; from it you shall be brought forth."
> O Children of Adam, We have sent down upon you a garment to hide your shame, and as adornment. But the garment of piety—that is best. These are some of God's revelations; perhaps they will remember.
> O Children of Adam, let not Satan seduce you as he drove out your two parents from the Garden. He stripped them of their garments to show them their shame. He and his clan can see you from where you cannot see them.
> We have assigned the devils as masters of those who do not believe. (7:24–27)

When Allah says that Satan "stripped them of their garments to show them their shame," He may mean either that Satan tore off the leaves they were using to cover themselves or that he deprived them of the concealing spiritual clothing that until then had hidden their private parts and precluded all sexual awareness. Even in the Book of Genesis, once the original innocent nudity has been lost, clothing quickly seems to become a blessing or at least the mitigation of a curse. When we read that Yahweh "made tunics of skins for the man and his wife and clothed them" (Genesis 3:21), just before banishing them forever, the wording implies that He dressed the bewildered two as if they were little children being introduced for the very first time to the use of actual clothing. By this point in Genesis no less than in the Qur'an, nakedness seems to bespeak vulnerability and deprivation rather than security or luxury. But in the Qur'an, much more explicitly and menacingly than in Genesis, the vulnerability of nakedness is specifically associated with humiliation at the hands of a cruel and cunning enemy.

In Italian Renaissance painting, nude figures presented in forced or antic poses are referred to by the suggestive term *ignudo,* which once seemed to me to differ from the standard term *nudo* in the way that ignoble (*ignobile* in Italian) differs from noble (*nobile*). In Michelangelo's Sistine Chapel, there are twenty *ignudi,* all of surpassing physical beauty but all with facial expressions of pensive sadness. Why? Perhaps, I thought, because by being exhibited in such oddly contorted poses, they are captives of a sort, coerced into performing an ignominious nude entertainment. Art historians may have good reason to scorn so presumptuous a projection upon Michelangelo's sanctified masterpiece. An Italian friend has also corrected my reading of the *nudo/ignudo* difference.[4] I share this amateur's reflection nonetheless to underscore the inherent ambivalence of human nudity. It may legitimately bear a score of different meanings—or none at all.

But Qur'an 7:10–27 is, in any case, about very much more than nudity. When Allah says to Adam and his wife, "Descend, enemies one to another!" he may well seem to announce the birth of marital strife in the world. But because Allah is so often speaking simultaneously to Muhammad and to all mankind, the war between the sexes may be no more than a microcosm for war in all its terrible forms. At Qur'an 2:30, opening one of the other Qur'anic accounts of creation, the angels object, when required to pay homage to Adam as Allah's "deputy," and predict that humankind will bring bloody violence upon the earth:

> And remember when God said to the angels: "I shall appoint a deputy on earth," and they answered: "Will you place therein one who sows discord and sheds blood while we chant Your praises and proclaim Your holiness?"

The angels are right, of course, about human violence. Allah replies to them that He has imparted knowledge to Adam beyond their ken, but He does not attempt to deny their prediction that human history will be a trail of tears and blood.

In Qur'an 7:24–27, Allah predicts that Adam and Eve, now that Satan has bared their private parts, will have "livelihood for a while," but then they shall die and be "brought forth." That is, they shall be brought forth from their graves on the "Day" referred to in Satan's initial request for reprieve—namely, Judgment Day, when the dead shall rise and come before Allah for their final reckoning. Allah ends this passage urging all mankind to don the raiment of reverent submission to Him for protection against Satan and his "tribe" of lesser devils.

Easily missed in this passage is the extent to which it conveys a message of mercy. True, Adam and his wife must "descend" from the heavenly garden, but because they have promptly and plainly admitted and repented of their sin, merciful Allah does not condemn them to eternal punishment in hell. In the Qur'an, Adam does not blame his wife the way he does in Genesis. The two of them confess together, neither blaming the other, and neither attempts to blame Satan. Accepting their repentance as sincere, Allah simply precipitates them into earthly existence where, after living a normal human lifetime and dying at its end, they will await His Last Judgment as indeed will all their descendants. They have every prospect, in other words, of eventually ascending to the heavenly garden from which He has sent them down. In effect, He has forgiven them this first sin. True, they must pay a price, but as they begin the life that awaits them down on earth, He has given them pardon and an immediate second chance.

In Qur'an 7:22, already quoted, when Allah remonstrates with Adam and Eve, "Did I not tell you that Satan was your undisguised enemy?" they might have replied, "No, you did not," for in this passage, though they have overheard Satan's initial declaration of enmity, Allah Himself has not warned them in His own words. In a complementary passage, however, Qur'an 20:117–119, Allah's warning is quite explicit:

> We said: "O Adam, this person is an enemy to you and your wife. Let him not drive you both out of the Garden, else you will be wretched. It is granted to you that you will not go hungry therein, nor naked. Nor will you be thirsty therein, nor swelter."

Though Allah never characterizes Himself as in a paternal, much less a maternal, relationship with His human creatures, His manner here is nonetheless like that of a parent who reminds the kids how good they have it here at home and urges them not to turn themselves heedlessly into runaways. And here, once again, we see the association of clothing with comfort and of nakedness with exposure.

In the Book of Genesis, Adam and Eve receive no warning to beware the Serpent and, after their sin, have no prospect of ever returning to the Garden of Eden. Yahweh has posted giant winged creatures with flaming swords to bar the way back, and He makes no reference, as He sentences them, to any afterlife, whether of compensating reward or further punishment. And this is just the beginning. Seething with anger, Yahweh announces that He will impose on Eve and her daughters the terrible pain of childbirth as part of her punishment. As for Adam, he is to suffer, for himself and all his descendants, a life sentence at hard labor followed by the death penalty:

> "Accursed be the soil because of you!
> Painfully will you get your food from it
> as long as you live.
> It will yield you brambles and thistles,
> as you eat the produce of the land.
> By the sweat of your face
> will you earn your food,
> until you return to the ground,
> as you were taken from it.
> For dust you are
> and to dust you shall return." (Genesis 3:17–19)

The Genesis narrator not only makes no reference to any afterlife but also holds out no other prospect of a restored relationship between creature and Creator. The human couple will proceed to reproduce, and Yahweh will, in fact, involve Himself in the lives of their offspring, but for all they know at the moment of their expulsion, He is done with them forever.

And, indeed, in a purely literary way, He might be said to leave them behind. A distinctive narrative feature of the Tanakh as the epic of Israel is that of multiple beginnings and endings. A story begins with Adam, then stops. Generations pass quickly until a second story begins with Noah, then stops. Further generations pass swiftly until a third story begins with Abraham, then stops; and so forth.

By contrast with the Adam and Eve of Genesis, sentenced as they are to true and final death without any prospect of restoration or afterlife,

Adam and his wife in the Qur'an are effectively immortal, as are all their descendants. In Qur'an 7:10–27, had the first couple not sinned, they might not only have lived forever in the heavenly garden with Allah but might never have reproduced at all. But once they have sinned, their new existential condition becomes no worse than the normal condition for all the "Children of Adam"—namely, birth, earthly death, then a final divine judgment, and afterward either eternal reward in the heavenly garden or eternal punishment in hell. When Satan tempts them, he falsely implies that Allah fears lest His human creatures might "become angels or turn immortal." But in fact, as Allah well knows, Adam and his wife are already destined to be immortal. Their immortality, however, is not in itself either a reward or a punishment; it is simply a part of the common human condition.

If Yahweh intended ever to forgive His sinful human creatures, why could He not have forgiven them immediately? This was the conundrum, the great unanswered question, that drove Milton to write *Paradise Lost* and *Paradise Regained*. Those two titles are, in fact, a brilliant, four-word summary of the vast Christian epic, according to which Christ, at long last, does restore to humanity the immortality that it lost through the "Original Sin" of Adam and Eve and does reopen the Gate of Paradise that the flaming sword of Yahweh had seemed to close forever.

How did this come about? In the lengthy concluding portion of *Paradise Lost,* Michael the Archangel explains to Adam, just before the first couple's expulsion from Paradise, how the Lord God will, in the fullness of time, enable the forgiveness of all human sins through the Crucifixion and Resurrection of Jesus Christ. Adam, for all the sorrow that attends his and Eve's expulsion from Paradise, is awestruck before this vision of how the Lord will in the end draw good from evil and, with Eve, he departs Paradise in a state of reverent resignation. *Paradise Lost* ends with the lines:

> They looking back, all th' Eastern side beheld
> Of Paradise, so late thir happie seat,
> Wav'd over by that flaming Brand, the Gate
> With dreadful Faces throng'd and fierie Armes:

Som natural tears they drop'd, but wip'd them soon;
The World was all before them, where to choose
Thir place of rest, and Providence thir guide:
They hand in hand with wandring steps and slow,
Through *Eden* took their solitarie way.[5]

Thus does Milton finally accomplish what in the prologue to *Paradise Lost* he had called on his "heavenly Muse" to assist him in undertaking:

…What in me is dark
Illumin, what is low raise and support;
That to the highth of this great Argument
I may assert Eternal Providence,
And justifie the wayes of God to men.[6]

The power of Milton's poetry is undeniable, but equally undeniable is the enormity of the theological task he undertakes. How can it have been just for Yahweh not to forgive His human creatures immediately, as Allah does, but only after centuries and only by way of the agonizing death of His only begotten Son?

What must strike us is the fact that Milton's epic is shaped by the same solution that shapes the Qur'an. Critics have endlessly pointed out that in Milton's Christian epic, the most compellingly realized character is Satan. But it served Milton's ultimate theological purpose well to make Satan as powerful as he did, for the more powerful Satan becomes, relative to God, the more easily God can be justified in taking so roundabout and costly a path to forgiveness. It took God so long, in other words, because, thanks to the power of Satan, He had a great deal to overcome. Satan thus helps Milton to "justifie the wayes of God to men."

Similarly in the Qur'an, the presence of Satan as a hugely powerful and omnipresent figure, an alternate source of Power, justifies the ways of Allah to men. It enables Him to be, in a similar way, a better and indeed an entirely good and ethical deity. When things go wrong, even stupendously wrong, Allah need never be even partly responsible. Between them, diabolical Satan and susceptible humankind are always available to blame. Satan will be as frequently and powerfully active in the New Testament as in the Qur'an, but he is only infrequently and weakly so in the Old Testament. As a result, Elohim or Yahweh must assume responsibility for evil as well as good in this earliest and longest of the three scriptural classics.

Thus, in Deuteronomy 32:39, Yahweh says:

> See now that I, I am he,
> and beside me there is no other god.
> It is I who deal death and life;
> when I have struck, it is I who heal
> (no one can rescue anyone from me).

And in Isaiah 45:6–7, Yahweh declares even more resoundingly:

> I am Yahweh, and there is no other,
> I form the light and I create the darkness,
> I make well-being, and I create disaster,
> I, Yahweh, do all these things.

In Genesis 2–3, the tempting Serpent is one of the creatures that Yahweh has created and placed in the garden. Does this not make Yahweh ultimately responsible for Adam and Eve's sin? Why would it not? If Yahweh knew that the Serpent would tempt them, did He not have a duty to warn them? Or was He surprised by what His snaky creature did? How much, in fact, does Yahweh know in the Book of Genesis? Is He omniscient from the start, or is He surprised by the consequences of His own actions? Christian theologians and Rabbinic sages have suffered over these questions for two millennia. Thanks to the presence of Satan in the qur'anic version, their Islamic counterparts suffer rather less. In the Qur'an, Allah does not have to ask, as Yahweh does at Genesis 3:11 (and not rhetorically), "Who told you that you were naked?"

In the Old Testament, Yahweh's unpredictability—His propensity for sometimes causing weal and sometimes woe—can make Him seem more godlike by being less knowable. He may seem less godlike when His knowledge seems only partial, but then, at such moments, He becomes even more unpredictable. Allah, by contrast, is never surprised by anything that anyone says or does or anything that happens and is far more dependably and predictably ethical and, above all, merciful. Allah is forceful, yes, but always to the same point and in the same way, and His rage is never so hot, as we shall see in the later chapters of this book, as to incinerate His mercy.

What is most shocking about the qur'anic creation story is the fact that Allah so readily grants Satan a reprieve that so jeopardizes humankind. And yet just such a reprieve appears briefly in the Gospel and is reprised at great and poetic length in Book Three of *Paradise Regained*. This second, shorter portion of Milton's two-part epic is a poetic expansion of the Gospel account of how the devil tempted Jesus for forty days in the desert. Thrice Satan sought to subvert Christ, the second time with a daring temptation to power. In Luke's version:

> Then leading him to a height, the devil showed him in a moment of time all the kings of the world and said to him, "I will give you all this power and their splendor, *for it has been handed over to me*, for me to give it to anyone I choose. Do homage, then, to me, and it shall all be yours." (4:5–8, emphasis added)

Milton seizes on the phrase "for it has been handed over to me," so reminiscent of Allah's license granted to Satan, and expands it into the third of the four books that constitute *Paradise Regained*. Book Three includes a sweeping geographical survey of the ancient world, all of which Satan claims to control diabolically from below. The "fiend," as Milton often calls him, concludes this survey by accurately depicting Judaea as a tiny pawn in the ongoing titanic struggle between two great empires—the Persian (Parthian) Empire in the east and the Roman in the west. He warns Christ that even if all Samaria and all Judaea should acclaim Him as Messiah and King of the Jews, His kingdom will not be secure unless He can have subdued one of these two empires in advance. Like a nineteenth-century European imperialist contemplating the partition of Africa, Satan shrewdly counsels Christ to pick off Persia (Parthia) first:

one of these
Thou must make sure thy own, the *Parthian* first
By my advice, as nearer and of late
Found able by invasion to annoy
Thy country, and captive lead away her Kings...[7] (362–366)

The Prince of Darkness is evidently, to a disturbing degree, the world's ultimate, if secret, powerbroker, and he can make Christ the emperor of Persia if Christ will but bow down to him. Satan knows that his power is not infinite and fears that in Christ he has met his match. But he is determined to delay his defeat as long as possible, and his resources are immense. Thereon hangs the tale in the New Testament (and in Milton's epic expansion of it) and in the Qur'an alike. Whatever may be said in theological terms of this enlargement of Satan's role, it is a brilliant literary turn. Temporarily checked only to win dramatically in the end, God becomes interesting in a new way. What is largely an inner conflict in the Old Testament becomes an outer conflict in both the New Testament and the Qur'an.

Half a millennium before the imparting of the Qur'an, a first-century, anonymous, extra-biblical Jewish work entitled *Life of Adam and Eve* told a story of rebellious angels expelled from heaven to hell for refusing to bow down before Adam. This work survives in two distinct and overlapping versions, one in Greek, the other in Latin; scholars believe a lost Hebrew original stands behind both. That the story of an angelic rebellion is attested as early as the first century does not mean that it may not have been current in the Middle East a good deal earlier and in other ancient venues than Palestine. Because, as already argued, the story answered some besetting questions, it was to make its way far and wide, living on in Jewish and Christian tradition alike through the Middle Ages down to its inclusion as context for *Paradise Lost* and *Paradise Regained*.

While at first glance the inclusion of Qur'an 7 and complementary passages in the Qur'an might seem merely to have continued and further extended the central legend of the *Life of Adam and Eve*, there is one key regard in which the Qur'an delivers here its sharpest correction of all. In the legend's central scene, as recounted in the *Life*, Adam speaks first, addressing Satan ("the devil" in the passage below):

> "What have I done to you, and what is my blame with you? Since you are neither harmed nor hurt by us, why do you pursue us?"
>
> The devil replied, "Adam, what are you telling me? It is because of you that I have been thrown out of there. When you were created, I was cast out from the presence of God and was sent out from the fellowship of the angels. When God blew into you the *breath of life* and your countenance and likeness were made *in the image of God*, Michael [the Archangel] brought you and made (us) worship you in the sight of God, and the LORD God said, 'Behold Adam! I have made you in our *image and likeness*.' And Michael went out and called all the angels, saying 'Worship *the image of the Lord God*, as the LORD God has instructed.' And Michael himself worshiped first, and called me and said, 'Worship *the image of God, Yahweh*.' And I answered, 'I do not worship Adam.' And when Michael kept forcing me to worship, I said to him, 'Why do you compel me? I will not worship one inferior and subsequent to me. I am prior to him in creation; before he was made, I was already made. He ought to worship me.' ... And the LORD God was angry with me and sent me with my angels out from our glory.... And we were pained to see you in such bliss of delights. So with deceit I assailed your wife and made you to be expelled through her from the joys of your bliss, as I have been expelled from my glory."[8]

The italicized phrases *breath of life* and *image of God* in the passage just quoted fuse allusions to, respectively, Genesis 2:7 (the creation of the first man) and Genesis 1:26 (the earlier creation of the first couple). In this relatively short passage, there are no fewer than four references to Adam being the image or the image and likeness of God.

Though the focus here is on the exalted character of Adam, the biblical passages in question are also legitimately read as characterizations of, respectively, Yahweh and Elohim. It is Elohim who says, at Genesis 1:26–27,

> "Let us make man in our own image, in the likeness of ourselves, and let them be masters of the fish of the sea, the birds of heaven, the cattle, all the wild animals, and all the creatures that creep along the ground."

> > God created man in the image of himself,
> > in the image of God he created him,
> > male and female he created them.

Few sentences in the entire Bible have been more aggressively parsed than these. Does Elohim create the male; and when the text reads, "in the image of God he created him," should we understand that it is only the male who is His image, despite the immediately following line? Or when the text reads "God created man," should we understand the creation of humankind, in which case the image is the species rather than the specimen and includes all the men and all the women who will ever live? From such questions are entire biblical theologies and biblical anthropologies spun out. Minimally, it seems beyond debate that this verse asserts that somehow Elohim may be known, however indirectly, through His human image and likeness.

A less abstract, more intimately physical connection between Yahweh Elohim and the first man is then asserted at Genesis 2:7:

> Yahweh God shaped man from the soil of the ground and blew the breath of life into his nostrils, and man became a living being.

But because *breath* and *spirit* are the same word in Hebrew, Yahweh Elohim ("Yahweh God," in the translation just quoted) breathes not just His physical life but also His spiritual life into His first human creature. And as there is thus something divine about the human spirit, so the study of mankind is at least a prologue to the study of God. Jesus will say boldly (John 14:9): "Anyone who has seen me has seen the Father."

But what, for Christians, is true of the Son of God par excellence is true to some extent of all human beings, according to Genesis 2:7—the more so for both Jews and Christians, once both began routinely to address their Creator as "Father."

Muslims take no such liberty. Nowhere in the Qur'an and scarcely anywhere else in Muslim tradition is any hint asserted of a familial relationship between deity and humanity. In Qur'an 7:10–27 and parallel accounts elsewhere in the Qur'an, Allah does order Satan to bow down to Adam, but He never presents Adam as an image of Himself. To appreciate the Qur'an, it is essential to hear the silence in that abstention, a silence that brings to my mind a poem, "God's Brother," by the American poet and playwright Dan O'Brien:

> We walked downhill
> from school; he was
> older than I
> was by ages. The hill
> was a runnel of shade
> and the great trees discarded
> their leprous bark down
> along the asphalt, curling
> and trod into dust. I told him
> of a boy who'd misbehaved
> at school again. What
> makes you think
> you're better than he is?
> he asked me.
>
> We walked
> in silence after that, wet leaves
> under our feet like water...
>
> Then as if to remind us both
> he said, You're not God,
> you know.[9]

A psychologically legitimate way for non-Muslims to engage the austerity of the Qur'an is to hear it saying, in myriad ways and yet simply: "You're not God, you know." You're not God. You're not God's son. You're not God's daughter. You're not God's brother or sister. Only God is God: *lā 'ilāha 'illā 'allāh*. Thus, in the Qur'an's corrected version, Allah's ground for commanding the angels' obeisance is decidedly not that Adam, much less Adam's wife, is somehow an image of God, deserving angelic respect or homage for that reason.

Is there any reason at all for Allah's commanding that obeisance other than sheer authority and prerogative? Allah, responding to the angels' complaint in Qur'an 2 that mankind will be corrupt and shed blood, insists:

> "I know what you do not."
> He taught Adam the names of all things. Then He displayed them to the angels and said: "Tell me the names of these things, if you are truthful."
> They said: "Glory be to You! We have no knowledge except what You taught us. You! You are All-Knowing, All-Wise."
> God said: "O Adam, reveal to them their names." When Adam revealed their names, God said: "Did I not tell you that I know the Unseen of the heavens and the earth? That I know what you make public and what you hide?" (Qur'an 2:30–33)

So it is because of the divine knowledge that Allah has imparted to him that Adam, God's "deputy," deserves angelic homage. In the Qur'an as also in the Old Testament, things and their names seem so intimately related that to know a thing's name means to know the thing itself and even to control it. Thus, to know all names here is tantamount to knowing all things—to knowing everything.[10] Adam, by his humble repentance, becomes the first Muslim. By his possession of divinely imparted knowledge, he becomes for his descendants the first messenger. But even as the first messenger, he is not the image or likeness of God.

But now what of Qur'an 38:72, quoted earlier, where Allah proposes to "give [Adam] the right shape and breathe into him of My spirit"? Does Allah's spirit within Adam not confer upon him a dignity that deserves angelic homage, however great or small his knowledge of "the names"? According to *The Study Quran,* one twelfth-century commentator, Rūzbihān al-Baqlī, did effectively defend that interpretation, but he is an exception to the rule:

> Insisting upon God's complete transcendence and the createdness of anything outside of God, most commentators seek to read *I breathed into him of My Spirit* figuratively. Some gloss *My Spirit* as "My Power"... or say that this is not God's Spirit, but that God refers to it as such as a means of honoring Adam.... [11]

In the practice of Islam, the Arabic word *shirk* names the cardinal sin of associating anything or anybody so closely with Allah as to compromise His *tawhid,* or unity. Whatever the text of the Qur'an might seem to say, pious Muslims cannot believe that Allah would ever have required *shirk* of any creature, angels included.

For much of modern literary criticism, the intrusion of a religious consideration like this upon the criticism, let alone the alleged original composition, of a work of literature is anachronistic and artistically objectionable. Yet Erich Auerbach, one of the greatest of all modern critics, made the appreciation of what he called "figural interpretation" central to his interpretation of all literature. The seventh chapter of Auerbach's masterpiece, *Mimesis: The Representation of Reality in Western Literature,* consists of a meditation on scenes from the twelfth-century French liturgical drama or "mystery play" *Le Jeu d'Adam,* also known as *Le Mystère d'Adam.* In one of these scenes, Adam, immediately after eating the forbidden fruit, turns to Eve and delivers a speech mingling frantic grief and desperate hope:

> Through your advice I have been brought to evil, from a great height I have fallen into great depth. I shall not be raised from it by man born of woman, unless it be God in His Majesty. What am I saying, alas? Why did I name Him? He help me? I have angered Him. No one will help me now except the Son who will come forth from Mary. To no one can I turn for protection, since in God we kept no faith. Now then let everything be according to God's will! There is no counsel but to die. [12]

Auerbach notes that from this speech, it is clear that Adam "has advance knowledge of all of Christian world history," but he cautions:

> One must, then, be very much on one's guard against tak-ing such violations of chronology, where the future seems to reach back into the present, as nothing more than evidence of a kind of medieval naïveté.... Everything in the dramatic play which grew out of the liturgy during the Middle Ages is part of one—and always of the same—context: of one great drama whose beginning is God's creation of the world, whose climax is Christ's Incarnation and Passion, and whose expected conclusion will be Christ's second coming and the Last Judgment.[13]

A literary appreciation of the Qur'an requires what Auerbach insists that the proper appreciation of this mystery play requires—namely, a recognition that when "the future seems to reach back into the present," we are not confronted with mere naïveté but with a figural interpreta-tion of history as "one great drama whose beginning is God's creation of the world, whose climax is" not Christ's Incarnation and Passion but God's revelation of the Qur'an to Muhammad, "and whose expected conclusion will be" not Christ's second coming but Muhammad's sec-ond coming (accompanied by Christ, actually, in developed Muslim tradition) "and the Last Judgment."

In a figural interpretation of history, Auerbach writes,

> every occurrence, in all its everyday reality, is simultaneously a part in a world-historical context through which each part is related to every other, and thus is likewise to be regarded as being of all times or above all time.[14]

In the chapters that follow, the Qur'an's corrections of the successive biblical episodes to be revisited will consistently be, in something like the sense that Auerbach captures, a succession of figural interpretations.

As regards the story of Adam and Eve, the story we have just been considering, if we regard "every occurrence, in all its everyday real-ity, [as] simultaneously a part of [the Muslim] world-historical context," then we may locate ourselves imaginatively within this context. We are not representations of Allah, to be sure, but we are, for all that, His representatives or deputies in the world, equipped for our sacred mission by the knowledge that He first imparted to our forefather, Adam. Satan is our enemy, coming at us from all sides and at any moment, but we have all the power we need to resist his deceptions and stay on the "straight path." If we do succumb, we know that just as Allah gave Adam and Eve their second chance, He will give us ours. Allah is like that: He can be counted on. He is not colorfully or dramatically unpredictable. He is not like you or me nor even, quite, like Yahweh. Agony awaits us if we defy Him, but He is on our side if we will let Him be. At Qur'an 50:16, He says:

> We created man and know what his soul murmurs to him,
> But We are nearer to him than his jugular vein.

Finally, at the end of the story and the end of time, what awaits us, as it awaited Adam and Eve even after their sin, is our return to the garden, the heavenly garden of paradise where it all began.

2

Adam's Son and His Brother

In the Bible, Adam and Eve do not start out as Adam and Eve. Those names do not occur at all in the first chapter of the Book of Genesis. On the sixth day of creation,

> God created man in the image of himself,
> in the image of God he created him,
> male and female he created them. (Genesis 1:27)

But on the seventh day, when Elohim rests, the couple still have no names.

Much that seemed done in Genesis 1 somehow has to be done over in Genesis 2, but in this second attempt at creation Yahweh moves early to breathe life into a human partner and to involve His partner, His creature, in the task of completing creation. Again, however, He gives him no name. He is simply "the man," and after all, does he need a name? He is the only one of his kind in existence.

When Yahweh decides that no animal is a suitable companion for "the man," He creates a suitable companion from the man's rib. The man then coins a term, not a name, for his companion—namely, "woman." In Hebrew, the word "woman," *'iššah,* is virtually identical with the phrase "her husband," *'išah.* So the man puns when he says, "She will be called *'iššah* because from *'išah* she was taken"—referring back, of course, to her creation from his rib. But she, no less than he, still lacks a proper name.[1]

The man, who at Yahweh's instigation has named all the animals in Eden, names the woman "Eve" only moments before the two of them are expelled from Eden, so, starting then, he has a name for her, but does she have one for him? Not yet, apparently: when they have their first post-Edenic coupling, he is still nameless: "The man had intercourse with his wife Eve, and she conceived and gave birth to Cain." Soon, she brings forth a second son, Abel.

In this chapter, we want to discuss the story of Cain and Abel in the Bible and in the Qur'an, but just as Adam and Eve do not start out named Adam and Eve in the Bible, so Cain and Abel are nameless in the Qur'an; they are just "Adam's two sons." Both accounts are quite brief. Let's begin with the qur'anic account:

> Recite to them the true story of the two sons of Adam, when they offered a sacrifice and it was accepted from one of them but not from the other.
>
> He said: "I shall slay you!"
>
> The other replied: "God only accepts from the devout. Were you to stretch forth your hand to kill me, I shall not stretch forth my hand to kill you, for I fear God, the Lord of the Worlds. I want you to bear my sin and yours, and thus become a denizen of the Fire, for this is the reward of wrongdoers."
>
> His soul tempted him to kill his brother, so he killed him and ended up among the lost. But God sent a raven clawing out the earth to show him how he might bury the corpse of his brother. He said: "What a wretch I am! Am I incapable of being like this raven and so conceal my brother's corpse?" And so he ended up remorseful.
>
> It is for this reason that We decreed to the Children of Israel that he who kills a soul neither in revenge for another, nor to prevent corruption on earth, it is as if he killed the whole of

mankind; whereas he who saves a soul, it is as if he has saved the whole of mankind. Our messengers came to them bearing clear proofs, but many of them thereafter were disobedient on earth. (5:27–32)

As we have already had occasion to see, the narrator in the Bible is typically an unidentified omniscient narrator who can recount the words and actions of God as well as those of human beings interacting with God as if seeing both from some elevated vantage point encompassing both. Moreover, these words and actions are typically spoken or performed as if on a stage before viewers who are not addressed while the performance is in progress. The invisible "fourth wall" that separates actors on a proscenium stage from the anonymous audience exists for many biblical narratives, including the story of Cain and Abel (Genesis 4:2–16). Neither the two human characters in the story, nor Yahweh, nor the narrator, ever directly addresses the readers or hearers of the story or even refers to them.

Who is this mysterious narrator? In pious Jewish tradition, he is Moses for Torah, the first five books of the Bible. By pious tradition Moses received them directly, and verbatim, from God. But this tradition only arose centuries after these books were written. Even for those who honor the tradition, the narrator is aesthetically, functionally, a hidden narrator, and the reader or hearer feels that he, too, is hidden, for though he watches the story unfold, the actors in the story never address him, and neither does Yahweh.

How very different all these conventions are in the Qur'an! The story of the two sons just quoted is a kind of public sermon on and against murder, and for the purposes of the sermon the names of the sons, or brothers, are irrelevant. Allah punishes murderers in hell; they become "denizens of the Fire." That's the moral of the story, and it is as if "the Abel character," as we might call him, turns to us in the audience as this didactic point is reached and warns us sternly, "God only accepts from the devout. Were you to stretch forth your hand to kill me, I shall not stretch forth my hand to kill you, for I fear God, the Lord of the Worlds. I want you to bear my sin and yours, and thus become a denizen of the Fire, for this is the reward of wrongdoers." The moral message of the passage, elaborated in what immediately follows, is clarified and heightened by being broken free from the complications that an enlarged, quasi-novelistic context could introduce.

Compare the opening of the story as told above with the opening in the Book of Genesis:

> The man had intercourse with his wife Eve, and she conceived and gave birth to Cain. "I have acquired a man with the help of Yahweh," she said. She gave birth to a second child, Abel, the brother of Cain. Now Abel became a shepherd and kept flocks, while Cain tilled the soil. Time passed and Cain brought some of the produce of the soil as an offering for Yahweh, while Abel for his part brought the first-born of his flock and some of their fat as well. Yahweh looked with favour on Abel and his offering. But he did not look with favour on Cain and his offering, and Cain was very angry and downcast. (4:1–5)

If Yahweh had been a little more gracious with Cain, could He have saved Abel's life? Does the trouble begin with Yahweh?

In this connection, we might well ask why the two of them are offering sacrifice in the first place. At this early point in the Bible, Yahweh has not commanded that any sacrifices be offered to Him. Where did Abel and Cain get the idea that they should do this sort of thing?

Prior even to that question, we might ask what they know of Yahweh and how they know it. Religiously speaking, how were they brought up? Staying only with what we know from the text, we can only note that they were brought up by a couple for whom and with whom Yahweh created Paradise, a couple who then disobeyed Yahweh just once, and who, having been given no opportunity to repent, were sentenced forthwith to death, they and all their offspring for all time. Eve, the boys' mother, and all her female offspring were sentenced as well to blighted sexuality. Their father, "the man," and all his male offspring were sentenced to blighted labor.

This is what Cain and Abel know. Knowing it, surely they might wonder what this Yahweh, this terrifying being, might do next? Would He grow even angrier and take from His four human creatures the little that they had left? Best, perhaps, to try to placate Him in advance—do something, anything, to win His favor, keep on His good side.

Even at this early point in the biblical narrative, the first four human beings have had a rich experience of divine anger, but has Yahweh had any experience of human anger? Moreover, does He realize that when He sentenced the first human couple to mortality, He introduced into His world the very possibility of murder? Does Cain's anger surprise Him? Will the spectacle of Abel's slaying, the world's first murder, surprise Him even more?

These questions carry us ahead in the biblical story, but such novelistic complications hold no interest at all for Allah when He addresses Muhammad (and us) through the unnamed good son in the qur'anic tale. It is, to repeat, the moral of that story that matters to Allah. Anything that distracts from that He elides. He allows no hint of divine responsibility for the human murder to intrude: "it [the sacrifice] was accepted from one of them but not from the other." That's all that Muhammad needs to hear to move the story forward. With a deft shift to the passive voice, Allah passes over in silence His possible role in what is about to happen. Allah has no need, either, to point out that these two sons are the *first* two children ever born to human parents, the first two humans whom He has not created directly. They are, you might say, strangers to Him—other people's children. Interesting, perhaps, but to what ethical point? Interesting to somebody, perhaps; not interesting to Allah.

Pregnant psychological complications like these, missing in the qur'anic account, continue in the biblical account. Yahweh's reaction to His first experience of human anger seems, on the one hand, almost puzzled and, on the other, touched with a troubled foreboding: something is about to go wrong, and it is as if even He cannot quite predict what it will be.

> Yahweh asked Cain, "Why are you angry and downcast? If you are doing right, surely you ought to hold your head high! But if you are not doing right, Sin is crouching at the door hungry to get you. You can still master him." (4:6–7)

Instead of taunting Cain with questions—"Why are you angry and downcast? If you are doing right, surely you ought to hold your head high!"—Yahweh could have counseled him: "You are doing right, so

hold your head high!" Cain might then have been consoled and reas-
sured by the deity he had sought to placate instead of darkly faulted by
Him. The moral of the story as a didactic fable is obscured when Yahweh simultaneously goads Cain toward action and warns him against
it. All the same, the plot gains considerable momentum from just this
chiaroscuro complication. Aesthetically, a more "appropriate" Yahweh
would be a less compelling character.

We the audience in this biblical theater have overheard Yahweh's
ominous comments to Cain, but Abel has not. Abel thus does not sense
what we sense when Cain says to him, "Let us go out." A moment of
suspense follows, and then the deed is done: "While they were in the
open country [out of Yahweh's sight], Cain set on his brother Abel and
killed him" (4:8).

In the Qur'an, as noted, Allah elides His role in either accepting or
rejecting either offering, and the occasion for any exchange between
Him and the son whose offering was not accepted disappears into the
elision. There is no suspense—no subtlety, no entrapment—in the
murder itself. There is only the rejected son's bald, cold, but entirely
undisguised declaration, "I shall slay you." In Genesis, Cain's anger
over his rejection may encompass both Yahweh and Abel. In the Qur'an,
his rage targets the favored brother and him alone. In Genesis, fraternal
deceit—a recurring plot motif in the Bible—moves the action forward.
In the Qur'an, no ruse, no deception, is called for.

But at this point we encounter a fork in the two-track road. In the
Bible, the murderous action takes place silently. If the action were taking place on a stage, it would be a kind of pantomime or perhaps, in the
manner of some Greek drama, an action taking place offstage, signaled
only by a cry. Not so in the Qur'an. With the defiance of a martyr, the
good son addresses his killer in a short but vivid speech whose last sentence is addressed past the killer to Muhammad and to us:

> "God only accepts from the devout. Were you to stretch forth
> your hand to kill me, I shall not stretch forth my hand to kill
> you, for I fear God, the Lord of the Worlds. I want you to bear
> my sin and yours, and thus become a denizen of the Fire, *for
> this is the reward of wrongdoers.*" (5:27–29, emphasis added)

Here—in the Qur'an as not in the Bible—Allah addresses the question of *why* Cain's offering was rejected. It was because Cain gave his gift without reverence, giving it grudgingly perhaps rather than willingly, or resentfully, without true submission to Allah. In the Qur'an, Allah is forthcoming, again, on another point that the Bible passes over in silence. Did Abel fight back when Cain attacked him? Did he see the attack coming? Allah answers those questions plainly: the reverent son—the one who truly fears "the Lord of the Worlds"—did indeed see the attack coming, and he did not fight back.

Given the worldwide preoccupation now with jihadi terrorism, discussed in the prologue to this book, it is striking for Christians reading this incident to come upon the Muslim scriptural celebration of a man who seems well nigh Christ-like in his nonviolence. A nearer scriptural analogy than Jesus, however, might be the seven Jewish brothers of the Second Book of Maccabees, each tortured to death in turn by a cruel Greek king, each confident of vindication. At the moment of his martyrdom, the fifth defies the king with the words:

> "You have power over human beings, mortal as you are, and can act as you please. But do not think that our {people} has been deserted by God. Only wait, and you will see in your turn how his mighty power will torment you and your descendants." (7:16–17)

Like the fifth Maccabee son, the good son in the Qur'an predicts torment—here, "the Fire"—for his slayer. Violent retribution there will be, but it is Allah—not the wronged human being—who will inflict it.

The puzzling prediction that the bad son is to "bear my sin [the good brother's] and yours" may mean, to paraphrase, "bear the sin of having killed me plus your other sins," but in his commentary on the Qur'an, Muhammad Asad offers an alternative explanation in a footnote to this verse. By attested Muslim interpretive tradition, he asserts:

> In cases of unprovoked murder, the murderer is burdened—in addition to the sin of murder—with the sins which his innocent victim might have committed in the past and of which he (the victim) is now absolved...

To the extent that this may have become an established understanding of this verse, those hearing it would be provided with yet another disincentive to commit so grave a crime. For his crime, the bad son "ended up among the lost," the sinner having actively brought his loss upon himself.

To digress for a moment, the Muslim tradition to which Asad alludes reflects a preoccupation common to Christians as well as Muslims with the consequences of unprepared death, death that a man may suffer without having had the opportunity to repent of his sins. For centuries, the Christian response to this worry was belief in Purgatory—a temporary hell where sinners who would indeed have repented had death not come without warning could suffer punishment for a time but then finally be admitted to heaven.

In Shakespeare's tragedy *Hamlet, Prince of Denmark,* the ghost of the murdered king, calling on his son to avenge him, speaks to him of his sufferings in Purgatory:

> I am thy father's spirit,
> Doom'd for a certain term to walk the night,
> And for the day confin'd to fast in fires,
> Till the foul crimes done in my days of nature
> Are burnt and purg'd away. (Act I, sc. v, lines 9–13)

He is suffering thus because by being murdered he was:

> Cut off even in the blossoms of my sin,
> Unhous'led, disappointed, unanel'd,[2]
> No reckoning made, but sent to my account
> With all my imperfections on my head. (Act I, sc. v,
>   lines 76–79)

By the Muslim tradition to which Asad refers, King Hamlet would have been spared this suffering, as the punishment for the sins the king had not yet repented of would have fallen on the head of Claudius, his brother and his murderer.

But as both scriptures now do, let us consider the corpse of the slain Abel.

In Genesis, Yahweh and Cain gaze together on the first dead body that either has ever seen, and Yahweh's initial reaction seems more stunned than wrathful:

> Yahweh asked Cain, "Where is your brother Abel?" "I do not know," he replied. "Am I my brother's guardian?" "What have you done?" Yahweh asked. "Listen! Your brother's blood is crying out to me from the ground." (4:9–10)

Did Cain know that when he "set on his brother Abel," he would end up killing him? Did he truly intend to strike a mortal blow? Might Cain himself not have wondered where Abel truly was as his dead brother lay before him? Did he fully comprehend what had happened? So often, the spontaneous human reaction to news of the death of a close relative is denial: "No, no, this can't be!" What had Cain done? Not Cain alone but even Yahweh might wonder.

But now Yahweh does just what Cain may most have feared. He takes away from him the little that he has left after his parents' expulsion from Eden. Cain's sacrifice was of the sort that in religious studies is called *propitiatory.* A propitiatory sacrifice is a preemptive sacrifice. Once, as a teenager, I suffered a little on-the-job accident, and my employer surprised me by thrusting upon me three or four twenty-dollar bills—a tidy bonus in 1958. I was puzzled, but that night my father explained: the boss was afraid that I might sue. To avert that, to render his young employee propitious, he made an eighty-dollar propitiatory sacrifice. This is what Cain did when he sacrificed some of the produce from his field to Yahweh. He gave Yahweh part of the crop in the hope that Yahweh would not commandeer the whole crop, or deny Cain access to the field itself. But now, in the aftermath of Abel's slaying, Yahweh does just what Cain most feared He would do. He takes from him the very possibility of agriculture in the following words:

> "Now be cursed and banned from the ground that has opened its mouth to receive your brother's blood at your hands. When you till the ground it will no longer yield up its strength to you. A restless wanderer will you be on earth." (4:11–12)

In effect, is Yahweh not sentencing Cain to death? Will the killer not starve if he cannot farm? Cain seems to think so, and would we really have been surprised if Yahweh had struck Cain dead as punishment for his crime?

> Cain then said to Yahweh, "My punishment is greater than I can bear. Look, today you drive me from the surface of the earth. I must hide from you, and be a restless wanderer on the earth. Why, whoever comes across me will kill me!" (4:13–14)

Why does Yahweh not reply with righteous indignation, "So be it!"? Perhaps because at this point in the story, no human being is around to kill Cain except Adam, Cain's father. Were Adam to kill his remaining and only son, would Cain's blood not cry out as loudly to Yahweh as Abel's does? For whatever reason, in the final lines of the episode, Yahweh chooses to deprive Cain of his livelihood and yet forbid his murder:

> "Very well, then," Yahweh replied, "whoever kills Cain will suffer a sevenfold vengeance." So Yahweh put a mark on Cain, so that no one coming across him would kill him. Cain left Yahweh's presence and settled in the Land of Nod, east of Eden. (4:15–16)

Yahweh's opposition to murder is clear. His administration of justice is much less clear and, in any case, includes no reference to any punishing "Fire" in an afterlife. Whatever punishment Cain is to suffer, even if it amounts to slow capital punishment, must be imposed during his earthly lifetime.

Meanwhile, may we not ask: Was rehabilitation entirely out of the question? Under what circumstances if any might Cain have been permitted to remain "on the earth" and cultivate it as before? Could he have repented of his sin, and could Yahweh have forgiven him?

As it happens, this very question carries us back again to the corpse and to the qur'anic telling of this tale as it concludes:

> But God sent a raven clawing out the earth to show him how he might bury the corpse of his brother. He said: "What a

wretch I am! Am I incapable of being like this raven and so
conceal my brother's corpse?" And so he ended up remorseful.

It is for this reason that We decreed to the Children of Israel
that he who kills a soul neither in revenge for another, nor to
prevent corruption on earth, it is as if he killed the whole of
mankind; whereas he who saves a soul, it is as if he has saved
the whole of mankind. Our messengers came to them bearing
clear proofs, but many of them thereafter were disobedient on
earth. (5:31–32)

Allah sends the guilty son a raven for two reasons, it would seem.
First, so that the innocent son's body may be buried. Second, so that
the guilty son may be induced to express grief and remorse—"What
a wretch I am!"—and end up remorseful. The innocent son was not
mistaken in predicting the "Fire" that awaited "wrongdoers," including
potentially his brother. Yet Allah, although He never tires of repeating in the Qur'an that He will punish those who deserve punishment,
is equally tireless in repeating that He is merciful with the repentant.
In this passage, we are led to believe that the killer may not suffer the
worst after all, for he has repented and done the right thing for his dead
brother.

The phrase "my brother's corpse" is literally, in the Arabic, "my
brother's nakedness," but the phrase does not mean that Abel died without clothing. It means that an unburied corpse is indecent, in the sense
that it needs what we ourselves, speaking English, call a "decent burial."
The qur'anic text does not state but strongly implies that the surviving
brother buried the dead brother. It is as if the raven, sent by Allah, has
conveyed the very idea that the decent and proper place for a corpse is
buried underground.

On this reading, Allah implies when He says, "*It is for this reason,*

that We decreed to the Children of Israel that he who kills a
soul neither in revenge for another, nor to prevent corruption
on earth, it is as if he killed the whole of mankind; whereas
he who saves a soul, it is as if he has saved the whole of mankind. (5:32)

In an earlier era, in other words, He had told the story of the two sons to the "Children of Israel," the Jews, in the same way that it is told here to Muhammad—namely, as a moral fable against the taking, and for the saving, of human life. Read in one way, the words just quoted can be understood to acknowledge the fact that this respect for human life has been and still is a part of Jewish tradition. It appears in the Talmud (Mishnah Sanhedrin 4:5), though it is not in the Bible. But Michael Lodahl in his book *Claiming Abraham: Reading the Bible and the Qur'an Side by Side,* citing the Talmud and discussing a contemporary Muslim commentator on Qur'an 5:32, writes: "His assumption, like that of virtually all traditional Muslim exegesis, is that this compelling principle—'whoever saves a life is like one who saves the lives of all mankind'—likely was in the original scriptures of the Jews but subsequently suppressed or removed."[3]

A more grievous charge comes in the final verse of the excerpt we are considering: "Our messengers came to them bearing clear proofs, but many of them thereafter were disobedient on earth" (5:32). Disobedient in what regard? The context seems clearly to indicate: disobedient in the taking of human life. Previous prophets—perhaps including Jesus—"came to them," Jews and perhaps Christians as well, "bearing clear proofs." The moral fable of the two sons is just such a "proof"— namely, a proof that murder is evil in Allah's eyes. And yet Allah reminds Muhammad in this verse that murder remains frequent among Jews and the Christians, as indeed it does, even if contemporary Jews or Christians might easily counter, Is it any less frequent among Muslims?

Allah's prohibition of murder is not absolute. The qualification "in revenge for another" reserves the right not just of self-defense but also of retaliation. As for the much broader qualification "to prevent corruption on earth," its ramifications are explored in the verses that follow. But as these seem generally to leave the story of the two sons behind, I have chosen not to extend the target excerpt past Qur'an 5:32.

As we compare the presentations of God in these two tellings of a single story, what differences and similarities come into view?

First of all, God clearly exercises the authority of an attentive judge in both accounts. Confronted with human crime, He does not look on with detached indifference, as if this need be none of His business. Yahweh's emotional involvement with the death of Abel seems greater in the biblical account than does Allah's in the qur'anic. Nothing in Qur'an 5 quite corresponds, in other words, to the agitation of "Your brother's blood is crying out to me from the ground" in Genesis 4. But if Allah's manner is less impulsive and more aloof or contained in the Qur'an, His solicitude, His care, seems distinctly greater there. As if demonstrating or applying to Himself the dictum that "he who saves a soul, it is as if he has saved the whole of mankind," Allah reaches out in Qur'an 5 to save the soul of even history's first murderer. He is, in a word, more *merciful* in Qur'an 5 than is Yahweh in Genesis 4.

In Genesis 4, Yahweh appears more compromised by his involvement with His human creatures than Allah does in Qur'an 5. What drove Cain to kill Abel? Was it Yahweh's rejection of his sacrifice? Genesis 4 does not rule that out. Qur'an 5:30 does rule it out: "His soul tempted him to kill his brother, so he killed him and ended up among the lost." The murderer perpetrates his crime entirely on his own; it is a crime of his passion and his alone. Allah—quite above the fray of human relations in Qur'an 5—had nothing to do with it.

Most striking of all, however, Yahweh in Genesis 4 directs his attention narrowly and exclusively to the human beings then in the world. Moreover, His only interlocutor is Cain. He does not look past the lifetimes of Cain and Abel, as Allah does in the Qur'an, or speak of the whole sweep of human history through time and beyond it into the afterlife. As Allah does that, He characterizes Himself as the Lord who addresses not only Muhammad nor only Muhammad's Muslim followers but also Jews, Christians, and humankind at large. Such is Allah's self-understanding in the Qur'an: He is always talking to everybody at once, and this makes Him seem more decisive, more certain in advance of the universal and permanent significance of all that He says and does. In Genesis, Yahweh seems to some extent a work of self-creation still in progress. In the Qur'an, by contrast, Allah seems a work already accomplished turning to the correction of a creation also accomplished but in need of the final revision that only He can provide.

3

Noah

If only because it is so often turned into a children's story, a children's play, or even, latterly, a delightful children's museum,[1] the story of Noah—the ark with the animals marching in two by two, the forty days and forty nights of rain, and the lovely rainbow when the rain stops—may be the most familiar single episode in the entire Bible. Yet in both the Bible and the Qur'an, Noah stands at the center of a story told effectively for adults only. In either account, God is a terrifying figure, not a consoling one, and yet He is terrifying for reasons that differ strikingly from one scripture to the other.

In the Qur'an, Allah mentions Noah again and again, often quite briefly, but His two longer accounts are particularly revealing. One occurs at Sura 71, the sura (chapter) named for Noah. In its entirety, this short sura—the story of a Noah without an ark—reads as follows:

> We sent Noah to his people:
>
> "Warn your people before there comes to them a painful torment."
>
> He said: "My people, I am to you a manifest warner, that you worship God, fear Him and obey me, and He will forgive you your sins and defer you to a stated term. When God's term arrives it cannot be deferred, if only you knew."

He said: "My Lord, I call on my people, night and day, but my call only makes them flee further away.

"Whenever I call them together that You may forgive them, they place their fingers in their ears, wrap themselves up in their garments, grow headstrong and swell in arrogance.

"So I invited them openly.

"Then I addressed them in public.

"Then I spoke to them in faint tones.

"I said: 'Ask your Lord to forgive you, for He is All-Forgiving, and He will let flow the sky in torrents upon you, furnish you with wealth and progeny, provide you with gardens, and cause rivers to flow for you.

" 'Why are you not in awe of God's majesty, though He created you at every stage?

" 'Do you not see how God created seven heavens, piled one upon another, setting the moon among them as an illumination and the sun a glowing lamp?

" 'God it was Who caused you to sprout from the earth—and what sprouting! Then He shall resurrect you therein—and what a raising He shall raise you! God it was Who levelled out the earth for you, that you may travel its diverse roads.' "

Noah said: "My Lord, they have disobeyed me and followed one whose wealth and progeny only increases him in loss."

And they practiced utmost guile.

They said: "Do not abandon your gods. Do not abandon Wadd, nor Suwā', Yaghuth, Yā'uq, nor Nasr."

Many have they led astray. Lord, increase the wicked in error!

Because of their sins, they were made to drown and herded into a Fire, finding none to come to their aid save God.

Noah said: "My Lord, leave no habitations on earth for the unbelievers. If You let them be, they will lead Your servants astray, and will beget nothing but the dissolute and the blaspheming. My Lord, forgive me, and forgive my parents, as also any who enters my house as a believer. And forgive believing men and believing women and increase not the wicked save in perdition." (Qur'an 71:1–28)

The story of Noah that Allah tells here finds its strongest biblical echoes not in the Genesis saga of Noah (Genesis 6–9) but in the stories of the various prophets of Israel. The Hebrew word for "prophet" is *nabi'*; Arabic, belonging to the same language family, uses the same word. Muhammad is the *nabi'* whom Allah sends to the people of Mecca, just as in the story just quoted Noah is the *nabi'* whom Allah sends to "his [Noah's] people." Noah, like Muhammad, warns his polytheistic people that they must convert to the worship of the one true God or suffer grave consequences. The biblical prophets warn the Israelites that if they *abandon* the worship of the one true God, they will suffer comparable consequences; often enough, the biblical prophets condemn Israel because the nation has in fact been guilty of just this desertion.

In short, the Noah of Qur'an 71 is less like the Noah of Genesis—who, within the Bible, is not a prophet at all—than he is like the prophet Jeremiah:

> In the days of King Josiah, Yahweh said to me [Jeremiah], "Have you seen what disloyal Israel has done? How she has made her way up every high hill and to every green tree, and played the whore there? I thought, 'After doing all this she will come back to me.' But she did not come back. Her faithless sister Judah saw this. She also saw that I had repudiated disloyal Israel for all her adulteries and given her her divorce papers. Her faithless sister Judah, however, was not afraid: she too went and played the whore. And with her shameless whoring, she polluted the country; she committed adultery with stones and pieces of wood. Worse than all this: Judah, her faithless sister, has come back to me not in sincerity, but only in pretense, Yahweh declares."
>
> And Yahweh said to me, "Disloyal Israel is upright, compared with faithless Judah. So go and shout words toward the north, and say:
>
> Come back, disloyal Israel,
> Yahweh declares,
> I shall frown on you no more,
> since I am merciful,

Yahweh declares.
I shall not keep my anger for ever.
Only acknowledge your guilt:
how you have rebelled against Yahweh your God,
how you have prostituted yourself with the Strangers
under every green tree
and have not listened to my voice,
Yahweh declares." (Jeremiah 3:6–13)

For the prophets of Ancient Israel, monotheism was like wedded monogamy, and polytheism was like the promiscuity of a wife who turns herself into a whore and sleeps with many men (= many gods). Beginning with Moses, Yahweh had warned Israel that though He had brought her out of exile and bondage and into this quasi-marital covenant with Himself, He would divorce her and send her back into bondage and exile if she were ever unfaithful to Him. That threat, though luridly evoked elsewhere in Jeremiah, is not mentioned in this passage, but it hovers in the background.

Yet Yahweh is merciful, just as Allah is merciful in Qur'an 71. He is a husband who yearns for reconciliation with His wife if she will but admit the truth that "you have prostituted yourself with the Strangers." If she will go that far, He will graciously forgive her and take her back as His wife. Yet she will not. In an adjacent passage, Yahweh laments in fury:

"Does a nation change its gods?
—and these are not gods at all!
Yet my people have exchanged their Glory [Yahweh]
for the Useless One! [Baal]
You heavens, stand aghast at this,
horrified, utterly appalled,
Yahweh declares.
For my people have committed two crimes:
they have abandoned me,
the fountain of living water,
and dug water-tanks for themselves,

cracked water-tanks
that hold no water." (Jeremiah 2:11–13)

The water tanks that hold no water are the gods that are no gods. True, the qur'anic and the biblical passages are as different as espousal and divorce are different. Through Noah, God warns Noah's people about what will happen *unless* they convert from worshipping Wadd, Suwā', Yaghuth, Ya'uq, and Nasr to worshipping God. Through Jeremiah, Yahweh warns Israel of what will happen *if and when* they stop worshipping Him and start worshipping Baal or other gods "that are not gods at all." In the first case, conversion is demanded; in the second, it is condemned. Yet in both passages, a warning is delivered, submission to the same God is at issue, and in both passages the warning is ignored. Noah's people continue in the worship of Wadd and company; Israel continues to choose "the Useless One" over "their [the Israelites'] Glory"—namely, the Glory of their God.

In both instances the deity then inflicts catastrophic mass punishment on the peoples that have rejected Him. In the Book of Jeremiah, true to His early word, Yahweh sends an invader who destroys Jerusalem and carries Jeremiah's people into a new exile and a new bondage. In Qur'an 71, Allah drowns Noah's people and then sends them to burn forever in hell: "they were made to drown and herded into a Fire." In other words, they died by drowning and then were punished in the fire of hell forever. Strikingly, there is no ark in this version of Noah's story, and there are no survivors except, apparently, Noah himself.

Such is the master plot of prophecy. A people—either by failing to convert (Qur'an) or refusing to stay converted (Bible)—is worshipping one or more false gods rather than the one true God. God sends His prophet to preach the truth, often paying major attention to the kings or leaders of the people, and to warn that unless the people hears and accepts the truth, God will punish them severely. A minority of the people, at most, heeds the prophet; more, or sometimes all, ignore, reject, or even attack him. The prophet assures them that God is merciful and will forgive even those who have sinned against Him if they will only repent and turn (or return) to Him. They do not repent, all but (at most) a tiny faithful remnant; they do not turn (or return) to Him; and God, as He had threatened, sends disaster upon them.

This plot is repeatedly re-enacted in the Bible and repeatedly recalled in the Qur'an, but it is not the plot of the biblical Noah story. In the latter story (Genesis 6–9), Yahweh proclaims disaster not at the end of the story but at the beginning. The story begins with Yahweh alone on stage, talking to Himself, as He does at the beginning of Genesis. Only after announcing His resolve to Himself does He announce it to Noah.

> Yahweh regretted having made human beings on earth and was grieved at heart. And Yahweh said, "I shall rid the surface of the earth of the human beings whom I created—human and animal, the creeping things and the birds of heaven—for I regret having made them."
>
> God said to Noah, "I have decided that the end has come for all living things, for the earth is full of lawlessness because of human beings.... For my part I am going to send the flood, the waters, on earth, to destroy all living things having the breath of life under heaven; everything on earth is to perish. But with you I shall establish my covenant and you will go aboard the ark, yourself, your sons, your wife, and your sons' wives along with you. From all living creatures, from all living things, you must take two of each kind aboard the ark, to save their lives with yours; they must be a male and a female." (Genesis 6:6–7, 13, 17–19)

You may have noticed that the deity's name changes from "Yahweh" to "God" in the passage just quoted. The Noah story as we have it in the received text of the Book of Genesis began as two stories, one of which knew the deity as Yahweh and the other as Elohim ("God" in Hebrew). Further complicating the textual situation, the redactor who combined the two has made his own editorial additions or enhancements to the story. As a result, the story of the building of the ark—the ship on which the designated survivors are to ride out the catastrophic flood—is repetitive and sometimes confusing. The great flood does come, however, as a welling up of the waters beneath the earth and a raining down of the waters above the earth. World genocide does follow. Then, at last, the waters recede, the survivors disembark, and life resumes.

Back on dry land, Noah—who has spoken not a word to this point in the story—offers Yahweh the burnt sacrifice of several animals, still never speaking a word.

> Yahweh smelt the pleasing smell and said to himself, "Never again will I curse the earth because of human beings, because their heart contrives evil from their infancy. Never again will I strike down every living thing as I have done." (8:21)

Once again, we encounter the mysteriously omniscient biblical narrator who knows what Yahweh says to Himself or, as the King James Version has it, says "in his heart." But how secure is this resolution of restraint? At Genesis 9:12–15, we read a declaration similar in intent but ominously different in its wording:

> "And this," God said, "is the sign of the covenant which I now make between myself and you and every living creature with you for all ages to come: I now set my bow in the clouds and it will be the sign of the covenant between me and the earth. When I gather the clouds over the earth and the bow appears in the clouds, I shall recall the covenant between myself and you and every living creature, in a word all living things, and never again will the waters become a flood to destroy all living things." (9:12–15)

As Yahweh, the deity promises never again to destroy the world. As Elohim, He promises only never to destroy it again *by water.* This is the distinction that enlivens a couplet heard in two exegetically alert Negro spirituals: "I Got a Home in That Rock" and "Mary, Don't You Weep":

> God gave Noah the rainbow sign:
> No more water, the fire next time.

The Fire Next Time is the title of a manifesto that the late, gifted black writer James Baldwin published to electrifying effect amid the 1960s groundswell of activism on behalf of racial justice. Interpretive alertness in the reading of scripture is not what people love most about Negro spirituals. For that matter, it's not what I love most about them. But whoever came up with "No more water, the fire next time" was both an exegete and a social prophet.

But back to Genesis:

What was the "lawlessness" that so troubled Yahweh Elohim that He had to destroy almost all life? We don't know. At this point in His story, as the Bible tells it, He has given no laws to the humans whom He expelled from Eden and who, it seems, have now greatly increased in number. *No laws, no lawlessness*, one might think. But what does this passage say about the mind of Yahweh Elohim? Does He only think to impose laws after seeing an action performed that He wants to forbid? The Noah story ends with an act of lawgiving, but the law is one that Yahweh Elohim might better have given in an earlier generation to Cain and Abel, or even to Adam and Eve:

> "Every living thing that moves will be yours to eat, no less than the foliage of the plants. I give you everything, with this exception: you must not eat flesh with life, that is to say blood, in it. And I shall demand account of your life-blood, too. I shall demand it of every animal, and of man. Of man as regards his fellow-man, I shall demand account for human life.
>
> He who sheds the blood of man,
>> by man shall his blood be shed,
> For in the image of God
>> was man created." (9:3–6)

Serious as it is, this question of lawlessness and lawfulness is not the only question about God that Genesis 6–9 leaves hanging in the air.

At the start of the story, we read: "But Noah won Yahweh's favor" (6:8). Why? What had he done to win Yahweh's favor? How does anyone win Yahweh's favor? It happens, apparently, but we don't know how or why it happens, and the fact that we don't raises the possibility that Yahweh is capricious enough to have chosen Noah at random, for no reason. If His character is such that He might save for no reason, might He not also destroy for no reason? As I said at the start of this chapter, God—Yahweh Elohim in the biblical account and Allah in the qur'anic account—is terrifying in both but for different reasons in each.

And what of the uncounted dead in the biblical version? Was there anything the drowned human beings, not to speak of the drowned animals, might have done to placate Yahweh and save their lives? Could they somehow have averted this genocide? All we know is that they, unlike those addressed by Noah in Qur'an 71 or by Jeremiah in the Book of Jeremiah, were given no opportunity to repent of whatever wrong they may have done and throw themselves on the mercy of the merciful Yahweh Elohim. No, Yahweh Elohim takes mankind by surprise, and in the Gospel of Matthew, Jesus underscores this very point with regard to the judgment that he himself will one day render as the "Son of Man":

As it was in Noah's day, so will it be when the Son of man comes. For in those days before the Flood people were eating, drinking, taking wives, taking husbands, right up to the day Noah went into the ark, and they suspected nothing till the Flood came and swept them all away. This is what it will be like when the Son of man comes. (Matthew 24:37–39)

In the Genesis account, Yahweh Elohim's motivations seem only lightly touched by morality and totally untouched by religious orthodoxy—that is, by anything like worshipping the right god rather than the wrong god or gods. Yahweh Elohim in Genesis 6–9 does not demand that human beings be monotheists rather than polytheists, or Yahwists rather than Baalists, or Muslims rather than Waddists, Suwā'ists, etc. Horrifying as the "convert or die" ultimatum of Qur'an 71 may be, it is vastly preferable to mass death inflicted without warning and without any ethical or confessional ground whatsoever. Better a grim choice than none at all.

After lingering this long over the Noah story as told in the Book of Genesis, it is time to look at the second, longer, and particularly revealing Noah story that Allah tells at Qur'an 11:25–49:

We sent Noah to his people, saying: "I am come to you as a clear warner. You are not to worship anything but God. I fear for you the torment of a grievous Day."

The chieftains of those who disbelieved among his people said: "We do not see you as anything but a human being like us. We do not see that any have followed you except our riff-raff, as it seems. We do not see that you have any advantage over us. Rather, we think you are liars."

He said: "My people, tell me this. If I am certain of my Lord, and He has brought me a mercy from Him which was hidden from you, are we to force you to accept it when you are averse to it?

"My people, I ask you no money for it: my wage falls only on God. I am not about to drive away those who believed: they shall encounter their Lord. But I see you are a people that do not understand.

"My people, who will take my side against God if I drive them away? Will you not recollect? I do not say to you that I possess the treasures of God. I do not know the Unseen, nor do I say I am an angel, nor do I tell those whom your eyes despise that God will not bring them good, for God knows best what is in their hearts. If I did so I would indeed be wicked."

They said: "O Noah, you have argued with us: indeed, you have exceeded the limit in argument. So now bring upon us what you threaten us with, if you are truthful."

He said: "It is God Who will bring it upon you, if He wills. Nor can you escape it. My counsel, should I wish to counsel you, will be of no benefit to you if God desires to confound you. He is your Lord, and to Him you shall return."

Or do they say: "He fabricated it?" Say: 'If I fabricated it, upon me falls my sinful act, and I am quit of your sinning.'"

It was revealed to Noah: "None shall believe from your people except those who have already believed, so do not feel sad because of what they do. Build the Ark where We can see you and with Our inspiration, and do not plead with me regarding those who are wicked. They shall be drowned."

Noah then builds the Ark. Whenever a group of notables of his people passed by, they would mock him.

He said: "If you mock us, we mock you as you mock. You will surely know upon whom shall fall a torment that will abase him, upon whom shall fall an everlasting torment."

And so it came to pass that when Our command went out, and water gushed forth to the surface, We said: "Load up on board two of every kind, and your family—except for those foretold—and those who believed." But the believers with him were few.

He said: "Go on board. In the name of God may it sail and anchor! My Lord is All-Forgiving, Compassionate to each."

And so it sailed with them amidst waves like mountains. Noah called out to his son, who had kept away: "My son, embark with us and do not remain among the unbelievers."

He said: "I shall find refuge on a mountain which shall protect me from the waters."

He said: "Today there is no protector from the command of God, except him to whom God shows mercy."

Then the waves came between them and he was among those who were drowned.

It was said: "O earth, swallow your waters! O sky, desist!" The waters subsided, the judgement was passed. The Ark settled upon Mount Judi and it was proclaimed: "Away with the wicked!"

Noah then called out to his Lord, saying: "Lord, my son is of my family. Your promise is the truth, and you are the fairest of judges."

He said: "O Noah, he is not of your family. It is an act unrighteous. So ask Me not for that of which you have no knowledge. I counsel you not to be foolish."

He said: "My Lord, I seek refuge in You lest I be one who asks You for what I have no knowledge of! If you do not forgive me and show me mercy, I shall surely be lost."

It was said: "O Noah, disembark in Our peace, and with Our blessings upon you and upon the nations with you. Other

nations We shall grant prosperity, and then there shall touch
them from Us a torment most painful."

These are reports of the Unseen which We reveal to you.
You knew them not, neither you nor your people, beforehand.
So be patient: the final outcome will vindicate the pious.

In idiomatic American English, the phrase "prophet of doom" is
roughly synonymous with "crank," if not also with "hoax." The prophet
of doom, we are to understand, usually turns out to be prophesying
a doom that never comes. Cooler heads supposedly know enough not
to be alarmed by such prophets. But, of course, sometimes doom does
come, and then the prophets once dismissed as cranks are belatedly
honored as brave visionaries, even saviors of their peoples.

At the opening of this second telling of the Noah story, as in Qur'an
71, Allah presents Noah as a prophet warning "his people" of "the torment of a grievous day" unless they convert to the worship of Allah
alone. But there is a rhetorical difference in how the two accounts por-
tray Prophet Noah in action. In Qur'an 71, Noah offers a positive incentive for why his people should worship only Allah. Allah rules over all
of nature, he argues; the false gods, by implication, lack this enriching
power. Accordingly, in Qur'an 71, if the people will but beg Allah's forgiveness for the sin of worshipping Wadd, Suwā', and the other false
gods mentioned, then the true God "will let flow the sky in torrents
upon you, furnish you with wealth and progeny, provide you with gardens, and cause rivers to flow for you" (71:11–12). In Qur'an 11, Noah offers
only the negative incentive of avoiding the "grievous Day." This is not
only the day of the punitive flood that Noah knows of and his hearers
do not, but also the day of final judgment that will consign the drowned
disbelievers to "the Fire."

In this second version of the Qur'an's Noah story, Allah stresses the
importance of accepting the messenger as well as the message. The
"chieftains of those who disbelieved among his people" reject Noah's
claim to his exalted calling: "We do not see you as anything but a
human being like us," attracting only "our riff-raff" as followers. The
socially leveling power of submission to Allah, its capacity to trivialize
differences of wealth and station, lives and breathes in this verse and
those that follow.

The notables insult Noah and his lowly followers: "we think you are liars." Noah is certain of his divine vocation: "I am certain of my Lord," and "He has brought me a Mercy from Him." That is, Noah knows in his heart that in the catastrophe that impends, he will be spared. What can he do? "Are we to force you to accept it when you are averse to it?"

This Noah will not and truly cannot do. *The Study Quran* in its comment on this verse (11:28) quotes what has become in recent years one of the more frequently cited single verses in the Qur'an—namely, Qur'an 2:256, "There is no compulsion in religion. Right guidance has been distinguished from error."

Yet Allah allows himself what he denies Noah or other mere prophets. According to an old nautical saw, "The ship that does not answer to the rudder will answer to the rock." Noah's people are like the ship: if they do not answer to his prophetic warning (the rudder), then they will answer to Allah's punitive flood (the rock). Their error—and their suffering—at that point will confirm Noah's truth; he can provide no earlier confirmation; all he can offer is his own good faith.

In the verses that follow (11:29–31), Noah, by arguing earnestly for his own prophetic legitimacy, argues simultaneously for the reality of both the peril of divine punishment and the availability of divine mercy. The depth of his feeling resounds in the thrice repeated "My people!" In delivering his warning message, he is not after their money: "I ask not of you any wealth in return for it; my reward lies only with God." And, by at least a difference in emphasis from Qur'an 71, he does not promise wealth or arcane knowledge if they accept his message: "I do not say to you that I possess the treasures of God. I do not know the Unseen, not do I say I am an angel…." His critics are right: he is only a fellow human being—a man like themselves, not an angel—but he does not scorn the "riff-raff" of believers whom they scorn, for Allah accepts those who submit to him, as these humble followers have done, and who is Noah to reject those whom Allah has accepted?

At this point, Noah's opponents, misconstruing the messenger as a magician, the agent of the very doom that he prophesies, challenge him to "bring it on": "So now bring upon us what you threaten us with, if you are truthful" (11:32). Noah clarifies resolutely but with a touch of menace:

He said: "It is God Who will bring it upon you, if He wills.
Nor can you escape it. My counsel, should I wish to counsel
you, will be of no benefit to you if God desires to confound
you. He is your Lord, and to Him you shall return." (11:33–34)

Then, at this point in Qur'an 11, there comes one of those moments in
which Allah interrupts himself to speak privately, as it were, to Muhammad
but also past Muhammad pointedly to us who are overhearing his
advice to his prophet. Allah says:

Or do they say: "He fabricated it"? Say: "If I fabricated it, upon
me falls my sinful act, and I am quit of your sinning." (11:35)

To paraphrase only very lightly, what Allah says, speaking past Muhammad
to us, is: "Do you think Muhammad made all this up? If so, so
much the worse for him. But if not, so much the worse for you."

Past this point, narrative momentum picks up. God tells Noah the
bad news that he will be able to save from the flood only the few whom
he has already converted to the worship of the true God. His stern
counsel to Muhammad is that he should

"not feel sad because of what they do. Build the Ark where We
can see you and with Our inspiration, and do not plead with
Me regarding those who are wicked. They shall be drowned."
(11:36–37)

In the Bible, Jeremiah gives full-throated expression to his distress at
the disaster that, in Yahweh's name and at Yahweh's command, he has
prophesied for Israel. To whom are all the questions in the following
verses addressed if not to the deity who is poised to bring disaster upon
his people Israel?

Incurable sorrow overtakes me,
my heart fails me....
The wound of the daughter of my people wounds me too,
all looks dark to me, terror grips me.
Is there no balm in Gilead any more?

Is there no doctor there?
Then why is there no progress
in the cure of the daughter of my people?
Who will turn my head into a fountain,
and my eyes into a spring of tears,
that I can weep day and night
over the slain of the daughter of my people?
    (Jeremiah 8:18, 21–23)

In the Qur'an, Noah directs no such laments, no "Jeremiads," at God as the floodwaters engulf his people, with the exception of one hesitant moment that we shall consider just below.

Noah builds the ark and loads on it his family, the animals two by two, and the few believers among his people. His opponents scoff. Noah replies, in effect, that he who scoffs last scoffs best. Shortly, the waters gush forth. Mountainous waves begin to heave. But at this juncture, Allah tells a story within the story that has no parallel in the Bible.

The ark has set sail when Noah sees that his son has "kept away." He is still ashore. Noah cries out: "My son, embark with us and do not remain among the unbelievers" (11:42). But the unbelieving son thinks he can save himself by riding out the flood on a mountaintop. The floodwaters rise; the son drowns. Presently Allah orders the floodwaters to recede, taking the corpses of the drowned with them. ("And it was proclaimed: 'Away with the wicked.'") And then Allah tells the story of a subtle confrontation between Himself and his prophet.

Noah's disbelieving son is dead and gone, but Noah, evidently still thinking about him, dares to speak of him to Allah: "Lord, my son is of my family." As a flat declarative sentence, this observation says almost nothing. But imagine an actor putting into these halting, perhaps choked out words the emotion of a father reeling from such a loss: "Lord…my son…A member of my own family…"

Is Noah not asking Allah to answer the questions, How is my son? What has happened to him? What *will* happen to him? But as if suddenly aware of the huge risk he has run in asking Allah to stoop to fill in these emotional and informational blanks, Noah hurries on to a sentence of preemptive praise: "Your promise is the truth, and you are the fairest of judges."

As Allah continues the story, he has had no difficulty reading between Noah's lines. He rebukes Noah, but gently:

> He said: "O Noah, he is not of your family. It is an act unrigh-teous. So ask Me not for that of which you have no knowledge. I counsel you not to be foolish." (11:46)

Noah is duly contrite, and the Noah story concludes with Allah's quali-fied blessing on the new community that Noah, his family, and the sur-vivors from the drowned town, with the salvaged animals, will build:

> "O Noah, disembark in Our peace, and with Our blessings upon you and upon the nations with you. Other nations We shall grant prosperity, and then there shall touch them from Us a torment most painful." (11:48)

The reference to future torment reflects Allah's knowledge that the message of Islam will be forgotten eventually so that He will have to send new messengers threatening new peoples with new punishments unless they renounce their new false gods and worship him.

This is to conclude the main Noah story, but the story-within-a-story calls for a further word of commentary. When Allah tells Noah that his son "is not of your family," he speaks past Prophet Noah to and about the future Muslim 'ummah or worldwide religious "people" (the meaning of the Arabic word). Theirs was and is not to be a community based on genealogy or consanguinity but on a shared commitment to submit to Allah as the only God and to accept Prophet Muhammad as truly His messenger.

For Christian readers, Qur'an 11:46, "he is not of your family," might well evoke several echoes from the New Testament. Most sharply, there is Mark 3:31–35:

> Now his mother and his brothers arrived and, standing out-side, sent in a message asking for him. A crowd was sitting round him at the time the message was passed to him, "Look, your mother and brothers and sisters are outside asking for you." He replied, "Who are my mother and my brothers?" And

looking at those sitting in a circle round him, he said, "Here are my mother and my brothers. Anyone who does the will of God, that person is my brother and sister and mother."

Paul, preaching Christianity years after Jesus's death, in an arc between Jerusalem and Rome, took Jesus's transfer of filial identity to the "family" of his followers and used it to transform God's covenant with Abraham into a covenant with all humanity as Abraham's spiritual descendants:

> There can be neither Jew nor Greek, there can be neither slave nor freeman, there can be neither male nor female—for you are all one in Christ Jesus. And simply by being Christ's, you are that *progeny* of Abraham, the heirs named in the promise. (Galatians 3:28–29; *The New Jerusalem Bible* italicizes progeny to signal Paul's allusion to Genesis 12:7, where Yahweh's promise to Abraham is made equally to his progeny.)[2]

Christianity and Islam, as world communities, are alike in being conceived not as natural communities but as intentional communities. It is obviously the case on a planet with 2 billion Christians and 1.5 billion Muslims that millions are "born into" one community or the other with, effectively, little choice about the matter. And yet neither world religious community began as birth-based, and neither has entirely forgotten its origins. The unique strength of such intentional communities is that anyone can join them; anyone can convert to them, for they are Abraham's spiritual progeny. The unique weakness is that anyone can quit them; anyone can apostatize. Birth-based communities cannot grow so easily, but neither can they shrink so easily. Thus, a Jew who is not a Judaist—not a practitioner of Judaism—is still a Jew. There's the difference.

As noted above, nothing in Genesis 6–9, the biblical Noah story, corresponds to the story of Noah's recalcitrant son. However, I cannot resist mentioning, as a minor comic interlude, Noah's recalcitrant wife in the late medieval mystery play *Noyes Fludd*. In this anonymous and slightly irreverent work of popular drama, Noah's wife is certainly not a disbeliever. She believes not only in God but also in Jesus and all the saints as well. And she has no doubt, either, that the Great Flood is coming. All the same, she absolutely will *not* come on board the ark unless she can bring her lady friends—her "gossips," as she calls them—with her. They are good women. She will not have them swept away in the flood.

To me, the work seems droller and wittier in the rhyming, rollicking Middle English than in any modernization.[3] For fun, however, here is one exchange between Noah and Mrs. Noah in my own rough-and-ready modernization:

NOAH.
Wife, come in. Why stand you there?
You're always forward, that I swear.
Come, in God's name; high time it were
    For fear lest we drown.

NOAH'S WIFE.
Well, sir, set up your sail
And row on out, hearty and hale,
For without any fail
    I will not out of this town.
Unless I have my gossips, every last one,
One foot further I'm not a-goin'.
They shall not drown, by Saint John,
    If I can save their life.
They loved me full well, by Christ.
Either them on your ship you hoist,
Or else row on out, Noah, in high haste,
    And get you a new wife.

If accommodation is occasionally made in the Tanakh, notably in the Book of Jonah, for levity of this sort, I detect none in either the New Testament or the Qur'an, and this second qur'anic account of the Noah story ends on an exceptionally sober and far-reaching note. In Qur'an 11:49, the last verse in our second long excerpt, above, Allah once again speaks directly to Muhammad, and what he says is a kind of enlargement on Qur'an 11:35, quoted earlier, where the charge of fabrication is addressed and refuted. In 11:49, God takes explicit note of the fact that there are elements in the story as just told that Muhammad could not possibly have known beforehand, or picked up from stories in general circulation:

> These are reports of the Unseen which We reveal to you. *You knew them not, neither you nor your people, beforehand.* So be patient: the final outcome will vindicate the pious. (11:49, emphasis added)

In Christendom, East and West, from the early Middle Ages through to the seventeenth century, the mildest among the sundry hostile characterizations of Muhammad (heretic, demoniac, maniac, Anti-Christ) was that he was a mere impostor—a false prophet whose alleged revelations were all indeed fabrications.

Qur'an 11:35, where Muhammad's opponents call him a fabricator, parallels very closely Qur'an 11:27, where Noah's opponents call him a liar. In Qur'an 11:49, Allah prepares Muhammad to respond to Meccan skepticism of this sort by turning the table on his critics. Regarding completely unprecedented elements in the Noah story as God has just told it to Muhammad, Allah says, in effect, that Muhammad should argue that this very novelty proves the authenticity of the revelation. In modern American slang, one way to underscore the authenticity of a report is to say of it, "You can't make this stuff up." Such is Allah's advice to Muhammad: Muhammad could neither have made such stuff up nor imbibed it from any human source. Yet Allah braces Muhammad against charges that will indeed be made. "So be patient," Allah says to him, for "the final outcome will vindicate the pious."

Allah makes his most far-reaching correction of the Jewish and Christian scriptures not through even significant details like the story of Noah's recalcitrant son but through two much broader, structural revisions.

First, Allah takes a crucial set of the major figures in the earlier scriptures—figures who, if we were to take those scriptures on their own terms, would fall into a variety of different categories: patriarchs, priests, Levites, judges, kings, generals, counselors, prophets, seers, scribes, and others—and recasts them all as prophets sent by Allah to warn their respective peoples of the punishment that will befall them unless they worship Him alone. To take the Old Testament at face value, Abraham is not a prophet. To take the New Testament at face value, Jesus is not a prophet. But for Allah in the Qur'an, this is evidently just where the early scriptures in the faulty form in which they survive have gone astray. Allah's retelling of these stories makes His claim clear: These figures *were* prophets, and Allah explains to Muhammad just *how* they were prophets.

Second, in thus fitting the biblical stories as Jews and Christians know them to this prophetic model, Allah makes them all congruent with the story of the very prophet he is addressing—Muhammad, "the Seal of the Prophets," the last prophet that the world will ever need. As in the Noah accounts reviewed in this chapter, so at other points in the Qur'an, as we shall see, Allah turns repeatedly to address Muhammad as the last and best of his prophets. And because the Qur'an is to be recited, Allah, when speaking *to* Muhammad, is also speaking *about* Muhammad to us. But as this happens, something easily missed but even more powerful is simultaneously under way. Allah is revising the portrayal of himself as extant in the earlier scriptures. No longer reckless, unpredictable, barely moral, highly emotional, the deity who addresses Muhammad is, yes, ferociously severe but predictably, consistently so, severe on terms that do not change and are revealed from the start. Yes, He is fully prepared to consign recalcitrant human beings to "the Fire" forever, a severity that Yahweh never contemplates. Yet he is also *eager*—not merely willing—to be merciful to all those willing to accept Him as God and to recognize His *nabi'* as both a true messenger and, in the case of Muhammad, the final, definitive messenger.

4

Abraham and His Father

Although Adam became the first Muslim by repenting immediately of his disobedience and submitting himself to the judgment (and punishment) of Allah, it is Abraham whom the Qur'an presents as the truly paradigmatic Muslim not just in his maturity but even in his youth. Like Muhammad after him, Abraham in the Qur'an not only submits to Allah but fearlessly champions Him against the pretenses of any alleged rival. And because Allah repeatedly expresses His warm approval of Abraham, almost His delight, Abraham is uniquely important as a vehicle for Allah's indirect self-characterization in the Qur'an.

A richly revealing passage, and a good place to begin, is Qur'an 21:51–73. Allah has been consoling Muhammad, His culminating messenger, that though "Messengers before you were mocked," Muhammad will be vindicated as those earlier messengers were: "But those who mocked them were overwhelmed by that which they used to mock" (21:41). And before long, Allah is reminding Muhammad in more detail of the tribulations and final vindication of Abraham:

> Before, We had bestowed right guidance on Abraham, and knew him well.
>
> This was when he said to his father and his people: "What are these idols that you keep ministering to?"
>
> They said: "We found our ancestors had worshipped them."

He said: "You and your ancestors are in manifest error."

They said: "Do you come to us with the truth, or are you jesting?"

He said: "Rather, it is your Lord, Lord of the heavens and earth, Who created them.

Of this I am witness.

By God, I shall confute your idols, once you depart and turn your backs."

So he smashed them into fragments, all but their greatest, hoping they would turn back to God.

They said: "Who did this to our gods? He must truly be wicked."

They said: "We heard a young man make mention of them, called Abraham."

They said: "Bring him out in full view of people, and perhaps they will give witness."

They said: "Is it you who did this to our gods, O Abraham?"

He said: "Rather, it was this greatest among them who did it.

Ask them, if they can speak."

They reconsidered within themselves, and said: "It is you who are the wicked ones."

But then—head over heels they were made to turn: "You know these do not speak."

He said: "Do you indeed worship, apart from God, that which has no power to benefit you in anything, nor harm you?

"Shame on you and on what you worship instead of God! Will you not come to your senses?"

They said: "Burn him, and uphold your gods, if ready to act thus."

We said: "O fire, be cool and comforting to Abraham."

And they intended him malice, but We made them the losers,

And We delivered him and Lot to the land We blessed for all mankind.

And We bestowed on him Isaac and Jacob, as an added
bounty from Us,
And all We created righteous.
And We made them leaders, guiding to Our commands.
And We inspired them to do righteous deeds,
To perform the prayer, and hand out alms,
And they were Our worshippers. (21:51–73)

Intergenerational conflict between fathers and sons is a universal theme in literature and, often enough, in religion as well. Rudyard Kipling wrote, in bitterness after his son's death in World War I, "If any question why we died, / Tell them, because our fathers lied." Wilfred Owen's "The Parable of the Old Man and the Young"—a poem heavy with Abrahamic echoes—is yet another World War I poem that makes the same bitter point.

It would be a mistake, however, to read Abraham's rebellion through this perennial psychological filter. For though there is boldness in the young man's words to "his father and his people," there is no bitterness. Allah makes it plain in innumerable statements throughout the Qur'an that those who do not worship Him as the one and only deity are doomed to suffer forever in hell, and so it is an act of mercy on Abraham's part to acquaint his people with their fatal error. Warning was an essential part of Muhammad's message to the people of Mecca, and so it was also for Abraham. Just as important, Abraham is not delivering this warning simply on his own authority. Allah has deputed him for this errand, giving him "right guidance" beforehand.

How did Allah impart judgment to Abraham? At Qur'an 6:75–79, He describes how He tutored Abraham to prepare him to challenge Azar, his father (called Terah in the Bible):

This is how We made Abraham see the kingdom of the heavens and the earth, so that he would have certain faith.
When night enveloped him he saw a star;
He said: "This is my Lord."
When the star set, he said: "I love not things that set."
When he saw the rising moon, he said:
"This is my Lord," but when it set, he said:

"If my Lord does not guide me, I shall be among those who go astray. When he saw the rising sun he said

"This is my Lord, for it is larger," but when it set he said:

"O people, I am quit of your idolatry. I have set my face towards Him Who created the heavens and the earth, pure in my worship, nor am I one who associates anything with God."

The term *hanīf,* untranslated in *The Study Quran,* is translated just above as "pure in my worship" and, in the Norton Critical Edition of the Qur'an, as "one by nature upright," where the phrase "by nature" perhaps reflects the Muslim view that pure monotheism is mankind's natural religion. Muslims would later use the term *hanīf* respectfully to designate non-Christian, non-Jewish, but pre-Muhammadan monotheists (there were such Arab monotheists in the Hijaz at the time of Muhammad's birth). Among all such proto-monotheists, the *hanīf* par excellence is Abraham.

But not to digress further about the Arabic term, what Allah means to call to Muhammad's mind, in recounting how He led Abraham from relative uncertainty into absolute certainty, is that "*This was Our argument* which We conveyed to Abraham against his people. We elevate in degrees whomsoever We wish. Your Lord is All-Wise, Omniscient" (6:83, emphasis added). Allah could have raised someone else up, but it was Abraham whom he actually did raise up and whom he armed with this cosmological argument so as the more effectively to bring the saving message to Azar and his people that "it is your Lord, Lord of the heavens and earth, Who created them. Of this I am witness" (21:56).

The challenge to Azar's people then is double: first, they must accept Allah and reject all rival gods as false; second, they must accept Azar's son Abraham as a witness bringing testimony about Allah. But their reaction to this challenge, in effect, is the scoffing and dismissive "Surely you jest. Surely you can't be serious." Ah, but Abraham, Allah's messenger, could not be more serious! He demonstrates that he will not be trifled with by breaking their idols into pieces when their backs are turned, "all but their greatest, hoping they would turn back to God." The meaning of this stratagem becomes clear as the story continues.

For when the people ask who has shattered the idols and young Abraham is implicated, he says that "it was this greatest among them who did it." If they doubt him, they should ask the other, wounded idols themselves: "Ask *them*, if they can speak." At first, the idolaters do so, proceeding as if indeed the idols could answer a direct question and even accusing them: "It is you who are the wicked ones." But then, "head over heels," they return to their prior suspicion of Abraham, coming to their senses and saying, "You know these do not speak."

With these words, of course, they have fallen into Abraham's trap, and in righteous and triumphant wrath he cries, "Shame on you and on what you worship instead of God!" In reply to this, they become a lynch mob, determined to burn this outrageous young heretic at the stake. "Burn him, and uphold your gods!" they cry. But Allah foils their plan, whether or not they quite realize that it is He who has done so. The sentence, "O fire, be cool and comforting to Abraham" is not addressed to them but to the fire, after all, and at no point does Allah say that Abraham was bound or placed on any kind of pyre. "We made them the losers," Allah says, but just how this was accomplished He leaves unclear.

What is quite clear, however, is that Allah is pleased with Abraham's zeal on His behalf. Allah rewards Abraham and his brother Lot with "the land We blessed for all mankind" and further rewards Abraham with his son Isaac and his grandson Jacob. These two Allah then makes leaders and teachers of Islam, like Abraham himself—guiding them forward as Allah guided Abraham before them.

But what of Azar? Did he accept the message that his son was bringing and accept him in the end as Allah's designated messenger? It would seem not. At Qur'an 26:83–95, we read a rather touching prayer to Allah in which Abraham seems to beg forgiveness for Azar, followed by a vivid picture of the judgment that must await the older man as an intransigent unbeliever. In A. J. Arberry's poetic translation:

> My Lord, give me Judgment, and join me
>   with the righteous,
> and appoint me a tongue of truthfulness
>   among the others.
> Make me one of the inheritors of the
>   Garden of Bliss,

and forgive my father, for he is one
  of those astray.
Degrade me not upon the day when they
  are raised up,
the day when neither wealth nor sons
  shall profit
except for him who comes to God with
  a pure heart.
And Paradise shall be brought forward
  for the godfearing,
and Hell advanced for the perverse.
It shall be said to them, "Where is that
  you were serving
apart from God? Do they help you
  or help themselves?"
Then they shall be pitched into it,
  they and the perverse
and the hosts of Iblis, all together.

There is a poignancy in this passage as Allah recalls to Muhammad how Abraham first begged forgiveness for Azar but then immediately went on to concede that Hell is inescapable for those, like Azar, who in their lifetimes did not worship Allah. In this prayer, we see how far indeed Abraham's rejection of his father stands from Kipling's bitterness. And though Allah, unless He exercises His mercy option on the Day of Judgment, fully intends to punish Azar with Hellfire for all eternity, He does not fault Abraham for his devotion to the old idolater whose faith Abraham himself has abandoned. At Qur'an 31:14–15, Allah says:

And We enjoined upon man to care for his parents—his mother carried him in hardship upon hardship, and his weaning lasts two years—and to say: "Give thanks to Me and to your parents, and to Me is your homecoming." And yet, should they press you to associate with Me that of which you have no knowledge, do not obey them, but befriend them in this life, in kindness. And follow the path of one who has turned in repentance to Me.

That Allah recalls to Muhammad both Abraham's prayer and Allah's own stern counsel is the more affecting when we recall that the orphaned Muhammad's uncle and foster father, Abu Talib, never managed to break with his ancestral faith. Although he defended Muhammad against the Prophet's enemies in Mecca, Abu Talib, like Azar, was headed for Hell as an unbeliever, absent, again, some exceptional intervention on Allah's part. Faith can hold families together. It can also tear them apart.

In the Gospel of Matthew (10:34–6), Jesus, quoting (in italic below) the Israelite prophet Micah, famously says:

> "Do not suppose that I have come to bring peace to the earth: it is not peace I have come to bring, but a sword. For I have come to set son against *father, daughter against mother, daughter-in-law against mother-in-law, a person's enemies will be the members of his own household.*"

The sword to which Jesus refers in this passage is not a sword of military conquest but of domestic turmoil and familial division. Speaking with divine authority, the Messiah intended to—and indeed he did—bring dissension to the greater Jewish household of his time. Muhammad would do no less in his time. Allah comforts Muhammad by telling him that as it was thus for the great Abraham, so it must ever be, whatever the cost: devotion to God must always trump devotion to family.

Granting that Abraham dealt kindly with his idolatrous father, did he for all that remain resident in Azar's household? In the Apocalypse of Abraham, a visionary Jewish text, originally written in Hebrew and roughly contemporary with the writing of the New Testament, Abraham's father is not just an idolater but an idol-sculptor and an idol-merchant. Young Abraham's exposure to the all-too-human manufacture and sale of supposedly divine images gives rise in him to a crisis of idolatrous faith. He then prays to (the real) God to reveal himself; and when God speaks, He instructs Abraham to leave his father's house. (Abraham's father is Azar in the Qur'an but Terah in the Bible and later Jewish texts.)

The text of the Apocalypse of Abraham reads, in English translation:

And it came to pass as I was thinking things like these with regard to my father Terah in the court of my house, the voice of the Mighty One came down from the heavens in a stream of fire, saying and calling, "Abraham, Abraham!" And I said, "Here I am." And he said, "You are searching for the God of gods, the Creator, in the understanding of your heart. I am he. Go out from Terah, your father, and go out of the house, that you too may not be slain in the sins of your father's house." And I went out. And it came to pass as I went out—I was not yet outside the entrance of the court—that the sound of a great thunder came and burned him and his house and everything in his house, down to the ground, forty cubits.[1]

At Qur'an 19:42–48, Allah recalls for Muhammad a story somewhat similar to that told in the Apocalypse of Abraham:

And mention in the Book Abraham; he was a man of deepest faith, a prophet.

Remember when he said to his father: "My father, why do you worship what does not hear, what does not see, what is of no use to you whatsoever?

"My father, there has come to me of Knowledge what did not come to you, so follow me and I shall guide you to a level path.

"My father, do not worship Satan: Satan has always been disobedient to the All-Merciful.

"My father, I fear a torment will touch you from the All-Merciful, and you become a follower of Satan."

He said: "Are you renouncing my gods, O Abraham? If you do not desist, I shall curse you. Leave me alone for a while."

He said: "Peace be upon you! I shall ask my Lord forgiveness for you, for He has always been kind to me. I shall keep aloof from you and from what you worship instead of God, and I shall call upon my Lord; perhaps by calling Him I will not be amiss."

Here, Abraham deals with Azar with the kindness that Allah pre-
scribes and even promises to beg Allah's forgiveness for him, but the rift
between them is deep, all the same, and will prove fatal in the end for
Azar, just as in the Apocalypse of Abraham it proved fatal in a different
way for Terah. In subordinating familial to creedal values, Abraham
in these passages is again like Jesus who, when interrupted among his
disciples by a report that his mother and his brothers were waiting for
him outside, said,

> "Who is my mother? Who are my brothers?" And stretch-
> ing out his hand towards his disciples he said, "Here are my
> mother and my brothers. Anyone who does the will of my
> Father in heaven is my brother and sister and mother." (Mat-
> thew 12:48–50)

Allah, in just this way, is pleased that Abraham has placed devotion to
Him so clearly above devotion to Azar, a point he makes even more
forthrightly at Qur'an 9:113–114, with unmistakable further reference to
Muhammad himself:

> It is not right for the Prophet {i.e., for you, Muhammad} and
> the believers to ask forgiveness for polytheists, even if they are
> relatives, once it has become clear to them that they are deni-
> zens of hell. When Abraham asked forgiveness for his father,
> this was only to fulfil a promise he had promised him. But
> once it became clear to him that he was an enemy of God,
> he washed his hands of him—Abraham was one who sighed
> much, and was self-restrained.

Abraham's sigh is understandable. Allah does not blame him for grieving that Azar must be damned and even praises him for his gentle,
restrained manner, but Abraham must and does submit to Allah's determination that all unbelievers, Azar included, are to be "denizens of
hell" forever. This was why Allah "had taken Abraham for an intimate"
(Qur'an 4:125) and rewarded him, as already noted: "When he abandoned them and what they worshipped instead of God, We bestowed

on him Isaac and Jacob, and each We made a prophet. And We granted them of Our mercy, and conferred upon them the highest praise on tongues of truth" (Qur'an 19:49–50).

The character of Abraham is sharply and consistently drawn in the Qur'an, but the focus of our inquiry is not Abraham per se, or any one personage who appears both in the Qur'an and in the Bible but rather God and how His character is indirectly revealed in the respective scriptures through His interaction with a series of these personages. In such a comparison, attention to formal or stylistic differences between the two scriptures can sometimes be surprisingly helpful.

In the Qur'an, Allah is omnipresent because He is the speaker at every moment. When a story is being recalled, He is, accordingly, the narrator. In Genesis, by contrast, when a story is being told the narrator is anonymous. As I said earlier, Jewish tradition, to be sure, honors Moses as the divinely inspired author of Torah, which comprises the five "Books of Moses," of which Genesis is the first. Page by page, however, the text of Genesis never presents Moses in that role. No, the anonymous narrating voice is taken for granted; always reliable, it is simply, automatically "there," as if the Bible were telling its own story.

In the Qur'an, both because Allah is never offstage and because He often refers to the very Qur'an that He is speaking into existence as a book, the character of the Qur'an as a spoken-and-then-written artifact seems to be at the front of Allah's mind. Allah is far more intensely and audibly involved in the Qur'an as scripture than Yahweh is ever involved in, say, the Book of Genesis as scripture. Put most simply, Allah cares more about writing than Yahweh does.

And yet within the stories that Allah tells about Abraham in the Qur'an, Allah rarely assigns Himself a speaking role. He is there as the narrator, to be sure, from start to finish; and yet within His narration He rarely or never says, "And then We said to Abraham," much less "And then I said to Abraham." Abraham's words to Allah are quoted directly on occasion; an example would be the prayer quoted above. Allah's conversations with Abraham are not quoted directly.

In Genesis, by contrast, the anonymous narrator often quotes Yahweh's words directly. On one occasion, repartee between Yahweh and Abraham becomes exceptionally lively and, on Abraham's part, only barely reverent. The occasion is Abraham's attempt to talk Yahweh out of destroying the sinful city of Sodom:

> Abraham stepped forward and said, "Will you really destroy the upright with the guilty? Suppose there are fifty upright people in the city. Will you really destroy it? Will you not spare the place for the sake of the fifty upright in it? Do not think of doing such a thing: to put the upright to death with the guilty, so that upright and guilty fare alike! Is the judge of the whole world not to act justly?" Yahweh replied, "If I find fifty upright people in the city of Sodom, I shall spare the whole place because of them."
>
> Abraham spoke up and said, "It is presumptuous of me to speak to the Lord, I who am dust and ashes: Suppose the fifty upright were five short? Would you destroy the whole city because of five?" "No," he replied, "I will not destroy it if I find forty-five there." Abraham persisted and said, "Suppose there are forty to be found there?" "I will not do it," he replied, "for the sake of the forty." (Genesis 18:23–29)

The bargaining continues down to the number ten. True, in the end Yahweh destroys Sodom after all, yet a deity who can be argued with and bargained with in this way can only seem less toweringly august and overpowering than one with whom such back talk is simply and utterly out of the question. For all his power and dynamism, Yahweh in the Bible is less absolute and overwhelming than is Allah in the Qur'an.

That said, nowhere in the qur'anic interaction between Allah and Abraham as reviewed above does Allah deliver for Abraham's private benefit a demonstration of his power as intimately terrifying as the one Yahweh stages at Genesis 15. There, the anonymous narrator begins with another candid dialogue between Abraham and Yahweh, as Abraham—at this point still named Abram—complains that Yahweh has not kept his fertility promise:

[Yahweh] then said to him, "I am Yahweh who brought you out of Ur of the Chaldaeans [in far-off Mesopotamia] to give you this country [Canaan] as your possession." "Lord Yahweh," Abram replied, "how can I know that I shall possess it?" He said to him, "Bring me a three-year-old heifer, a three-year-old goat, a three-year-old ram, a turtledove and a young pigeon." He brought him all these, split the animals down the middle and placed each half opposite the other; but the birds he did not divide. And whenever birds of prey swooped down on the carcasses, Abram drove them off....

When the sun had set and it was dark, there appeared a smoking firepot and a flaming torch passing between the animals' pieces. That day Yahweh made a covenant with Abram in these terms:

"To your descendants I give this country,
from the River of Egypt to the Great River,
the River Euphrates, the Kenites, the Kenizzites, the Kadmonites, the Hittites, the Perizzites, the Rephaim, the Amorites, the Canaanites, the Girgashites, and the Jebusites." (15:7–11, 17–21)

What kind of covenant is this? It is a covenant that reveals the characteristic concern of Yahweh as distinct from the characteristic concern of Allah. Yahweh is a fertility god; Allah is a theolatry god. The rare and archaic English word *theolatry*—meaning god-worship as *idolatry* is idol-worship—effectively names Allah's characteristic concern both that He Himself be worshipped and that no other god be worshipped and thus "associated" with Him. Yahweh, by strong contrast, never demands worship from Abraham or expresses any indignation that another being might be receiving the worship due only to Him. The matter of worship seems not to be on His mind at all. Yahweh's concern is elsewhere—namely, on human fertility, at first, and later on Abraham's fertility.

In Genesis 1, Elohim commanded the first human couple to be fruitful and multiply and rule the earth. By Genesis 15, the promise implied in that command has been both narrowed and intensified: narrowed to Abraham but intensified inasmuch as Abraham's is to be a truly miraculous fertility, in return for which Abraham will enter an unbreakable covenant with Yahweh, binding himself to absolute obedience under pain of death.

Both these elements—both the fertility and the covenant of obedience—are present in the ritual performed at Genesis 15. The several animals that Abraham obediently bisects are not simply sacrificed. Because this is a covenant ritual, their bisection and the divine flame that passes between their body parts function together to mime the horror that will befall Abraham should he ever dare to break covenant with Yahweh. This horror, note well, is to occur not in an afterlife but during Abraham's own lifetime. Unlike Allah, who speaks so often of the afterlife and the excruciating hellfire that awaits those who have not worshipped Him while alive on earth, Yahweh never alludes to any punishment coming after death, or any reward either.

Abraham's reward for fidelity to his covenant with Yahweh is to be not eternal bliss in a heavenly garden but rather a splendidly lengthy human lifetime enriched by the grand possession of all the land from the Nile in Egypt to the upper Euphrates. Yahweh has thus promised Abraham that he will rule over the entire eastern end of the Mediterranean coastlands, populating this vast territory with the fruit of his now miraculous loins and dominating any and all peoples already inhabiting the land: Hittites, Canaanites, Girgashites, and so forth.

Yahweh's goal, however, is not some quasi-imperialist lust for territory for its own sake. After all, Yahweh is already "the judge of the whole world," as Abraham rightly calls Him in the passage quoted above. Land (with subjugated peoples to work the land) has a merely instrumental value for Him: it serves to foster the fertility of the one man, Abraham, whom "I have singled . . . out to command his sons and his family after him to keep the way of Yahweh by doing what is upright and just, so that Yahweh can carry out for Abraham what he has promised him" (18:19).

Even doing what is upright and just functions instrumentally to promote the beyond-all-human-reckoning fertility that Yahweh has promised Abraham:

> "I shall make your descendants like the dust on the ground; when people succeed in counting the specks of dust on the ground, then they will be able to count your descendants too!" (13:16)

"Look up at the sky and count the stars if you can. Just so will your descendants be," he told him. Abram put his faith in Yahweh and this was reckoned to him as uprightness. (15:5–6)

"For my part, this is my covenant with you: you will become the father of many nations. And you are no longer to be called Abram; your name is to be Abraham, for I am making you father of many nations. I shall make you exceedingly fertile. I shall make you into nations, and your issue will be kings." (17:4–6)

Why does Yahweh so desire Abraham's fertility? Why, for that matter, does He desire fertility in the first place? Why did Elohim so direct the creation of the world itself that its very climax should be the fertility and world dominion of Adam and Eve? These questions really have no answers. Rather than the conclusion of an argument, they are the premise. Many consequences flow from God's determination, first, that humankind should reproduce without hindrance and, later, that Abraham and his people should reproduce so miraculously as to dominate all the other peoples in the land that Yahweh has promised them. As for the origin of this determination, this the Bible leaves hidden in the unknowable mind of God. Did Yahweh Elohim create the world out of love for His human creatures, or special love for Abraham and his offspring? Perhaps the latter, but if so, the Bible never says so: it leaves us in wonderment.

So it is as well with Allah's desire for exclusive human worship. Why might it not be beneath Allah to be troubled by whether mere human beings—His own lowly creatures, "created…from dust, then from a sperm, then from a blood clot, then from a morsel," as we read at Qur'an 22:5—should worship Him or not? But the matter clearly does trouble Him, and the consequences of the trouble reverberate on virtually every page of the Qur'an. Does Allah desire human worship for humans' sake? Perhaps so, but if so, the Qur'an never clearly says so. It leaves us in wonderment, facing an all-shaping desire that simply must be taken on its own terms.

Allah and Yahweh are one in the expectation that their human creatures should submit their wills to the divine will, but Allah does not anticipate that this submission should lead to any other-than-normal fertility in His servant Abraham. Nor is it on His agenda that Abraham should rule over other peoples in the Levant. What matters is only that Abraham should formally and publicly acknowledge Allah as God, should accordingly repudiate any rival claims to divinity, and should fearlessly bring this message to his people. Abraham's reward for doing all this will come not in this life but in the glory of his afterlife.

Strikingly, Abraham's world in the Qur'an is a populous world that is generally both polytheistic and idolatrous. In the Bible, by contrast, the nomadic Abraham wanders across what seems a much emptier landscape, never once encountering an idolater or a declared polytheist. Moreover, at Genesis 14, Abram takes part in a bread-and-wine ritual conducted by the priest-king of Salem, a ritual in which it is unclear whether the *'el 'elyon* or "God Most High" being honored is identical or not with Yahweh. The ritual, involving bread and wine, seems appropriate to an agricultural people, while Abram is a herdsman, reckoning his wealth by the size of his herds and conducting rituals (as at Genesis 15) that involve the sacrifice of animals rather than of crops. It is at least conceivable, then, that Abram—by no means yet in control of any of the land that Yahweh has promised him—is practicing here a kind of politically pragmatic religious diplomacy and that Yahweh is prepared to tolerate this. One cannot imagine the literally and violently iconoclastic Abraham of Qur'an 21 engaging in any such dubious tolerance of polytheism, nor can one imagine Allah ever countenancing it.

With regard to fertility, it is not that Allah does not recognize it as a human good, but in His interactions with Abraham, Allah makes fertility a good that follows rather than precedes the good of proper theolatry. It is only after commissioning and training Abraham as His messenger and then observing with gratification how bravely and well Abraham has challenged Azar and his people that Allah says, in a passage already quoted: "And We bestowed on him Isaac and Jacob, *as an added bounty from Us* (21:72, emphasis added). Fertility is a reward, an added gift, for correct and zealous theolatry. Moreover, it is not by their sheer, miraculous numbers that Abraham's offspring are to bear witness that Allah is great but rather by their exemplary work as practitioners of Islam in upright living, prayer, and almsgiving, crowned by the worship of Allah alone:

> . . . to do righteous deeds,
> To perform the prayer, and hand out alms,
> And they were Our worshippers. (21:73)

For Yahweh, it is the other way around, fertility then theolatry. Yahweh first promises Abram land and offspring in "a country which I shall show you; and I shall make you a great nation" (Genesis 12:1–2). Only after Abraham has arrived in the land where Yahweh has led him does it come about that he "built an altar to Yahweh and invoked the name of Yahweh" (12:8). Divinely promised (if not yet delivered) fertility comes first as the premise; human worship follows as the consequence. Abraham's trust that Yahweh will keep his promise corresponds, in Genesis, to Abraham's zeal for Allah's claim to unique and universal worship in the Qur'an. As quoted already, "Abram put his faith in Yahweh, and this was reckoned to him as uprightness" (Genesis 15:6).

The covenant or alliance between Allah, on one side, and Abraham, Isaac, and Jacob, on the other side, is thus essentially *about* theolatry: Allah demands worship, for reasons of His own; His human worshippers provide it. The covenant between Yahweh and Abraham is essentially *about* fertility: Yahweh, for reasons of His own, promises fertility; Abraham builds a worshipful altar in testimony to his trust that fertility will follow.

As this chapter opened with a confrontation between Abraham and his father, Azar, in Qur'an 21, we must not conclude before inquiring into the state of Abraham's relationship with his father, Terah, in the Bible.

Abraham does leave Terah's house in the Bible. As Abram, he dutifully answers Yahweh's call that he leave his country, his kindred, and his father's house (12:1) and be guided by Yahweh to the land of Canaan. Nowhere, however, is it suggested that in this departure he was also breaking with his father's god(s). In Genesis 11:31, we read that Terah took Abram and his wife along with Abram's nephew, Lot, who is Terah's grandson, "and made them leave Ur of the Chaldaeans to go to the land of Canaan." True, the family stops just short of Canaan in Haran; but when Abram departs Haran for Canaan, it is as if he is completing the family's originally intended journey as its representative. Later, as we shall see, Abraham will send back to Haran to find a spouse for his son,

Isaac. All this is context for Yahweh's statement at Genesis 15:7 "I am Yahweh who brought you out of Ur of the Chaldaeans," indicating indirectly that Yahweh had been with Terah, too, on that earlier journey from Ur to Haran. In any case, between Abram's departure from Haran and Terah's death there, years pass, but no further interaction between father and son is recorded in the Bible.

Many centuries later, a Rabbinic commentary-by-expansion on the Book of Genesis would tell a quite different, conflict-filled story about Abraham and Terah, one that has many elements in common with the Qur'an's story of Abraham and Azar as recalled above. Chapter 38 of *Genesis Rabbah*, a large work concluded not long before the birth of Muhammad, is nominally an expansion of Genesis 11:27–28:

> Terah fathered Abram, Nahor and Haran. Haran fathered Lot. Haran died in the presence of his father Terah in his native land, Ur of the Chaldaeans.[2]

Why, the ever-curious Rabbis asked, did Haran die? And the answer they provided, matching much of the Qur'an's account of Abraham's rebellion against Azar, includes the story of Abraham smashing his father's idols and then claiming, as in the Qur'an, that the largest idol must have smashed the smaller ones. *Genesis Rabbah* then introduces the figure of Nimrod, a legendary Mesopotamian king, who has Abraham thrown into a bonfire, defying his god to save him. The Lord does save Abraham, but when Haran—Terah's brother and Abraham's uncle—decides that he, too, will now declare his faith in Abraham's God and when he, in turn, is thrown into the fire, God does not save him, and so the Rabbis have an answer to their question: why did Haran die? This answer does, of course, raise further questions, but such ever is Rabbinic commentary.

Nimrod appears in many later Arabic legends as well, but our comparison is not of the full sweep of Jewish tradition with the full sweep of Muslim tradition but only of the Bible with the Qur'an. That already limited comparison is more limited still in the current chapter, which addresses only Abraham and only his relationship with his father in the two scriptures. Within that limited comparison, we may conclude that the relationship between Abraham and his father is central in the

Qur'an because Allah's central preoccupation there is theolatry, and Azar is an idolater, while the same relationship is marginal in the Book of Genesis because Yahweh's central preoccupation there is fertility, and because Terah, whether or not he worships Yahweh, shares through his son in Yahweh's promise of miraculous fertility. Later in the Bible, notably in His relationship with Moses, Yahweh will develop a preoccupation with theolatry that matches or exceeds Allah's in this chapter, but it remains true that neither idolatry nor polytheism figure in Yahweh's relationship with Abraham, so long as we confine our attention to the Bible itself.

In the Bible and in the Qur'an alike, however, whatever the importance of Abraham's relationship to his father, what will matter still more—and say more about the character of God—is Abraham's relationship to his two sons, Ishmael and Isaac. To this subject we now turn.

5

Abraham and His Sons

The birth of a child and the high hopes that precede childbirth. The death of a child and the wreckage of hope that follows. The eleventh-hour rescue of a child in mortal danger. The selfless devotion of a young child to a parent in distress.

Few themes in all literature have more primal power than these, and these are the themes that, in both the Bible and the Qur'an, shape the story of Abraham and his two sons: the elder, Ishmael (with his mother, Hagar); and the younger, Isaac (with his mother, Sarah).

We begin, this time, with the Bible, again in the Book of Genesis, where not just years but decades have passed in Abram's life since Yahweh promised him offspring as numerous as the dust on the ground and an empire stretching from Syria to Egypt. Abram is eighty-five years old and childless. His wife, Sarai, is apparently barren. In desperation, she has given her slave Hagar to Abram as a concubine, and Hagar has quickly become pregnant. Now, however, Hagar no longer defers as a slave to her mistress, and Abram allows the furious Sarai to so mistreat Hagar that, still pregnant, she flees into the desert, facing almost certain doom both for herself and her unborn child.

An angel then finds Hagar near a spring in the desert, commands her to return to her mistress, and goes on, consolingly:

"Now, you have conceived and will bear a son,
and you shall name him Ishmael,
for Yahweh has heard your cries of distress." (Genesis 16:11)

Ishmael is a sentence-name, like many Hebrew names, and means "God has heard."

So Hagar returns home, gives birth to Ishmael, and thirteen years pass. Abram is approaching ninety-nine, and Sarai has turned ninety, when Yahweh Elohim appears to Abram under the mysterious title El Shaddai (perhaps "God of the Mountain Peaks"), changes his name from Abram to Abraham, changes Sarai's to Sarah, imposes male circumcision as a new sign for the already existing covenant, and then astonishes Abram/Abraham with the announcement that Sarai/Sarah will conceive after all:

"I shall bless her and moreover give you a son by her. I shall bless her and she will become nations: kings of peoples will issue from her." ... "Yes, your wife Sarah will bear you a son whom you must name Isaac. And I shall maintain my covenant with him, a covenant in perpetuity, to be his God and the God of his descendants after him." (Genesis 17:16, 19)

How does Abraham receive this prediction? *The New Jerusalem Bible* translates: "Abraham bowed to the ground, and he laughed, thinking to himself, 'Is a child to be born to a man one hundred years old, and will Sarah have a child at the age of ninety?'" (17:17) I prefer here the Jewish Publication Society translation, which opens: "Abraham threw himself on his face and laughed...."

Fertility can be miraculous in two ways. It can be, as already promised, so great as to defy all human calculation. Or, as now announced, it can occur in blatant defiance of the well-known laws of nature. Women of ninety do not conceive. A man of eighty-five might impregnate a much younger woman; such was Abram when he impregnated Hagar. But now? At ninety-nine? The prospect is laughable indeed. Abram will eventually be honored for his faith, but in this scene, his spontaneous reaction is a guffaw.

Quickly, however, it becomes evident that something quite serious is at issue. Abraham, still trusting Yahweh/Elohim's promise, has been expecting for thirteen years now that this promise would be realized through his son and heir, Ishmael. Even after hearing Elohim's declaration that Sarah will conceive and that his line is henceforth to continue through another son, still to be born, Abraham remains genuinely incredulous. He clings to his thought that young Ishmael is still likely to be his only heir: "May Ishmael live in your presence!" he implores Elohim; "That will be enough!" (17:18)

Elohim then backs partway off. Ishmael, too, he concedes, will father a great nation:

> "For Ishmael too I grant you your request. I hereby bless him
> and will make him fruitful and exceedingly numerous. He
> will be the father of twelve princes, and I shall make him into
> a great nation." (17:20)

And yet Elohim insists: "But my covenant I shall maintain with Isaac, whom Sarah will bear you at this time next year" (17:21).

A tension enters the story at this point, for all the males of Abraham's household, slave as well as free, are to be brought into the covenant by circumcision, which Elohim has declared to be "the sign of the covenant between myself and you" (17:11). Ishmael, too, Abraham's heir, even though the son of a slave mother, is marked with the sign of the covenant. In fact, underscoring the intimacy of the link between the father and son, the narrator reports:

> Abraham was ninety-nine years old when his foreskin was
> circumcised. Ishmael his son was thirteen years old when his
> foreskin was circumcised. Abraham and his son Ishmael were
> circumcised on the very same day. (17:24–26)

How can Ishmael not be a son of the covenant? But then, too, if the covenant is essentially about fertility, does it matter whether Ishmael is included in the covenant or not since fertility seems to be promised equally to both heirs? Tension remains because although the two are both promised fertility and even greatness, they are not promised it *in the same place*. There is a territorial or national component to Yahweh's covenant with Abraham that is absent from Allah's.

Meanwhile, the renamed Sarah, despite what must have been her astonishment at this sudden mass circumcision, has not yet been told that she is to conceive. Abraham, it would seem, has done nothing lately to make her doubt that her childbearing years are over for good. Then, as the aged patriarch rests at the entrance to his tent, under the shade of an oak tree, Yahweh appears to him, or three men appear to him, or Yahweh and two men, or Yahweh and two angels: the Hebrew of Genesis 18–19 is mysteriously fluid as references to Yahweh, His message, and His messengers (angels) alternate so unpredictably as to blend together. In any case, Abraham recognizes that this is (or these are) no ordinary visitor(s), and he prepares a lavish meal for them with Sarah's help. The visitors eat, and then the focus shifts to Sarah:

> "Where is your wife Sarah?" they asked him. "She is in the tent," he replied. Then his guest said, "I shall come back to you next year, and then your wife Sarah will have a son." Now Abraham and Sarah were old, well on in years, and Sarah had ceased to have her monthly periods. Sarah was listening at the entrance of the tent behind him. So Sarah laughed to herself, thinking, "Now that I am past the age of childbearing, and my husband is an old man, is pleasure to come my way again?" But Yahweh asked Abraham, "Why did Sarah laugh and say, 'Am I really going to have a child now that I am old?' Nothing is impossible for Yahweh. I shall come back to you at the same time next year and Sarah will have a son." Sarah said, "I did not laugh," because she was afraid. But he replied, "Oh yes, you did." (18:9–15)

Sarah knows her own body. She knows her husband's, too, all too well. But Yahweh is making a point: Ishmael's birth was perhaps remarkable, but Isaac's will be truly miraculous—a biological impossibility that nonetheless will come to pass. When fertility is miraculous, Yahweh Elohim owns it.

The Qur'an tells a similar story at 11:69–76 but with some intriguing differences or corrections:

> Our envoys came to Abraham, bearing glad tidings.
>
> They said: "Peace!"
>
> He said: "Peace!"
>
> At once he brought forth a roasted calf. When he saw that their hands did not stretch forth to it, he was in doubt about them and harboured some fear of them.
>
> They said: "Fear not. We were sent to the people of Lot."
>
> His wife, standing by, laughed, so We brought her glad tidings of Isaac, and after Isaac, of Jacob.
>
> She said: "Alas for me! Am I to give birth, me an old woman, and here is my husband, an old man? That would indeed be a marvel!"
>
> They said: "Do you marvel at the command of God? May the mercy of God and His blessings descend upon you, O members of the house! He is All-Praiseworthy, All-Glorious."
>
> When fear left Abraham, and glad tidings came to him, he began to argue with Us regarding the people of Lot. Abraham was gentle, sighing much, penitent.
>
> "O Abraham, make no mention of this matter. The command of your Lord is come and they—there shall come to them a torment irreversible."

Allah is present in this story as its narrator but, as usual, He assigns Himself no speaking role in the story. His messengers/angels visit Abraham and his (unnamed) wife. He Himself does not.

When an Arab host entertains strangers, he serves them food as a sign of friendship. As a sign of answering friendship, they must consume it. For should they ignore it, they would be taken to have done so pointedly in order to decline the proffered friendship with the food. Are these visitors then enemies? What are their intentions toward their host, Abraham, and his family?

In Genesis 18, Abraham's visitors do consume the food he lays before them. In Qur'an 11, they do not, but only because they are *angelic* messengers (ancient commentaries have reasoned) and so require no human nourishment. Abraham, not yet recognizing their nature, begins to fear hostile intentions on their part. They reassure him that, yes, their intentions are hostile but toward the people of Lot, Abraham's nephew, and his people rather than toward Abraham and his. At this point, Abraham's wife laughs, evidently in relief that she and her husband are not in danger after all. So far, nothing has yet been said about her coming pregnancy. When that word is imparted, her reaction is equal parts wonderment and blank dismay. In the Book of Genesis, Sarah laughs at the ludicrous but nonetheless agreeable prospect of sexual pleasure with her aged husband. In the Qur'an, the unnamed wife moans at the daunting prospect of pregnancy and childbirth at her advanced age. The same sentiment is the more vividly conveyed in a briefer but parallel telling of this episode at Qur'an 51:29–30:

> His wife came forward, in utter amazement, scratching her face and saying: "A barren old woman!"
> They said: "Thus spoke your Lord; He is All-Wise, All-Knowing."

The striking of the face is a sign of extreme alarm and dismay, but the never-named wife must accept whatever lies ahead, for "Thus spoke your Lord."

As Abraham realizes that these Allah-sent angels have brought good news for him and his house and bad news only for his nephew Lot and Lot's house, Abraham begins to plead for divine mercy upon his relatives, just as we saw him earlier pleading for mercy for his own father. Allah, once again, praises Abraham as full of sighs and tenderness, and yet, once again, the message for him is that from Allah's decrees there is no appeal, even for family: "O Abraham, make no mention of this matter. The command of your Lord is come and they—there shall come to them a torment irreversible."

The biblical account continues as Isaac is born, circumcised, and weaned. In an era when infant mortality was common, it was a cause for celebration when a newborn survived long enough (perhaps two years) to be weaned. To celebrate Isaac's weaning, Abraham holds a great celebration during which Sarah sees Ishmael, now about fifteen years old, playing with little Isaac. This demonstration of their affectionate brotherhood and so their presumed equality as Abraham's sons and heirs revolts her, and she demands that Abraham disown Hagar and Ishmael and, more drastically, send them out into the desert to die. Abraham is distressed at the thought of doing away with his own firstborn son, but Yahweh reassures him that he may accede to Sarah's deadly wishes, for Yahweh will intervene to save Hagar and Ishmael, and eventually to turn Ishmael, after all, into a great nation.

Hagar knows nothing of this as she is sent off with just some bread and a skin (a leather canteen) of water. Sarah knows nothing of it either. In the desert of Beersheba, Hagar's water runs out. She believes that she is now facing death. Worse, her teenage son is dying more quickly than she is. She beds him down under a bush, and "Then she went and sat down at a distance, about a bowshot away, thinking, 'I cannot bear to see the child die.' Sitting at a distance, she began to sob" (21:16).

Ishmael, under his bush, is weeping as well, but then Elohim

> heard the boy crying, and the angel of God called to Hagar from heaven, "What is wrong, Hagar?" he asked. "Do not be afraid, for God has heard the boy's cry in his plight. Go and pick the boy up and hold him safe, for I shall make him into a great nation." Then God opened Hagar's eyes and she saw a well, so she went and filled the skin with water and gave the boy a drink.
>
> God was with the boy. He grew up and made his home in the desert, and he became an archer. He made his home in the desert of Paran, and his mother got him a wife from Egypt. (21:17–21)

And just where is Paran? In the Bible, Ishmael is understood to be the ancestor of the Arabs: *Arab* and *Ishmaelite* are virtually synonymous. The Arab homeland is understood to be well south of the town of Beersheba, traditionally the southern boundary of the territory inhabited by the twelve tribes of Israel. But what the Bible calls "the desert of Beersheba" is effectively the desert that *begins* at Beersheba and runs south from there. It was somewhere in that desert that Hagar was visited by the angel and led to the life-saving spring. Ishmael came of age in that area, and his Egyptian mother found a wife for him in Egypt.

Ishmael had not known what Abraham knew about Yahweh Elohim's intent to save his life and guarantee his grand future. Had he known, he would not have wept so under that bush. Did he resume contact with his father as he grew and as he traveled on? A parallel tradition, echoed rather than formally recounted in the Qur'an, suggests strongly that he did and that, in fact, Abraham had a hand in Ishmael's eventual settling in the Hijaz, the desert region adjacent to Mecca, where, in Muhammad's time, the hallowed Ka'aba—often called simply "the House" or "the Sacred House"—was located. At Qur'an 14:35–39, we read:

Remember when Abraham said: "My Lord, make this land safe, and avert from me and my offspring the worship of idols.

"My Lord, they have led astray so many people. Whoso follows me is of my number; whoso disobeys me, You are All-Forgiving, Compassionate to each.

"Our Lord, I have settled some of my progeny in a valley where no vegetation grows, near your Sacred House, our Lord, that they may perform the prayers. So turn the hearts of some towards them, and grant them some nourishment; perhaps they will render thanks.

"Our Lord, you know what we conceal and what we proclaim. Nor is anything concealed from God on earth or in heaven.

"Praise be to God Who granted me, though old, Ishmael and Isaac! My Lord hears full well all supplications."

In the foreword to this book, we noted that Allah presumes a broad familiarity on Muhammad's part with the tales told in the Bible. In the largely oral culture of the Hijaz, this familiarity would have come from repeated hearing rather than from reading and may have been more deeply rooted in local memory for that very reason. Typically, Allah reminds Muhammad of one or another of these already familiar tales and provides some of the highlights without troubling to provide a fully detailed account. Among such tales, if there were one that, above all others, Muhammad, like almost any other Arab of his time, could be presumed to know well, it would surely be the story of the descent of the Arabs of his home region from Abraham and Hagar through their son, Ishmael. Allah thus does not need to retell the story of Hagar for Muhammad's benefit. Moreover, He can trust that Muhammad will easily hear Allah's allusion to Abraham's having settled Hagar and Ishmael in the Hijaz, even if the first step in the settlement seemed to the two of them to be a traumatic abandonment.

To repeat, what Muhammad knows—and Allah knows he knows—of the Bible does not come from *reading* the Bible. According to a long-standing tradition, Muhammad was illiterate. But the religious culture of the Hijaz mingled Jewish and Christian lore with Arab tribal polytheism in a rich oral tradition that "canonized" its own versions, often elaborated, of received material. Allah sometimes corrects these, but sometimes, as above, he simply incorporates them into his message to Muhammad, signaling his intentions with just the briefest of allusions.

So it happens that we read in the Qur'an at 2:158:

> Al-Safa and al-Marwa are among the rites of God. As for him who performs the Greater Pilgrimage to the Sacred House or else the Lesser, no blame shall attach to him if he circumambulates them.

Al-Safa and al-Marwah were two hills near Mecca between or around which pilgrims would reenact Hagar's desperate search for water in a formal ritual of lapping back and forth. The ritual, like the story of Hagar and Ishmael in the Hijaz, predated the lifetime of Muhammad and so predated the Qur'an. Was it then still legitimate after the coming of Muhammad? This was evidently a question that arose. Yes, Allah reassures Muhammad and his early followers, the old ritual is still legitimate, incorporated as it was and is not only into the Muslim haj (the Greater Pilgrimage which is to be made only at a designated time each year) but also into the related, simpler *'umrah* (the lesser pilgrimage that Muslims may make at any time).

Our intent here is not per se to discuss Islam's pilgrimage rituals but only to note the felt presence in the Qur'an, despite formal silence, of the story of Abraham, Hagar, and Ishmael—this tale of the birth of Abraham's firstborn son; of the early near-death experience of that son and his mother in the desert; and finally of their dramatic divine rescue.

The biblical story of Abraham and his sons continues, after the departure of Hagar and Ishmael, with the birth of Isaac. Then, "some time later,"

> God put Abraham to the test. "Abraham, Abraham!" he called. "Here I am," he replied. God said, "Take your son, your only son, your beloved Isaac, and go to the land of Moriah, where you are to offer him as a burnt offering on one of the mountains which I shall point out to you." (Genesis 22:1–2)

Abraham has complied with Elohim's every command so far, but has Elohim done His part? Has He provided the promised miraculous fertility? Abraham, having repeatedly complained of his childlessness, is now one hundred years old and has exactly two sons, one of whom he may never see again. Is his commitment to Yahweh Elohim weakening? But then, too, viewing the matter from Elohim's side, has Abraham ever given Him any but an entirely conditional, quid pro quo commitment? Elohim, having forcefully limited His covenant commitment to Isaac and his future offspring, now brings the matter to a brutal head and demands that Abraham give Isaac back.

Fertility, we said earlier, was what this covenant was *about*. But what if Elohim now takes away the fertility, depriving Abraham of any descendants through Isaac and, it would seem, canceling His side of the covenant? Will Abraham obey this command? Will he pass this test? And why is the test necessary? What has Abraham done to rouse doubt in Elohim's mind?

Or is this, perhaps, a paradoxical test—that is, a test you can only pass by failing it? Since Elohim has already forbidden murder, will Abraham, paradoxically, pass the test by *disobeying* Elohim? At Genesis 9:6, Elohim has solemnly proclaimed to Noah, in the aftermath of the great flood:

"He who sheds the blood of man,
      by man shall his blood be shed,
for in the image of God
      was man created."

Isaac, still young enough to be living at home with his parents, is a man-child created in the image of Elohim. If Elohim orders him murdered, is He to be believed, or, as Abraham might well ask, in tones of incredulity: "What is this—some kind of test or something?" Which of Elohim's two commands is Abraham to obey? Is Abraham even dealing with the same deity at all? Without ever declaring in so many words any compliant willingness to sacrifice Isaac, Abraham begins silently to go through the motions:

> Early next morning Abraham saddled his donkey and took with him two of his servants and his son Isaac. He chopped wood for the burnt offering and started on his journey to the place which God had indicated to him. On the third day Abraham looked up and saw the place in the distance. Then Abraham said to his servants, "Stay here with the donkey. The boy and I are going over there; we shall worship and then come back to you." (22:3–5)

Worship: a most interesting word choice. It neither excludes nor necessarily includes sacrifice. The core meaning of the Hebrew root involved is simply *bow down*: obeisance, yes, but not necessarily obedience.

Abraham and his party have journeyed for three full days, beginning, apparently, from Beersheba at the southern extreme of later Israelite territory, but in what direction have they traveled? Later Jewish tradition identifies Mount Moriah with the Temple Mount in Jerusalem, but what if they were traveling southward, in the same direction that Hagar and Ishmael may have traveled, rather than northward toward Jerusalem? Abraham knows that once before, Elohim had seemed to sentence a son of his to death and then saved him after all. Will He do so again?

Tension builds as the Genesis story continues:

Abraham took the wood for the burnt offering, loaded it on Isaac, and carried in his own hands the fire and the knife. Then the two of them set out together. Isaac spoke to his father Abraham. "Father?" he said. "Yes, my son," he replied. "Look," he said, "here are the fire and the wood, but where is the lamb for the burnt offering?" Abraham replied, "My son, God himself will provide the lamb for the burnt offering." And the two of them went on together. (22:6–8)

Who is testing whom here? In Hebrew, Abraham's sentence "God himself will provide" is identical to "Let God himself provide"; the verb, in Hebrew, may be either a future or what is called in Hebrew grammar a jussive—that is, a third-person imperative. Abraham may either be challenging God to provide an actual lamb or delicately concealing from Isaac that he is to be the sacrificial lamb. Suspense builds, for the words can be read either way.

And, by the way, which of the two—Abraham or Isaac—is undergoing the real test of faith here? The biblical text implies that Isaac—young, naïve, and trusting—has no inkling of what is in store for him, but it by no means rules out the possibility that he does in fact have some inkling. If he does, is he a willing or a horrified and unwilling victim?

The anonymous narrator of Genesis leaves this question unanswered, but Allah answers it in the Qur'an. In Sura 37, Allah states that He has rewarded Abraham for his zeal in attacking the idolatry of Azar and his people with the birth of a "gentle son." But then, when that son

was old enough to accompany him, he said: "My son, I saw in a dream that I was sacrificing you, so reflect and give me your opinion."

He said: "Father, do as you are commanded and you shall find me, God willing, steadfast." (37:102)

Here, Allah sharply corrects the biblical account: Abraham does *not* conceal from his son the divine command that has come to him in a dream. And the son, for his part, does *not* proceed in oblivious trust, like Isaac in the Book of Genesis, but—being old enough to take a reflective and responsible part in the sacrifice—declares a forthright willingness to give up his life if such is Allah's will. Like his father, he submits to his divine Lord—good Muslims both.

In Jewish interpretive tradition, the focus over centuries of time would shift gradually from Abraham to Isaac as persecuted Jews saw their traumatized trust in God mirrored in Isaac's traumatized trust in Abraham.[1] This shift is evident in *The Lessons of Rabbi Eliezer* (*pirkêy de rabbi 'eli'ezer*), a work written in Hebrew and brought to completion, probably after a long period of expansion and repeated revision, in the early ninth century. In this work, Isaac, facing his own immolation, cries out:

> O my father! Bind for me my two hands, and my two feet, so that I do not curse thee; for instance, a word may issue from the mouth because of the violence and dread of death, and I shall be found to have slighted the precept, "Honor thy Father." (Exodus 20:12)[2]

Given the relatively late date of this work and its possible origin in Mesopotamia under Muslim rule, it may well reflect the influence of the Qur'an.

As a boy, I was quietly disturbed at a rather young age by the word *infant* carried in the word *infantry,* and there does seem something curiously modern in the shift of emphasis from the sacrificing father to the sacrificed son. Wilfred Owen was clearly devastated by the sacrifice in World War I of "half the seed of Europe, one by one." From the depths of the war in Vietnam, Leonard Cohen expressed a kindred emotion in his 1969 "Story of Isaac."

The biblical account continues:

> When they arrived at the place which God had indicated to him, Abraham built an altar there, and arranged the wood. Then he bound his son and put him on the altar on top of the wood. Abraham stretched out his hand and took the knife to kill his son.
>
> But the angel of Yahweh called to him from heaven. "Abraham, Abraham!" he said. "Here I am," he replied. "Do not

raise your hand against the boy," the angel said. "Do not harm him, for now I know you fear God. You have not refused me your own beloved son." Then looking up, Abraham saw a ram caught by its horn in a bush. Abraham took the ram and offered it as a burnt offering in place of his son. Abraham called this place "Yahweh provides," and hence the saying today "On the mountain Yahweh provides." (Genesis 22:9–14)

In this entire episode, Abraham says nothing but "Here I am," and he says that twice—the first time when Elohim calls to him and demands the sacrifice of his only and beloved son; the second time when the angel of Yahweh calls to him and revokes the command. If Yahweh Elohim knows that Abraham "has not refused me your own beloved son," it is not because of anything that Abraham has actually said. As for what may be Isaac's condition after this ordeal, the angel has nothing to say. An undercurrent of darkness and mystery runs through this tale, surely accounting for much of the endless Jewish and Christian commentary that it has attracted over the centuries.

In the Qur'an, Allah brings the story to a kind of surprise conclusion as follows:

> When both submitted to the will of God, he bent his head down and on its side.
> And We called out to him: "O Abraham, you have made your vision come true."
> Thus do We reward the virtuous.
> That was indeed a conspicuous ordeal.
> And We ransomed him with a mighty sacrifice,
> And conferred honour upon him among later generations.
>
> Peace be upon Abraham! Thus do We reward the virtuous.
> He was one of our faithful worshippers.
> And We gave him glad tidings of Isaac, a prophet and man of virtue. (37:103–112)

No wood, no binding, no knife, and no inscrutable silence on Abraham's part: Abraham places his son's face sideways lest their eyes should meet, and on the spot Allah accepts this as submission and cancels the sacrifice. Allah "ransoms" Abraham's son by providing a substitute sacrifice for the two of them and perhaps other guests to consume in a great celebration, the celebration memorialized today in Islam's annual Eid al-Adha (Feast of the Sacrifice).

In literary terms, the biblical account has foreshadowing, irony, ambiguity, and suspense, with perhaps its most electrifying moment coming in the very last line. The qur'anic account aims at none of these effects, but then Allah never aims for effect. He is not attempting to entertain Muhammad but only to remind him of stories Muhammad already knows, each of them recalled to make essentially the same point: the supreme importance of submission, *'islam,* to Allah.

I do not mean to suggest that Genesis 22, as originally composed, was a mere entertainment. Child sacrifice is clearly attested to in Canaanite archeological evidence. If no Israelites had ever engaged in the same practice, Yahweh would not have needed to forbid it as He does in the Book of Leviticus: "You will not allow any of your children to be sacrificed to Molech, thus profaning the name of your God. I am Yahweh" (18:21). Centuries later, King Josiah of Judah would not have had to campaign to stop that very practice in Jerusalem (2 Kings 23:10).

The structure of the Genesis story might well be borrowed from a Canaanite myth in which Molech demanded the sacrifice of a child, a Molech worshipper performed the sacrifice, and Molech was pleased. Here, the story begins in the same way but then, at the crucial moment, is reversed. It could thus quite conceivably be a myth consciously designed to counter an earlier myth. Over time, while the key elements of the story survived, its moral may have changed several times over, for successive interpretive communities.

But not to deprive the qur'anic version of all suspense or mystery, it certainly does leave the hearer with one large question: who is the unnamed son of this sacrifice? One plausible way to read the phrase "glad tidings of Isaac," which comes in the aftermath of the "submission," is as an allusion to the passage already considered—namely, the passage in which Allah gave Abraham and his wife the news that Isaac would be born. But then if Isaac, the younger son, is still to be born, it can only be the older son, Ishmael, who has just acquitted himself so nobly in the sacrifice story, or so some Muslim commentators have reasoned, according to *The Study Quran*. The editors add, however: "Others understand this verse as a separate statement affirming that Isaac was the subject of the sacrifice and was to be given the gift of prophethood."

In the Book of Genesis, the story that Jewish tradition calls the Akedah (Hebrew, "binding") of Isaac ends only after the angel of Yahweh calls to Abraham once again, this time with a final message from Yahweh:

> "I swear by my own self, Yahweh declares, that because you have done this, because you have not refused me your own beloved son, I will shower blessings on you and make your descendants as numerous as the stars of heaven and the grains of sand on the seashore. Your descendants will gain possession of the gates of their enemies. All nations on earth will bless themselves by your descendants, because you have obeyed my command." (22:16–18)

To this, the taciturn Abraham makes no reply at all but simply turns back to his waiting servants and heads homeward to Beersheba. Yahweh has promised nothing whatsoever in the aftermath of this traumatic episode that He had not already promised. Nothing, initially, was required of Abraham except his obedience to the command to "leave your country, your kindred and your father's house" (12:1). At this climactic moment, once again nothing but obedience has been required, but are we to conclude that Abraham has once again obeyed, or is it rather that Yahweh has blinked and countermanded His own command without ever learning whether Abraham would commit the sin of parricide rather than break covenant with Him?

The Akedah contains in microcosm the entire saga of Israelite and later Jewish history, for what is the antithesis of miraculous fertility if not genocide? Is it not the annihilation of immense populations, to the point that the very annihilation becomes proverbial, the antithesis of the promised proverbial fertility, fertility so wondrous that "all clans on earth will bless themselves by you" (12:3)?

Abraham in the Akedah and Moses in Egypt are related as thesis and antithesis. Had Abraham slain Isaac, the myriad Israelite descendants miraculously saved from Pharaoh's pursuing army would never have been born. It would be as if they had gone up in smoke, dying with Isaac on Abraham's sacrificial pyre.

Isaac's birth to a postmenopausal, ninety-year-old woman was a miracle, as great a miracle as a virgin birth. It happened only because of divine intervention. Isaac's survival—the loosing of his bonds that day on Mount Moriah—came about through another act of divine intervention. And because the only afterlife recognized in the Book of Genesis is life extended through one's offspring, the life restored to Isaac when the knife was taken from his neck was restored as well to Abraham.

Intriguingly, the text does not say that Abraham *and Isaac* rejoined the servants and then returned together to Beersheba. Did Isaac, once unbound, flee homeward alone to rejoin his mother, Sarah, and tell her what happened? Sarah dies in the following chapter, and later, when Isaac marries, we read (Genesis 24:67): "He married Rebekah and made her his wife. And in his love for her, Isaac was consoled for the loss of his mother."

Did the old woman die of shock? How many years had passed between the *akedah* and his marriage? How old was he on that fateful day? The Bible does not tell us. *The Lessons of Rabbi Eli'ezer* offers a guess: "Isaac was thirty-seven years old."[3]

Any younger, and he might have lost his faith. But unmarried at that age? Hardly typical for that time and place, historians would maintain, but then, too, Isaac lived an exceptional life in so many ways.

Centuries later, the first Christians would identify faithful trust as that which God had shown himself to desire most from mankind from Abel down to Abraham and on down to their own trusting faith in the resurrection of Jesus. Of Abraham, the Letter to the Hebrews says:

> It was by faith that Abraham, *when put to the test, offered up Isaac.* He offered to sacrifice *his only son* even though he had yet to receive what had been promised, and he had been told: *Isaac is the one through whom your name will be carried on.* He was confident that God had the power even to raise the dead; and so, figuratively speaking, he was given back Isaac from the dead. (Hebrews 11:17–19, with internal quotes from other biblical books italicized)

In the Letter to the Romans and the Letter to the Galatians, Paul relativizes the entire Mosaic Covenant—whose intent was and is by upright living to maintain Israel's covenant with God—by noting that Abraham lived long before Moses, and yet God said of him, in a line already twice quoted, "Abram put his faith in Yahweh, and this was reckoned to him as uprightness" (Genesis 15:6). Paul thus leaps back over Moses and centuries of righteous Israelite life within the Mosaic Covenant to Abraham's faith-based path to the same righteousness. He then sees the impossibly glorious fertility promise to Abraham fulfilled not in physical descendants but in Paul's own new and growing throng of converts, spiritual descendants of Abraham—those who are sons of Abraham through faith rather than by birth:

> *Abraham*, you remember, *put his faith in God,* and this was reckoned to him as uprightness. Be sure, then, that it is people of faith who are the children of Abraham. And it was because scripture foresaw that God would give saving justice to the gentiles through faith, that it announced the future gospel to Abraham in the words: *All nations will be blessed in you.* So it is people of faith who receive the same blessing as Abraham, the man of faith. (Galatians 3:6–9, quoting Genesis 15:6 and 12:3 in italic)

What Paul does in this way to his fellow Jews, Allah does to Jews and Christians alike, and to all disputes between them over Abraham, when he addresses them together as what He calls "People of the Book":

> O People of the Book, why do you dispute concerning Abraham? The Torah and Evangel {Gospel} were revealed only after his time. Will you not be reasonable? Consider. It was you who argued about a matter of which you have knowledge. Why then do you argue about a matter of which you have no knowledge? God knows and you do not know. Abraham was neither a Jew nor a Christian, but a man of pristine faith, a Muslim, nor was he an idolater. Of all mankind, those most deserving of Abraham are his followers, and this prophet

standing before you {Muhammad}, and those who believe.
God is the Patron of believers. (3:65–68)

Here, with exceptional clarity, Allah identifies the submission of Abraham with that of Muhammad, relativizing all that lies between the two. Another, more powerful such identification is made—with a plausible link to the tale of Abraham, Ishmael, and the suspended sacrifice—at Qur'an 2:124 and following:

Remember when his Lord tested Abraham with certain rulings and how Abraham fulfilled them.
    God said: "I shall appoint you an exemplar to mankind."
    Abraham said: "And also my descendants."
    God said: "Evildoers shall not enjoy My covenant."
    Remember when We set up the House as a place frequented by mankind, a sanctuary: "Take the station of Abraham as a place of worship." And We thus commanded Abraham and Ishmael: "To sanctify My House for those who circle around it, those who seclude themselves in it and those who bow and prostrate themselves in prayer."

Remember when Abraham said: "Lord, make this city a sanctuary and bless its people with sustenance, those of them who believe in God and the Last Day."
    God said: "As for him who disbelieves, I shall grant him brief enjoyment and then shall consign him to the torment of the Fire, a wretched fate indeed."

Remember when Abraham and Ishmael were raising up the foundations of the House:

"Our Lord, accept this from us,
You are All-Hearing, All-Knowing,
Our Lord, make us surrender ourselves to You,
And from our descendants a nation which surrenders itself
    to You.

Show us our holy rituals,
And forgive us. You are All-Forgiving, All-Merciful.
Our Lord, send them a messenger, of their number,
Who shall recite to them Your verses,
Teaching them the Book and the Wisdom,
And who shall purify them.
You are the Almighty, the All-Wise."

Who can willfully abandon the religion of Abraham unless it
    be one who makes a fool of himself? (2: 124–130)

Here, again, the identification of the "religion of Abraham" with the
message of Muhammad is complete. But note well: Abraham has been
made an exemplar *"to mankind."* The Ka'aba, built by Abraham and
Ishmael, has been made "a place frequented *by mankind."* Accordingly,
the message of Muhammad, so powerfully identified with Abraham, is
for mankind as well.

And yet, in a special way, it remains a message for the Arabs. Just
as Yahweh claims sovereignty over all mankind but delivers His scripture in Hebrew and makes His covenant only with Israel, locating it
not on the planet as a whole but only in the Promised Land, so Allah,
too, claims universal sovereignty but gives his revelation in Arabic and
organizes his worship around one very particular spot in Arabia. At
the outset of his prophetic career, Muhammad instructed his followers that the direction (Arabic, *qiblah*) of their prayers should be toward
Jerusalem. Later, Allah instructed him that Muslim prayers should be
directed, instead, toward "the House," in Mecca. This redirection, this
new *qiblah,* was a crucial moment in the individuation of Islam as neither a new form of Judaism nor a new form of Christianity but a distinct
new community with, geographically as well as spiritually, a new orien-
tation. Jews turned toward Jerusalem—Zion, the City of David—when
they prayed. Christian churches were oriented toward the sunrise, a
symbol of Christ's resurrection. Each of the two has its own *qiblah.* But
Allah was now taking Muhammad in a new direction:

We have seen you turning your face from side to side in the
    heavens,

So We will now turn you towards a direction that will please
you:
Turn your face towards the Sacred Mosque.
Wherever you may be, turn your faces towards it.
Those granted the Book know that this is the truth from
their Lord.
God is not unaware of what they do. (Qur'an 2:144)

Speaking through Muhammad to Arabs newly converted to Islam,
Allah says at another point in the Qur'an:

Behold the revelations of the Manifest Book!
We have sent it down as an Arabic Qur'an; perhaps you will
understand.
We narrate to you the fairest of narratives, through what We
revealed to you—this Qur'an.
And yet before it you were heedless. (12:2–3)

Among the fair narratives, that of the heroic joint submission of Abraham and his son stands supreme. Historic in the Hebrew Bible, sym-
bolic in the New Testament, their ordeal becomes both paradigmatic
and foundational in Islam, linked as it is both to the Arabic Qur'an and
to the supremely hallowed desert oasis in Arabia to which, around the
world, millions of Muslims still direct their prayers, their theolatry, five
times a day.

6

Joseph

According to a venerable Spanish proverb, God writes straight with crooked lines (*Dios escribe derecho con renglones torcidos*), but how crooked does God allow the lines to become before he begins straightening them? This is the question that will shape our consideration of Yahweh Elohim and of Allah in the story of Joseph.

A famous few lines from Shakespeare's *Hamlet* make the same point as the Spanish proverb and invite the same question:

> Our indiscretion sometime serves us well
> When our deep plots do pall, and that should teach us
> There's a divinity that shapes our ends,
> Rough-hew them how we will. (Act V, sc. ii, lines 8–11)

To use Shakespeare's language, how rough may we hew before divinity shapes? At this point in the play, the murderous and usurping King Claudius of Denmark has sent his nephew, Prince Hamlet, the son of Claudius's slain predecessor on the throne, to England. Hamlet's shipboard traveling companions, Rosencrantz and Guildenstern, are carrying a letter from Claudius to the King of England. Indiscreetly and secretly, Hamlet opens the letter and discovers that Claudius has asked the English king to have Hamlet executed. In appropriately flowery diplomatic language, Hamlet then writes a substitute letter instructing the English king to execute the letter's bearers, Rosencrantz and Guildenstern themselves. Hamlet seals this substitute letter into the very envelope that Claudius's unsuspecting agents are carrying, and in due course the King of England does as requested.

The death of Rosencrantz and Guildenstern is not the end of the tragedy, however. Hamlet's letter was just one of the crooked lines, and in the play's final scene he himself will die. But is even his death the play's true conclusion? What awaits him in the afterlife, "from whose bourn / No traveller returns," in which he so firmly believes? Where does the "divinity that shapes our ends" end its shaping? Hamlet's dying words are: "The rest is silence."

In the biblical saga, after the departure of Hagar and Ishmael, little is said about him and nothing about her. The narration continues through Isaac, who fathers two sons, one of whom, Jacob, acquires the sobriquet Israel. Jacob/Israel then fathers twelve sons by two wives and their respective maidservants, whom he takes as concubines: these twelve are to be the eponymous patriarchs of the future twelve tribes of Israel. Among the twelve, leaving aside the toddler Benjamin, Jacob favors the seventeen-year-old Joseph—born to his favorite wife, Rachel—over the other ten, born to the concubines and to his less favored wife, Leah.

> Jacob loved Joseph more than all his other sons, for he was the son of his old age, and he had a decorated tunic made for him. But his brothers, seeing how much more his father loved him than all his other sons, came to hate him so much that they could not say a civil word to him. (Genesis 37:3–4)

Bitter rivalry between the wives, now transferred to their respective sons, is the context for a "rough-hewed" indiscretion by the teenaged Joseph that puts the plot in motion.

> Now Joseph had a dream, and he repeated it to his brothers, who then hated him more than ever. "Listen," he said, "to the dream I had. We were binding sheaves in the field, when my sheaf suddenly rose and stood upright, and then your sheaves gathered round and bowed to my sheaf." "So you want to be king over us," his brothers retorted, "you want to lord it

over us?" And they hated him even more, on account of his dreams and of what he said. He had another dream which he recounted to his brothers. "Look, I have had another dream," he said. "There were the sun, the moon and eleven stars, bowing down to me." He told his father and brothers, and his father scolded him. "A fine dream to have!" he said to him. "Are all of us then, myself, your mother and your brothers, to come and bow to the ground before you?" His brothers held it against him, but his father pondered the matter. (37:5–1)

In both the Bible and the Qur'an, God sometimes speaks through dreams, but it is clear not just from the brothers' reaction but also from Jacob's that they take this dream to come from nowhere loftier than a cocky teenager's imagination. A grave sin? Hardly. Rather, a boyish indiscretion that merely sets old Jacob to thinking.

This indiscretion, however, is a last-straw affront to the brothers. Out in the pastureland with their father's flocks and far from his tent, the brothers see Joseph approaching and are suddenly seized with a murderous impulse:

"Here comes that dreamer," they said to one another. "Come on, let us kill him now and throw him down one of the storage-wells; we can say that some wild animal has devoured him. Then we shall see what becomes of his dreams." (37:19–20)

Reuben, the eldest brother, persuades them to throw Joseph into a dry well but not to kill him immediately. Having disposed of Joseph for the moment, the brothers then settle down to eat. But a caravan of Ishmael-ite (Arab) traders happens along, and Judah says to his brothers:

"What do we gain by killing our brother and covering up his blood? Come, let us sell him to the Ishmaelites, then we shall not have laid hands on him ourselves. After all, he is our brother, and our own flesh." His brothers agreed. (37:26–27)

In Egypt, the traders sell Joseph to Potiphar, "one of Pharaoh's officials and commander of the guard" (37:36). Back home, the brothers plunge

Jacob into long days of mourning by dipping Joseph's decorated tunic in goat's blood, leading the old man to believe that his favorite son is dead, dragged off and devoured by a wild beast.

To this point in the biblical account, the anonymous narrator has not offered the story of Joseph as in any way an exemplary story, and he has assigned Yahweh Elohim neither a speaking role in it nor any other kind of intervention. Human action, indiscreet or impulsive as it may be, excusable or inexcusable, seems to be all that is driving the action forward.

The same story assumes a strikingly different character as Allah tells it in the Qur'an:

Remember when Joseph said to his father: "O father, I dreamt of eleven stars, and of the sun and moon. I dreamt they were bowing down before me."

He said: "My son, do not relate your dream to your brothers, else they will contrive and plot against you. Satan to man is a manifest enemy. Thus will your Lord choose you and teach you the interpretation of reports, and perfect His grace upon you and upon the family of Jacob, as He perfected it upon your ancestors before you, Abraham and Isaac. Your Lord is Omniscient, All-Wise."

In the story of Joseph and his brothers there were clear signs to those who seek answers.

Remember when they said: "Joseph and his brother are more dear to our father than we are, though we are a band. Our father is in manifest error. So kill Joseph or drive him away to some land, and the face of your father shall be wholly yours, and after him you shall be a virtuous community."

One of them said: "Do not kill Joseph but throw him into the darkness of the well, where some travellers will pick him up—that is, if you carry through that deed."

They said: "O father, why is it that you do not trust us with Joseph, though we care for him? Send him with us tomorrow to roam and play, and we will surely guard him well."

He said: "It grieves me that you take him away, and I fear
the wolf might eat him when you are not minding him."
They said: "Were a wolf to eat him, we being a band, we
would most surely be good for nothing!"

When they set out with him, and all agreed they would hurl
him into the darkness of the well, We revealed to him: "You
shall acquaint them with this act of theirs at a time when they
shall recall it not." (12:4–15)

In the biblical account, there is the divine actor, on the one hand,
and there are the human actors, on the other. In the qur'anic account,
there are the divine actor and the human actors, and then there is the
demonic actor: a two-character play becomes a three-character play in
which Satan has the godlike power to enter and influence human minds
and manipulate the course of events. As the biblical narrator tells the
story, the brothers' envy is self-explanatory. As Allah tells it, Satan did
what he could to lead the brothers into sin.

The biblical narrator would have us believe that Jacob sent Joseph
to join his brothers in the field never guessing that he was sending his
favorite son into danger. Allah, who honors Jacob as a prophet, tells us a
different story. Allah portrays Jacob as fully aware of the brothers' malice, warning Joseph in advance to beware the ten and not tell them the
dream that Joseph has just told his father. As for that dream itself, Allah
again corrects the Bible: Jacob is not offended by it, merely concerned
that Satan and the brothers—the two mentioned in the same breath—
will use it against Joseph.

Jacob goes on to predict that Joseph too will become a prophet:
"Thus will your Lord choose you and teach you the interpretations of
reports." And Allah further indicates that His final goal in managing
the events of the Joseph episode as He does is to offer "clear signs to
those who seek answers" (12:7). What happens to Joseph and his brothers
is happening, in other words, *so that* their story can eventually be part
of the Qur'an.

The biblical story of Joseph is a tour de force of Hebrew narrative
art, one of the subtlest and most elegant narrative set pieces in the
entire Bible. Betrayal and deceit in which the anonymous, omniscient

narrator and we the readers know the truth while one or another of the human actors in the story—Jacob or Joseph or, later, Judah—does not is intrinsic to its power. As we wait, repeatedly, for one actor or another to learn what we already know, suspense mounts, declines, mounts again, declines again, and so forth.

But where is Yahweh Elohim through all this suspense? Joseph—betrayed by his brothers, trapped at the bottom of a pit, awaiting in anguish what lies ahead—is a man whose plight would seem to cry out for the sort of prayer that we hear so often in the Psalms, where "the pit" is sometimes a powerful symbol for human despair and divine delay.

Such a psalm is Psalm 69, where we read:

> It is for you I bear insults,
> > my face is covered with shame,
> I am estranged from my brothers,
> > alienated from my own mother's sons;
> for I am eaten up with zeal for your house,
> > and insults directed against you fall on me.
> ....
> Rescue me from the mire before I sink in;
> > so I shall be saved from those who hate me,
> > from the watery depths.
> Let not the waves wash over me,
> > nor the deep swallow me up,
> nor the pit close its mouth on me. (Psalm 69:7–9, 14–15)

Powerful lines, but in the Book of Genesis, Joseph may be consumed with dread but is not "consumed with zeal" for Yahweh's house. He has shown, as yet, no sense at all of divine election or vocation. The reader is left wondering not only whether Joseph will beseech Yahweh Elohim to come to his rescue but also whether Yahweh Elohim will respond. As these background questions remain unanswered, a hum of theographical suspense grows behind the more obvious elements of narrative suspense.

But suspense is simply not a game that Allah plays in the Qur'an. Joseph, for whom Jacob has already provided some considerable, tension-relieving sense of what lies ahead, is visited by Allah Himself while he is still in the pit and before he has ever been sold into slavery in Egypt. Allah tells him, reassuringly, "You shall acquaint them with this act of theirs at a time when they shall recall it not" (12:15). Allah tells Joseph, in effect: To their great surprise, you will have the last word.

As the biblical story continues, the anonymous narrator does begin to mention Yahweh, even rather insistently:

> Now Joseph had been taken down into Egypt. Potiphar the Egyptian, one of Pharaoh's officials and commander of the guard, bought him from the Ishmaelites who had taken him down there. Yahweh was with Joseph, and everything he undertook was successful. He lodged in the house of his Egyptian master, and when his master saw how Yahweh was with him and how Yahweh made everything he undertook successful, he was pleased with Joseph and made him his personal attendant; and his master put him in charge of his household, entrusting him with all his possessions. And from the time he put him in charge of his household and all his possessions, Yahweh blessed the Egyptian's household out of consideration for Joseph; Yahweh's blessing extended to all his possessions, both household and estate. So he left Joseph to handle all his possessions, and with him there, concerned himself with nothing beyond the food he ate. (39:1–6)

Yahweh, Yahweh, Yahweh—five mentions within just six short verses. But at this point does Joseph know all that the omniscient biblical narrator knows? And what does the narrator intend by the words "[Joseph's] master saw how Yahweh was with him and how Yahweh made everything he undertook successful"? Even in the terms of a narrative within which miracles do occur and God regularly does speak, we may well ask what it was that Potiphar actually saw? Did he see the God of Abraham, Isaac, and Jacob in action? Is that what the narrator intends? Or did he simply see a charismatic Joseph exceeding all human expectations?

The word *charisma*—from the Greek for "grace" or "divine favor"— connotes an ability or a power beyond the human. When we say, even in English, that someone is "gifted," we imply that the gift had a giver whether or not we ever stop to ask who the giver might have been. Here, Yahweh Elohim is the giver, but does Potiphar see anything more than Joseph's gifts? In the Qur'an, Allah comments:

> Thus did We establish Joseph firmly on earth, in order that We might teach him the interpretation of reports. God's decree will prevail, but *most people* do not know.

> When he grew to full manhood, We granted him sound judgment and knowledge—thus do We reward those who act righteously. (12:21–22, emphasis added)

"Most people," presumably including Potiphar (known in the Qur'an only as "the man from Egypt"), saw the effects of divine favor but not divinity itself. They lack the eyes to see the wonder unfolding before them.

As the story proceeds, we learn that administrative ability is not Joseph's only gift:

> Now Joseph was well built and handsome, and it happened some time later that his master's wife cast her eyes on Joseph and said, "Sleep with me." (Genesis 39:7)

Joseph refuses out of loyalty to Potiphar, who has treated him so well and trusted him so completely, but also because of Elohim: "How could I do anything so wicked, and sin against God?" (39:9)

Potiphar's wife's attempt to seduce Joseph continues day after day. One day,

> she caught hold of him by his tunic and said, "Sleep with me." But he left the tunic in her hand, took to his heels and got out. (39:12)

Hell hath no fury like a woman scorned. When Potiphar returns home, his wife (unnamed in the biblical account) turns bitterly on Joseph and,

holding up Joseph's dropped tunic as evidence, accuses him of assault-
ing her. The outraged Potiphar then has Joseph clapped forthwith in
the dungeon that, as commander of the guard, he maintains beneath his
own residence.

Allah gives this episode a sharply different ending. Joseph's master finds Joseph innocent and his own wife guilty in a seduction story
that includes a slightly bawdy chase scene. The action begins as "The
woman in whose house he dwelt sought to seduce him and shut firm the
doors upon them: she in whose house he was staying sought to lure him
from himself":

> She said: "Come to me!" He said: "God forbid! He is my lord
> and has treated me hospitably. Sinners do not prevail." For she
> was about to possess him, and he to possess her, were it not
> that he saw the proof of his Lord.
>
> Thus did it turn out, so that We might avert from him sin
> and debauchery. He was one of Our faithful worshippers.
>
> They raced to the door, and she tore his shirt from behind.
> They found her master by the door.
>
> She said: "What is the punishment for one who intended
> evil against your wife except to be imprisoned or suffer pain-
> ful torment?"
>
> He said: "It was she who attempted to seduce me."
>
> A witness from her family witnessed as follows: "If his shirt
> is torn from the front, then she is telling the truth and he is
> lying. But if his shirt is torn from behind, then she is lying and
> he is telling the truth."
>
> When he saw that his shirt was torn from behind, he said:
> "This is woman's cunning; indeed, your cunning is great.
> O Joseph, mention this matter to no one; and you, woman,
> ask forgiveness for your offence, for you have truly been sin-
> ful." (12:23–29)

Allah's account ends with the too familiar "she said/he said," but as the
evidence favors the man, the master's anger is directed mainly at the
woman. By contrast, the biblical narrator's account ends abruptly with

"she said": Joseph is permitted no reply, and Potiphar's fury is directed at him alone.

Among other differences in these two accounts (differences of detail, such as the biblical lost tunic as opposed to the qur'anic torn shirt), one of some significance is that Allah allows candidly that Joseph was attracted to the woman, ready in human terms to "possess" her, even though he repelled her advances. About this, the biblical narrator has nothing to say. Essentially, however, the two accounts agree that Joseph resisted the woman's advances both out of loyalty to his Egyptian master and out of adherence to God's law. Satan, interestingly, is *not* an actor in this scene, but Allah is actively and declaratively engaged in it, bolstering Joseph's virtue and, in asides, making His interpretive points for the benefit of Muhammad. Yahweh Elohim, for all we know at this point, is involved, if at all, only invisibly and behind the scenes.

The next chapter in either account is the tale of Joseph in prison. In the Bible, Joseph is behind bars simply because Potiphar has put him there. In the Qur'an, the story is noticeably more complicated. After Joseph's master has largely exonerated him, Allah reports that his erstwhile seductress, even as she admits her sin, paraded Joseph before a gathering of the "women in the city," who swooned over his unearthly beauty: "He is no human being! He is nothing but a noble angel" (12:31)! So smitten were they, Allah says, that instead of cutting the food that she has served them, they end up cutting their own hands. Implied is that, like so many raving maenads, they were about to yield to their longing en masse, and she is fully prepared to be their ringleader:

> She said: "Here he is, the one you reproached me with! I attempted to seduce him but he resisted my seduction. And yet, if he does not do what I order him, he will assuredly be imprisoned and suffer humiliation." (12:32)

Faced with the choice between imprisonment and consent to an orgy, Joseph replies:

> "My Lord, prison is dearer to me than what they invite me to do. If You do not ward off their guile from me, I shall long for them, and so become a man of base desires."

His Lord answered his call and averted their guile from
him—He is All-Hearing, Omniscient. (12:33–34)

Once the signs of Joseph's God-given resolve become unmistakable, the
women turn on him and do manage to have him imprisoned. But this, it
would seem, is clearly a part of Allah's plan.

In the Bible, the story of Joseph seems to tell itself as one event leads
to, or provokes, the next. Joseph's imprisonment is caused by Potiphar's
believing his wife's false accusation, which was caused by her fatal
attraction to Joseph, which was caused by Joseph's beauty, which was
a gift from Elohim. Once in prison, events are set in motion again by
Joseph's skill in interpreting dreams, a skill he might not have been
called on to exercise had events not led to his imprisonment in the first
place.

In the Qur'an, Allah, the divine narrator, has shared His understanding of Joseph's future with Jacob, His prophet, who, as we saw, has shared
much of it with Joseph. Someday, Jacob has confided to Joseph, Joseph's
"interpretation of reports" will be Allah's great gift to him, and someday, too, Joseph's resolute decency will be a lesson to all inquirers—
inquirers, we may assume, about Muhammad's message. Allah thus not
only tells the story but also controls the story as it unfolds, revealing as
much of it in advance to His successive messengers as He chooses.

It is while he is in prison that Joseph begins to grow into his vocation
as a prophet of Allah to the polytheist Egyptians:

Entering the prison with him were two young men.
One of them said: "I dreamt I was pressing grapes."
The other said: "I dreamt I was carrying on my head bread
from which the birds were eating. Tell us its interpretation, for
we see you are a virtuous man." (12:36)

Joseph confirms that, yes, he has the Allah-given power to interpret
events but then proclaims his allegiance to "the religion of my forefathers, Abraham, and Isaac and Jacob." As for what they believe:

"My fellow prisoners, are many and diverse gods better, or is
the One Omnipotent God? What you worship instead of Him

are merely names that you and your ancestors coined, and for which no authority has come from God. Sovereignty belongs solely to God. He commands that you worship none but Him. This is the upright religion, but most mankind have no understanding." (12:39–40)

Sermons delivered in prison—and Joseph's speech to his fellow prisoners is the longest he will give in the Qur'an's Joseph story—can be as welcome and as life-giving as water in the desert or as desolating as the sight of land receding from view to a ship lost at sea. Decades ago, as a student in Rome, I attended a sermon in the lofty day room of a crumbling juvenile prison. Looming above the preacher hung a huge oil painting of the crucifixion and above it "God is love." The canvas of the painting was so old that it hung in folds upon which dust had accumulated over the years. Daylight streamed down on the dust from barred windows up near the barrel-vaulted ceiling, far beyond the reach of the boys gathered miserably below. One of the boys, effeminate and mocked for it by the others, had the cruel nickname *Biancaneve*—Italian for "Snow White." The scene could not have been more depressing. And yet many years later, I visited an American friend serving time for a drug offense in a low-security Northern California prison. How cheered and buoyed he was by my surprise visit to that seminormal and yet joyless place! I had brought him nothing and could do nothing at all to help him. I left humbled, troubled, and yet glad I had gone.

Prison can be a place of either brutal or tender truth. I think of King Lear's words to his daughter Cordelia—both doomed—as they are led off in hostile custody:

Come, let's away to prison:
We two alone will sing like birds i' th'cage;
When thou dost ask me blessing, I'll kneel down
And ask of thee forgiveness. So we'll live,
And pray, and sing, and tell old tales, and laugh
At gilded butterflies, and hear poor rogues
Talk of court news; and we'll talk with them too—
Who loses and who wins; who's in, who's out—

And take upon 's the mystery of things
As if we were God's spies. (Act V, sc. iii, lines 8–17)

Joseph in the Egyptian prison is like God's spy telling the mystery of things to his two fellow prisoners:

"My fellow prisoners, as for one of you, he shall serve his master wine to drink; as for the other, he shall be crucified and the birds shall eat from his head. The issue is settled upon which you seek my opinion."

To the man he imagined was about to be released from the two of them, he said: "Mention me to your master." But Satan caused him to forget the mention of this to his master, and he languished in jail for several years. (12:41–42)

In the Bible, the narrator tells of a closely parallel pair of dreams, adding the detail that it was the king of Egypt's cupbearer who had the wine dream and the king's baker who had the bread dream. And the two biblical dreamers do not turn to Joseph because of his charismatic virtue as the qur'anic pair does. The interpretation is set in motion by Joseph himself, who has been assigned as a kind of Hebrew valet to the two royal Egyptian functionaries:

When Joseph came to them in the morning, he saw that they looked gloomy, and he asked the two officials who were in custody with him in his master's house, "Why these sad looks today?" They replied, "We have each had a dream, but there is no one to interpret it." "Are not interpretations God's business?" Joseph asked them. "Tell me about them." (40:6–8)

The long speech that Allah recounts, Joseph exalting the religion of his forefathers and belittling the religion of Egypt, here shrinks to just one sentence, and that sentence no more than a leading question: "Are not interpretations God's business?"

After delivering the first, welcome interpretation to the cupbearer, the biblical Joseph adds:

"But be sure to remember me when things go well with you, and keep faith with me by kindly reminding Pharaoh about me, to get me out of this house. I was kidnapped from the land of the Hebrews in the first place, and even here I have done nothing to warrant being put in the dungeon." (40:14–15)

Joseph's interpretations quickly are confirmed by events, but "the chief cup-bearer did not remember Joseph; he had forgotten him" (40:23). Call the cupbearer's neglect ingratitude, call it indifference, call it excusable human fallibility—Satan has nothing to do with it as the biblical narrator tells the story. Another detail of expository difference: Joseph in the biblical account gives at this point his first defense of his innocence in Egypt and makes his first reference to his brothers' heartless betrayal of him in Canaan: "I was kidnapped in the land of the Hebrews."

Joseph is freed from prison in both the Bible and the Qur'an when Pharaoh has a troubling double dream that his courtiers (in the Bible, his "magicians and wise men") are unable to interpret. Pharaoh's cupbearer remembers Joseph, seeks him out in prison, and has him interpret Pharaoh's dream: seven fat cows devoured by seven lean ones, then seven plump ears of grain devoured by seven shriveled ones. Joseph explains, both in the Bible and in the Qur'an, that the dreams portend seven years of plenty followed by seven of famine. In both accounts, Joseph is eventually granted Pharaoh's own authority to manage the storage of grain during the years of plenty against the great need that will come, and does, in the years of famine.

In the Qur'an, however, Allah tells Muhammad that Joseph refused to go before Pharaoh until Pharaoh had first called to account the women who had accused Joseph, including his old master's wife. Only after they confess their guilt and confirm Joseph's innocence is he prepared to assume his task as Egypt's quartermaster, yet even then Joseph does not claim that his chastity is his own meritorious achievement: "I do not declare my soul innocent: the soul ever urges to evil, except when my Lord shows mercy. My Lord is All-Forgiving, Compassionate to each" (12:53).

After Joseph's elevation to high office, Allah offers a comment on the story to this point:

This is how We established Joseph firmly in that land, to live
therein wherever he wished. We cast Our mercy upon whomsoever We wish, and We do not neglect the reward of the righteous. But the reward of the hereafter is better for those who
believe and are pious. (12:56–57)

As in the story of Adam and Eve, the afterlife, "the Hereafter," appears
at a pivotal moment in the Qur'an's Joseph story; it never appears in the
Bible's.

The final half of the Joseph story in the Qur'an, its final two-thirds
in the Bible, is the story of Joseph, his brothers (now including Benjamin), and their father, all of them eventually in Egypt. Both accounts,
each in its own way, come to a moving, emotional climax, each climax
especially revealing of the two scriptures' different characterizations of,
respectively, Yahweh Elohim and Allah.

In the biblical account, famine in the biblical "land of the Hebrews"
drives the ten elder brothers to Egypt in hopes of procuring food. They
leave behind only the aged Jacob and his youngest son, Benjamin, now
a teenager about as old as Joseph was when his brothers sold him to the
Arab traders. Arrived in Egypt, the ten encounter but do not recognize
Joseph, now speaking Egyptian and dressed as Pharaoh's all-powerful
viceroy. The Bible's omniscient narrator and we, his readers, know that
Joseph, unbeknownst to his brothers, understands every word that they
are saying among themselves in Hebrew.

Feigning hostility, Joseph accuses them of being spies and imprisons
them for three days. On the third day, however, he offers them a deal:
he will provision them but hold Simeon as a hostage. If and when the
other nine return to him bringing their youngest brother—Benjamin,
Joseph's only full brother—with them, he will take this as proof that
they are honest traders and not spies. At that point, he says, he will both
release Simeon and grant them a second caravan of provisions. They
accept the deal, saying among themselves but within his hearing:

"Clearly, we are being punished for what we did to our brother.
We saw his deep misery when he pleaded with us, but we
would not listen, and now this misery has come to us." (42:21)

This is the first mention in the Bible that Joseph, in misery, actually pleaded with his brothers not to kill him or sell him into slavery. He knew they hated him, but until that moment, he had never guessed how much. Now, as he overhears them recalling their crime, he "turned away from them and wept" (42:24). He returns to them only after regaining his composure.

Joseph then orders their donkeys loaded with provisions and secretly has the money they have paid him returned to them in the saddlebags. They are disconcerted when they discover this: will it later be held against them? But they complete their homeward journey, and wrenching exchanges then ensue between them and their father, Jacob, about Joseph's demand for Benjamin. "You are robbing me of my children," Jacob moans; "Joseph is no more; Simeon is no more; and now you want to take Benjamin. I bear the brunt of all this" (42:36)!

First, Reuben tries to break the impasse and fails:

> "You may put my two sons to death if I do not bring him back to you. Put him in my care and I will bring him back to you." But {Jacob} replied, "My son is not going down with you, for now his brother is dead he is the only one left. If any harm came to him on the journey you are undertaking, you would send my white head down to Sheol with grief!" (42:37–38)

Sheol is the Semitic underworld—not a hell of punishment, much less a heaven of reward, but a realm only of ghostly powerlessness, a nonexistence barely short of nothingness. In simpler language, Jacob is saying simply, "If harm comes to Benjamin, it will kill me."

Meanwhile, however, the famine in the land is grievous and only getting worse. At length, Judah tries one last time:

> "Send the boy with me, and let us be off and go, if we are to survive and not die, we, you, and our dependents. I will go surety for him, and you can hold me responsible for him. If I do not bring him back to you and produce him before you, let me bear the blame all my life." (43:8–9)

At this, Jacob wearily succumbs: "May El Shaddai {another name for Yahweh} move the man to be kind to you, and allow you to bring back your other brother {Simeon} and Benjamin. As for me, if I must be bereaved, bereaved I must be" (43:14).

So, the eleven go down again to Egypt; Joseph receives them more hospitably than the first time; and, when Benjamin is identified for him, he is again overcome with emotion and says, "God be good to you, my son" (43:29). Joseph is twice Benjamin's age, just old enough to be his father. As on the previous visit, he orders his brothers' donkeys to be laden with provisions, the brothers' money again to be clandestinely returned to them atop the provisions, and in addition his own ceremonial drinking cup to be concealed in Benjamin's saddlebag. As the brothers head homeward, Joseph's agents accost them and, after a search, demand that Benjamin, the apparent thief, be returned to Egyptian custody.

At this point, Judah throws himself on Joseph's mercy, deferential to a rhetorical extreme but most effective when he says—inadvertently, because, of course, he does not realize that he is speaking to Joseph— something that pushes Joseph over the emotional brink:

> "So your servant our father said to us, 'You know that my wife bore me two children. When one of them left me, I supposed that he must have been torn to pieces, and I have never seen him since. If you take this one from me too and any harm comes to him, you will send my white head down to Sheol with grief.' If I go to your servant my father now, and we do not have the boy with us, he will die as soon as he sees that the boy is not with us, for his heart is bound up with him, and your servants will have sent your servant our father's white head down to Sheol with grief.... Let your servant stay, then, as my lord's slave in place of the boy, I implore you, and let the boy go back with his brothers. How indeed could I go back to my father and not have the boy with me? I could not bear to see the misery that would overwhelm my father." (Genesis 44:27–31, 33–34)

In the criticism of classical Greek literature, *anagnorisis* is the term used for the climactic recognition of previously unrecognized relationships or their previously unguessed meaning. The moment in Sophocles's tragedy *Oedipus Rex* when Oedipus recognizes that Jocasta, his wife, is also his mother and that he has murdered her husband, his own father, is perhaps the paradigmatic instance of *anagnorisis*. In a flash, everything changes for everybody.

Here, Joseph is moved by emotions that he can no longer conceal as he hears for the first time of what Jacob was told about his abduction so many years ago and of how very deeply Jacob loves Joseph's little brother, Benjamin, born late to their mother, Rachel, who died in childbirth, on a dark day that Joseph must surely recall.

> Then Joseph could not control his feelings in front of all his retainers, and he exclaimed, "Let everyone leave me." No one therefore was present with him while Joseph made himself known to his brothers, but he wept so loudly that all of the Egyptians heard, and the news reached Pharaoh's palace. (45:1–2)

Then comes the true *anagnorisis*:

> Then Joseph said to his brothers, "Come closer to me.... I am your brother Joseph whom you sold into Egypt. But now, do not grieve, do not reproach yourselves for having sold me here, since God sent me before you to preserve your lives. For this is the second year there has been a famine in the country, and there are still five years to come without ploughing or harvest. God sent me before you to assure the survival of your {people} on earth and to save your lives by a great deliverance. So it was not you who sent me here but God, and he has set me up as a father to Pharaoh, as lord of all his household and governor of the whole of Egypt." (45:4–8)

Dios escribe derecho con renglones torcidos. In the end Joseph's interpretation of what has happened coincides exactly with Allah's. Elohim has been in charge all along: "It was not you who sent me here but God." But the biblical narrator is not quite done telling his story, and Joseph must underscore his interpretation of it one more time.

As the eleven brothers, their father with them, draw near to Egypt, Jacob sends Judah ahead to bring word to Joseph, and at this point in the narration the narrator begins pointedly calling Jacob "Israel," using the sobriquet given him by a mysterious night visitor whom he wrestled to a draw years earlier:

> Israel sent Judah ahead to Joseph, so that Judah might present himself to Joseph in Goshen [on the eastern outskirts of Egypt]. . . . Joseph had his chariot made ready and went up to Goshen to meet his father Israel. As soon as he appeared he threw his arms round his neck and for a long time wept on his shoulder. Israel said to Joseph, "Now I can die, now that I have seen you in person and seen you still alive." (46:28–30)

There in Goshen, Israel the patriarch settles with his people, adopting Joseph's two sons as his own, and just before his death delivering a long, poetic, son-by-son blessing that functions analogously as a kind of musical reprise. But once Jacob/Israel is dead, will Joseph turn on his brothers after all?

> Seeing that their father was dead, Joseph's brothers said, "What if Joseph intends to treat us as enemies and pay us back for all the wrong we did him?" So they sent this message to Joseph: "Before your father died, he gave us this order, 'You are to say to Joseph: Now please forgive the crime and faults of your brothers and all the wrong they did you.' So now please forgive the crime of the servants of your father's God." Joseph wept at the message they sent to him.
>
> Then his brothers went to him themselves and, throwing themselves at his feet said, "Take us as your slaves!" But Joseph replied, "Do not be afraid: is it for me to put myself in God's place? The evil you planned to do me has by God's design been turned to good, to bring about the present result: the survival of a numerous people. So there is no need to be afraid; I shall provide for you and your dependents." In this way he reassured them by speaking affectionately to them. (50:15–21)

The biblical narrator is not the only writer of art fiction ever to bring a powerfully emotional story to what seems its resolution only to bring the tension rushing back, and then back again, before truly concluding. I think here of the extended, sometimes explosive codas that conclude certain of Beethoven's piano sonatas. Yet in Allah's account, the *anagnorisis* comes much more quietly and simply than in the Bible. Allah lingers over no sequence of copiously tearful scenes among Joseph, his father, and his brothers. The center of gravity in the Egyptian story as He tells it is not the brothers' protracted failure to recognize Joseph. Joseph's ability to overhear and understand the brothers when they speak Hebrew plays no part in it at all.

In the Qur'an, moreover, Jacob is blind, as he is not in the Bible. Joseph, knowing this, instructs his brothers to take a shirt of his with them when they return home for the first time, confident that his father will recognize Joseph's scent on the shirt. Jacob does so, his sight is restored on the spot, and it is at *that* point of high emotion that the brothers break down and confess, indeed much earlier and more readily than they do in the Bible, where initially only Benjamin meets Joseph's tears with his own. The brothers plead:

> They said, "Father, ask forgiveness for our sins, for we were sinners."
> He said, "I shall ask forgiveness for you from my Lord. He it is Who is All-Forgiving, Compassionate to each." (12:97–98)

In a poem inspired by a qur'anic correction of the Bible, the great Persian poet Jalal al-Din Rumi, makes the miracle of the sight-restoring fragrance of Joseph in the nostrils of Jacob a metaphor for the mystical allure of the divine in the human soul:

> If someone asks you about *houris* [heavenly lovers], show your
>   face and say, "Like this."
> If someone speaks of the moon, rise up beyond the roof and
>   say, "Like this."
> When someone looks for a fairy princess, show your face
>   to him.

When someone talks of musk, let loose your tresses and say,
   "Like this."
If someone says to you, "How do clouds part from the
   moon?"
Undo your robe, button by button, and say, "Like this."
If he asks about the Messiah, "How could he bring the dead
   to life?"
Kiss my lips before him and say, "Like this."
When someone says, "Tell me, what does it mean to be killed
   by love?"
Show my soul to him and say, "Like this."
If someone out of concern asks you about my state,
Show him your eyebrow, bent over double, and say, "Like
   this."
The spirit breaks away from the body, then again it enters
   within.
Come, show the deniers, enter the house and say, "Like this."
In whatever direction you hear a lover complaining,
That is my story, all of it, by God like this.
I am the house of every angel, my breast has turned blue like
   the sky—
Lift up your eyes and look with joy at heaven, like this.
I told the secret of union with the Friend to the east wind
   alone.
Then, through the purity of its own mystery, the east wind
   whispered, "Like this."
Those are blind who say, "How can the servant reach God?"
Place the candle of purity in each one's hand and say, "Like
   this."
I said, "How can the fragrance of Joseph go from town to
   town?"
The fragrance of God wafted down from His Essence and
   said, "Like this."
I said, "How can the fragrance of Joseph give sight back to
   the blind?"
Your breeze came and gave light to my eyes—"Like this."[1]

When the brothers return to Egypt for a second time, Jacob and his wife, Joseph's mother (who is not deceased in the Qur'an, as she is in the Bible), come with them. The old couple prostrate themselves before Joseph (a fulfillment, omitted in the Bible, of Joseph's sun-and-stars dream), and all ends roughly as it does in the Bible. There is one note-worthy difference, however, in Joseph's theological peroration, strongly analogous though it is to the one already quoted from the Bible:

> He said: "Father, this is the interpretation of my former dream; now my Lord has brought it to pass. He was gracious to me when He delivered me from prison and brought you from the wilderness, after Satan had sowed conflict between me and my brothers. My Lord turns with kindness to whomsoever He wills. He is Omniscient, All-Wise." (12:100)

Historically, Muhammad—born in Mecca but driven to flee with his first followers to Medina in the historical *hijra*—returned to Mecca in triumph in 630, striking fear into the hearts of his erstwhile persecutors. But on that occasion, Muhammad gathered the city leaders and elders together and recited to them from Sura 12, the Joseph Sura, reassuring them most especially with the first words of 12:92, the verse with which Joseph sent his brothers home to their father bearing Joseph's shirt with them:

> *"No blame shall fall upon you; today, God forgives you, for He is the most merciful of those who show mercy.* Take this shirt of mine and throw it over my father's face, and he will see again, and bring me your family, one and all." (12:92–93, emphasis added)

In the final moments of the qur'anic account, Joseph addresses himself to Allah in a prayer of gratitude that has no equivalent in the biblical account:

> "My Lord, You have granted me power and taught me the interpretation of reports. Creator of the heavens and earth!
> "You are my Protector in this world and in the hereafter.

"Let me die a Muslim and make me join the company of the
virtuous!" (12:101)

As in the Bible, so here: the providential power of God is ultimately
supreme. Joseph prays for Allah to accept him as a Muslim, in this
world and the world to come. In the Bible, Joseph never mentions the
world to come.

The emotional peak of Sura 12 of the Qur'an, however, comes not in
any scene or series of scenes, however moving, among the human actors
but rather in the heartfelt speech with which Allah concludes the sura,
conveying to Muhammad the full and final meaning of this story, the
only story that occupies an entire sura of the Qur'an. I am not a Muslim,
but something that I can only call the sincerity of Allah comes through
in this speech—something that makes it seem close to the essence of
the Qur'an, the essence of the message that Muhammad, Allah's messenger, is to deliver. Early in the sura, Allah has commented: "In the
story of Joseph and his brothers there were clear signs to those who
seek answers" (12:7). Now, at the sura's end, He spells out for Muhammad what the inquirers might learn from the story of Joseph, if they but
would, and what Muhammad himself must take away from it.

A key part of Allah's message to Muhammad consists precisely of
corrected versions of biblical stories, such as the story of Joseph, stories
that Muhammad already knows in a general way but has not previously
heard from Allah himself and could not have known in this form without Allah's revelation. In the climactic speech below, Allah begins and
ends with precisely this point:

> This account of something that was beyond the reach of thy
> perception We [now] reveal unto thee, [O Prophet:] for thou
> wert not with Joseph's brothers when they resolved upon what
> they were going to do and wove their schemes [against him].
> Yet—however strongly thou mayest desire it—most people
> will not believe [in this revelation], although thou doest not
> ask of them any reward for it: it is but [God's] reminder unto
> all mankind. But [then]—how many a sign is there in the
> heavens and on earth which they pass by [unthinkingly] and
> upon which they turn their backs!

And most of them do not even believe in God without [also] ascribing divine powers to other beings beside Him. Do they, then, feel free from the fear that there might fall upon them the overwhelming terror of God's chastisement, of that the Last Hour might come upon them of a sudden, without their being aware [of its approach]?

Say [O Prophet]: "This is my way: Resting upon conscious insight accessible to reason, I am calling [you all] unto God—I and they who follow me."

And [say:] "Limitless is God in his glory; and I am not one of those who ascribe divinity to aught beside Him!"

And [even] before thy time, We never sent [as Our apostles] any but [mortal] men, whom We inspired, [and whom We always chose] from among the people of the [very] communities [to whom the message was to be brought].

Have, then, they [who reject this divine writ] never journeyed about the earth and beheld what happened in the end to those [deniers of the truth] who lived before them?—and [do they not know that] to those who are conscious of God the life in the hereafter is indeed better [than this world]? Will they not then use their reason?

[All the earlier apostles had to suffer persecution for a long time;] but at last—when those apostles had lost all hope and saw themselves branded as liars—Our succour attained to them: whereupon everyone whom we willed [to be saved] was saved [and the deniers of truth were destroyed], for, never can Our punishment be averted from people who are lost in sin.

Indeed, in the stories of these men there is a lesson for those who are endowed with insight.

[As for this revelation,] it could not possibly be a discourse invented [by man]: nay indeed, it is [a divine writ] confirming the truth of whatever remains [of earlier revelations], clearly spelling out everything, and [offering] guidance and grace unto people who will believe. (12:102–111; all bracketed words original)

I quote here the earnest translation of Muhammad Asad, born Leopold Weiss in what is now Ukraine, a Jewish convert to Islam whose account of the moment of his conversion in his memoir *The Road to Mecca* concludes with his sudden conviction: "Out of the *Koran* spoke a voice greater than the voice of Muhammad."[2] In Asad's translation, I hear him straining at every point—especially in his many bracketed, explanatory insertions—to make his English readers hear what he hears as he listens not so much *to* as *through* the Arabic of the Qur'an. One of his translation's remarkable features is that neither Arabic nor English was his native language, but for him, clearly, the substantial linguistic challenges of the translation were just the beginning. He is straining to translate a voice beyond the Arabic and beyond even Muhammad, a voice that he finds fearsome and yet entirely reasonable and entirely merciful as well, a voice offering "guidance and grace unto people who will believe."

Joseph and His Brothers is the title of a magnificent, unsurpassed four-volume novel that Thomas Mann, the giant of modern German literature, considered his masterpiece. As I conclude this two-track walk through these two scriptural tellings of Joseph's story, what comes to mind is an imagined subtitle for Mann's masterpiece: *Joseph and His Brothers: A Tale of Guidance and Grace.*

7

Moses

"Who is God?" may be a question finally impossible to answer. Somewhat more easily within range, especially if we confine our attention—as in this book we do—to the Qur'an and the Bible alone, is the question "What does God want?" That question is an especially fruitful one to ask as we consider God in conversation and interaction with the remarkable and elusive figure of Moses, the man who, on a mission from God and with God's help, led the Israelites out of bondage in Egypt and through the desert to the Promised Land.

Or was that really what God wanted when he sent Moses into Egypt to confront its god-king, Pharaoh? Might God have wanted something else, something more important to Him than Israelite liberation? In the Qur'an, Allah mentions Moses more often than any other biblical figure. Moses's story—like the story of Abraham—matters to Him. He tells it several times, with variations, and alludes to it many more times. Allah, as we have already seen, makes all of the biblical figures that he mentions precursors of Muhammad, each with a distinct emphasis. He makes Abraham paradigmatic of submission to Allah. As for Moses, Allah makes him a paradigmatic warner (of Egypt) and a paradigmatic messenger (receiving his message, Torah, on a mountain, just as Muhammad received his). Yes, along the way Allah sees to it that Israel is liberated, but this liberation is a corollary or secondary consequence of Allah's primary mission for His prophet and messenger Moses, which is the spread of true religion.

To put the difference as briefly as possible, Yahweh Elohim wants to defeat Pharaoh; Allah wants to convert him. True, in the Qur'an, Pharaoh and the Egyptians do suffer defeat and Israel does escape across the Red Sea. True, conversely, in the Bible, Pharaoh and the Egyptians do at least fleetingly approach conversion. In broad outline, then, the story being told is the same in either scripture. But within that story, what Yahweh Elohim wants and what Allah wants retain their distinctive and illuminating emphases.

The biblical Book of Exodus opens with all the Israelites still in Egypt, just as they were at the end of the Joseph story, which concludes the Book of Genesis. The Israelites have multiplied in Egypt beyond all human reckoning. They now outnumber the Egyptians themselves. But things are beginning to change ominously for them:

> Then Joseph died, and his brothers, and all that generation. But the Israelites were fruitful and prolific; they became so numerous and powerful that eventually the whole land was full of them.
>
> Then there came to power in Egypt a new king [Pharaoh] who had never heard of Joseph. "Look," he said to his people, "the Israelites are now more numerous and stronger than we are. We must take precautions to stop them from increasing any further, or if war should break out, they might join the ranks of our enemies." (Exodus 1:6–10)

Pharaoh instructs the attending midwives to kill all the Israelites' male newborns, but the midwives demur claiming that the Israelite women

> "are hardy and give birth before the midwife can get to them." For this, God was good to the midwives, {the narrator continues} and the people went on increasing and growing more powerful....

> Pharaoh then gave all his people this command: "Throw every new-born boy into the river, but let all the girls live." (Exodus 1:19–20, 22)

This tug-of-war between the two, now equally large rival populations continues for many years: the divinely assisted fertility of the Israelite women against the Egyptian ruler's desperate and murderous attempt to reduce the burgeoning Israelites' power by enslaving them.

At length,

> the king of Egypt died. The Israelites, groaning in their slavery, cried out for help and from the depths of their slavery their cry came up to God. God heard their groaning; God remembered his covenant with Abraham, Isaac and Jacob. God saw the Israelites and took note. (Exodus 2:23–25)

Remember what Yahweh Elohim originally wanted when he commanded Abram, "Leave your country, your kindred and your father's house for a country which I shall show you" (Genesis 12: 1). He wanted fabulous fertility for Abram, later Abraham, and He wanted the resulting great nation to take possession of one particular land, Canaan, which He proceeded to show Abram. Superhuman fertility is still what Yahweh Elohim wants for His people.

Why does He want it? Why for this people rather than for another? He does not say, and we do not know, but there can be no doubt at all that He does indeed still want it. Temporarily, Yahweh Elohim's people are stalled in Egypt, but their fertility—much according to His plan—is so stunning that within just two lifetimes, they as immigrants have overtaken the host Egyptian population in number. Egypt's Pharaoh is now trying to frustrate Yahweh Elohim's plan, to roll back Israelite fertility, or even, over time, to exterminate Israel. Yahweh Elohim's counterreaction is no surprise: this Pharaoh must be stopped and put decisively in his place. And because Yahweh Elohim's fertility plan for His chosen people is to be realized in Canaan, where the twelve sons of Israel (Jacob) were taking root when famine struck, a time must soon come when they leave Egypt and return to Canaan. They will return, however, now transformed from a clan into a nation as populous as Egypt.

This is the point at which Allah begins the story of Moses in Qur'an 20, the longest and most elaborate telling of a Moses story in the Qur'an:

> Has there come to you the narrative of Moses?
>
> When he saw a fire, he said to his family: "Stay behind. I have glimpsed a fire; perhaps I will bring you a brand from it, or find at the fire guidance."
>
> When he drew near it, a voice called out to him: "Moses! It is Me, your Lord. Remove your sandals. You are in the sacred valley, Tuwa. I have chosen you, so listen to what is being revealed.
>
> "It is Me, God: there is no god but I. So worship Me and perform the prayer for My remembrance.
>
> "The Hour is coming—I am about to reveal it—so that every soul is rewarded for what it has achieved.
>
> "Let him not turn you away from it, he who does not believe in it and follows his base desires, else you will perish."
>
> "And what is that in your right hand, O Moses?"
>
> He said: "It is my staff; I lean upon it, and tend my sheep with it, and I have other uses for it."
>
> He said: "Throw it down, O Moses."
>
> He threw it down, and behold, it turned into a serpent, swiftly crawling.
>
> He said: "Pick it up and fear not; We shall return it to its former state.
>
> And tuck your hand into your armpit and it shall come out white, but without harm—another miracle. Thus will We show you some of Our greatest wonders.
>
> "Go to Pharaoh: he has grown tyrannical." (20:9–24)

Here, in commissioning Moses, Allah makes no mention of Israel or its distress. For the offenses of Pharaoh, "he has grown tyrannical" suffices. The bulk of Allah's speech to Moses consists of a summary of the true religion that Moses must preach to Pharaoh:

—that Allah is one;
—that worship of Allah is required;

—that prayer is required;

—that Judgment Day ("the Hour") is coming, though Allah wants it to come without notice so that all may be recompensed for just the sort of lives they are living when the fateful moment comes; and

—that those who believe in Allah must not be led astray by unbelievers who follow only their own whims and passions lest the believers, too, should perish.

Allah does intend that Moses should lead the Israelites out of bondage, out of Egypt, and on to a land that He has promised them, but this theme—so overwhelmingly central in the long, continuous story told by the anonymous narrator of the books of Genesis, Exodus, and beyond—is decidedly muted here as also in other parallel accounts in the Qur'an. Thus, Qur'an 26:10–11: "Remember when your Lord called out to Moses: 'Go forth to that wicked people, the people of Pharaoh—will they not fear Me?'" For Allah, the Egyptians' core offense is that they do not worship the one true God. Their oppression of the Israelites is just one instance of the wrongdoing expected of unbelievers. Whence Allah's tone in the opening words of a third qur'anic telling of the Moses story:

> We are reciting to you some reports of Moses and Pharaoh, the very truth to a people who believe.

> Pharaoh had grown high and mighty on earth. He had turned its inhabitants into diverse classes, holding a group among them to be weak, slaughtering their progeny and debauching their womenfolk. He truly was a corrupter. (28:3–4)

Egypt is a land of factional strife in Sura 28, and the Israelites, again unnamed, are just "a group among them." Pharaoh's overall offense is that he "had grown high and mighty" and "was a corrupter."

Allah's desire that all mankind should worship Him, pray to Him, and await His judgment on them is the motivating desire on His part that drives the qur'anic narratives forward, just as Yahweh's desire for the fertility of Abraham and his descendants drives the biblical narrative forward. Why ever does He desire human homage? Why should He not want, as do the gods of some classical Greek philosophies, to have nothing at all to do with humankind? To this question, Allah gives no answer in the Qur'an; nowhere, in fact, is that question even asked. But that such is indeed His desire is beyond doubt and must be accepted as the premise that animates the oratorically surging, page-by-page, sentence-by-sentence forward momentum of the Qur'an as a work of literature. No wonder, then, that the heart of Allah's commission to Moses regarding Pharaoh and his Egyptian subjects is that they should all repent and, to echo Allah's speech to Moses, should acknowledge that He is God and there is no God but Him.

We have had occasion before to note Allah's quite deliberate way of forestalling suspense in narration before it has a chance to build up. Many other kinds of literary narrative seek to build suspense. Qur'anic narrative often seeks the very opposite. This can be true both of the larger elements in a given narrative and of the smaller ones. Contrast Allah's manner in Qur'an 20, as just quoted, with the manner of the anonymous narrator of the Book of Exodus as he builds suspense both within the overall structure of Moses's call and within Yahweh's presentation of the two "signs" that Moses is to employ to convince skeptics that he is backed by divine power.

In the Exodus story, Moses sees not a fire but a burning bush and draws near out of simple curiosity rather than, as in the Qur'an, in search of either a helpful brand (to kindle another fire) or of "guidance." The Bible gives no early clue to what will happen once Moses reaches the burning bush. The biblical narrator carefully avoids "spoilers." Then Yahweh speaks from the burning bush:

> "Come no nearer," he said. "Take off your sandals, for the place where you are standing is holy ground. I am the God of your ancestors," he said, "the God of Abraham, the God of Isaac, and the God of Jacob." At this Moses covered his face, for he was afraid to look at God.
>
> Yahweh then said, "I have indeed seen the misery of my people in Egypt. I have heard them crying for help on account of their taskmasters. Yes, I am well aware of their sufferings. And I have come down to rescue them from the clutches of the Egyptians and bring them up out of that country, to a country

rich and broad, to a country flowing with milk and honey, to the home of the Canaanites, the Hittites, the Amorites, the Perizzites, the Hivites and the Jebusites. Yes indeed, the Israelites' cry for help has reached me, and I have also seen the cruel way in which the Egyptians are oppressing them. So now I am sending you to Pharaoh, for you to bring my people the Israelites out of Egypt." (Exodus 3:5–10)

Yahweh identifies himself not by claiming, as Allah does, that He alone is God, but rather by linking Himself to Moses's ancestors and, by implication, to what He has done for them. Yahweh continues, announcing that He has noticed the suffering of His people at the hands of the cruel Egyptians and that He intends to free them and bring them to "a country flowing with milk and honey." Contrast this speech with the speech quoted above in which Allah recites what is required of Moses *as a Muslim* and thus what he must preach to Pharaoh. In short, Allah addresses Moses principally as a prophet of the eternal, unchanging message of Islam, while Yahweh addresses him as the designated leader of an oppressed people. The difference matters hugely to the unfolding of the story.

As Allah tells that story, Moses approached the fire ready for guidance: an early clue, for, indeed, in what follows Moses unhesitatingly embraces the mission he has been given, asking Allah only to strengthen his spirit, grant him eloquence, and recruit his brother, Aaron, as reinforcement. No suspense or tension arises between Moses's initial openness and his later, willing compliance. It is quite otherwise in the Book of Exodus where tension arises as Moses initially resists Yahweh's call to lead the Israelites out of Egypt. "Suppose they will not believe me," Moses objects,

> "or listen to my words, and say to me, 'Yahweh has not appeared to you'?" Yahweh then said, "What is that in your hand?" "A staff," he said. "Throw it on the ground," said Yahweh. Moses threw it on the ground; the staff turned into a snake and Moses recoiled from it. Yahweh then said to Moses, "Reach out your hand and catch it by the tail." He reached out his hand, caught it, and in his hand it turned back into a staff. "Thus they may

believe that Yahweh, the God of their ancestors, the God of Abraham, the God of Isaac and the God of Jacob, has appeared to you."

Next, Yahweh said to him, "Put your hand inside your tunic." He put his hand inside his tunic, then drew it out again: and his hand was diseased, white as snow. Yahweh then said, "Put your hand back inside your tunic." He put his hand back inside his tunic and when he drew it out, there it was restored, just like the rest of his flesh. (Exodus 4:1–7)

In the Exodus version, Yahweh provides these demonstrations, these signs, only *after* and *because* Moses has tried to fight off Yahweh's great commission. Moses's resistance builds suspense; Yahweh's reaction momentarily relaxes it, or remands it to its later, intended exercise before the allegedly skeptical Israelites. In the Qur'an, no such tension ever arises, for the demonstrations come *before* Moses has spoken at all. The Exodus version proceeds cinematically, as it were. God tells Moses to pick up the serpent, and—as we, the readers, look on—Moses recoils, not knowing that the serpent will turn back into his staff. Vicariously, we experience something of his moment of anxiety and suspense. By contrast in the Qur'an, Allah *tells* Moses beforehand that the snake will change back. Again, in the Exodus version, we look on as Moses withdraws his hand from his tunic and finds it leprously "diseased, white as snow," and we share the tension (and his presumed horror) as he does not yet know that Yahweh will restore his hand to health and to its normal color. In the Qur'an, whiteness and health are associated, and the two insertions and withdrawals of the hand are collapsed into one. More to the point, Allah again *tells Moses in advance* that his hand will come out healthy. Where the Exodus narrator builds suspense, Allah forestalls it. In Allah's way of retelling a Bible story for Muhammad's benefit, the moral of any story permeates it from the beginning. Entertainment merely distracts from that moral point.

Not to digress further on a matter of style, the conduct of Moses and of Yahweh Himself during Moses's confrontation with Pharaoh and the Egyptians demonstrates clearly that Yahweh is out for as smashing a victory as possible, while Allah's goal is conversion, even of Pharaoh himself. Yahweh seems to have no intention of ever becoming Egypt's God. Allah has every such intention.

The qur'anic narrative of Sura 20 continues as Moses with Aaron at his side confronts Pharaoh with Allah's message. Allah sends the two of them off with encouragement:

> "So go forth, you and your brother, with My signs, and do not
>   neglect My remembrance.
> Go to Pharaoh: he has grown tyrannical,
> And speak gently to him; perhaps he will remember or be in
>   awe of Me."

> They said: "We fear he might fly into a rage against us, or grow tyrannical."
>   He said: "Fear not. I am with you, listening and seeing. Go to him and say: 'We are the messengers of your Lord. Send out with us the Children of Israel, and do not torment them. We bring you a wonder from your Lord, and peace be upon him who follows right guidance. To us has been revealed that torment shall fall upon him who denies and turns away.'"

> He said: "Who is your Lord, O Moses?"
>   He said: "Our Lord is He Who gave each thing its likeness in form, and then guided it."
>   He said: "What of earlier ages?"
>   He said: "Knowledge of them is with my Lord in a Book. My Lord neglects nothing, nor does He forget."

> It is He Who made the earth level for you, and marked out in it highways for you, and made water descend from the sky, through which We caused to come forth pairs of diverse plants. Eat, and pasture your animals—in this are signs for those possessed of reason.
>   From it We created you, to it We shall return you, and from it We shall once more resurrect you.

And We showed him all Our wonders, but he called them lies, and disbelieved.

He said: "Did you come to drive us out of our land, through your magic, O Moses?

"We will indeed bring you magic to match it.

"So set a date for us and you, not to be missed by us or you, at a place midmost between us." (20:42–58)

Just as Allah provided Abraham the arguments to use against his father and his people, so here, too, Allah is involved every step of the way. When Moses expresses fear that Pharaoh will "fly into a rage against us," Allah actually dictates the first words that Moses is to say, having first counseled Moses to "speak gently" to Pharaoh: "perhaps he will remember or be in awe of Me."

The meaning of "remember or be in awe" appears in Moses's answer to Pharaoh's tentatively open first question: "Who is your Lord, O Moses?" With the touch of gentleness that Allah has urged, Moses characterizes Allah to Pharaoh as "He Who gave each thing its likeness in form, and then guided it," and so forth. At just this point, Allah interrupts the narration and, addressing himself to Muhammad or through him to us, concludes that "in this are signs for those possessed of reason." Allah's point is that Pharaoh might well have seen Allah's signs in natural reality itself and so been prompted to "remember or be in awe." It is in this sense that Muslims think of Islam—spontaneous submission to God—as mankind's "natural" religion.

Pharaoh's first reaction, however, like Azar's (Abraham's father's), is to invoke his forebears and their quite different beliefs. If they were so mistaken, what has happened to them? Their fate, Moses says, is "with my Lord in a Book." *The Study Quran* takes this Book to be the "Preserved Tablet" referred to elsewhere in the Qur'an as including a record of all human good and evil deeds. Islam's Preserved Tablet is alternately the Qur'an itself or something like the Book of Life that appears at various points in both the Old and the New Testament, notably at Exodus 32:33, below, and in the New Testament at Revelation 20:11–12:

Then I saw a great white throne and the One who was sitting on it.... And another book was opened, which is the book of life, and the dead were judged from what was written in the books, as their deeds deserved.

Glossing Moses's reply to Pharaoh's question at Sura 20:52, Muhammad Asad writes: "I.e., [Allah] alone decrees their destiny in the life to come, for He alone knows their motives and understands the causes of their errors, and He alone can appreciate their merits and demerits."

Pharaoh seems at first to be drawn into a thoughtful consideration of Allah's message as delivered by Moses, but then suspicion overtakes him: Moses is out "to drive us out of our land, through your magic." But Pharaoh has magicians too, and so it is time for a duel. Before turning to that scene, however, we must contrast Allah's initial commission to Moses with Yahweh's. Yahweh says to Moses:

> "Look, I have made you as a god for Pharaoh, and your brother Aaron is to be your prophet. You must say whatever I command you, and your brother Aaron will repeat to Pharaoh that he is to let the Israelites leave his country. *But I myself shall make Pharaoh stubborn* and shall perform many a sign and wonder in Egypt. Since Pharaoh will not listen to you, I shall lay my hand on Egypt and with great acts of judgement lead my armies, my people, the Israelites, out of Egypt. And the Egyptians will know that I am Yahweh when I stretch out my hand against the Egyptians and lead the Israelites out of their country."

> Moses and Aaron did exactly as Yahweh had ordered. (Exodus 7:1–6, emphasis added)

Yahweh does not want to convert Pharaoh into a Yahweh-worshipper. He does not want to *tell* Pharaoh anything through Moses. Very much to the contrary, Yahweh is going to see to it personally that Pharaoh remains stubborn so that He can *show* Pharaoh in no uncertain terms just who He is. As subsequent events in the biblical narrative will make only too clear, Yahweh wants to do all this by inflicting maximum violence not upon Pharaoh alone but also upon all Egypt. Egypt, the oppressor, must suffer all the oppression it has visited on Israel and then some. Yahweh is out for revenge.

Both the biblical and the qur'anic account continue with a staffs-to-serpents duel between Pharaoh's magicians and God's delegates. As Allah tells the story, Moses, challenged by Pharaoh to name his date and time, replies:

> "Your appointment is on the Feast of the Pageant, and all people must be gathered there, in the morning."

> Pharaoh retired, gathered together all his cunning and came back.
> Moses said to them: "Wretches! Do not lie in God's name, or He will ravage you with a torment; liars shall surely fail."
> So they argued among themselves over their plan of action, and consulted in secret.
> They said: "These two are sorcerers who intend to drive you out of your land by their sorcery, and do away with your customary practice. So muster your cunning and go forth in single file. Today, whoso comes out on top will surely prosper."

> They said: "O Moses, either you cast, or we cast first."
> He said: "No, you cast first."
> And it was as if their ropes and staffs appeared to him, through their sorcery, to be swiftly crawling.
> In his heart Moses sensed fear.
> We said: "Fear not; you shall indeed be the victor. Cast down what is in your right hand and it shall swallow what they devised. They merely devised a sorcerer's deception, but the sorcerer shall not prosper, wherever he may be."

> The sorcerers were hurled to the ground, prostrate.
> They said: "We believe in the Lord of Aaron and Moses."
> He said: "You believe in him before I grant you leave? He is merely the greatest among you, the one who taught you sorcery. I shall cut your hands and feet, alternately, and I shall crucify you on the trunks of palm trees. And you will surely know which of us is more grievous in torment and more-lasting!"

They said: "We will not prefer you to what has come to us by way of clear proofs, nor to Him Who created us. Decree what you wish to decree: your decree runs only in this present life.

"We believe in our Lord that He may pardon our sins, and what you forced upon us of sorcery. God is better and more abiding." (20:59–73)

How did whatever Moses had in his right hand devour the sorcerers' "swiftly crawling" ropes and staffs? Allah does not linger over the details. Instead, He jumps to the remarkable conclusion of the duel: the stunning conversion of the sorcerers to the worship of Allah and their even more stunning zeal for Him against Pharaoh's vow to have them mutilated and crucified. Pharaoh may well have proceeded to martyr his magicians; Allah does not indicate whether he did or not. But no matter: the former magicians now have their gaze fixed on the afterlife, to which, as they boldly remind Pharaoh, his rule does not extend.

The elements of this scene—a torturing tyrant, subjects holding to their faith despite the agony of torture, and his subjects' confidence that their vindication will come in the afterlife—might well remind a Bible reader of the Second Book of Maccabees. There, a Greek tyrant who, like Pharaoh, claims to be divine, has demanded that seven Jewish brothers and their mother eat pork, thus renouncing the Jewish law and submitting to him. All refuse. Six, in turn, are tortured hideously and put to death. The seventh, scorning the tyrant's attempt to bribe him, addresses him as "unholy wretch and wickedest of villains" (7:34) and concludes his gallows speech with a vision of what awaits the torturer and the tortured in the afterlife:

"Our brothers, having endured brief pain for the sake of ever-flowing life have died for the covenant of God, while you, by God's judgement, will have to pay the just penalty for your arrogance. I too, like my brothers, surrender my body and life for the laws of my ancestors, begging God quickly to take pity on our nation, and by trials and afflictions to bring you to confess that he alone is God." (2 Maccabees 7:36–37)

It is to just this kind of fearless trust in Allah's justice and His power that Moses and Aaron have converted Pharaoh's sorcerers—standing in, we may well say, for all of Pharaoh's subjects. Their conversion is what Allah really wants. This was the message that He wanted Moses and Aaron to bring. They brought it, and the common people, in the person of these magicians, have heard it.

The staffs-to-serpents duel takes place in the Book of Exodus as well and ends, as in the Qur'an, with Moses and Aaron's serpents devouring those of the Egyptian magicians. Pharaoh, however, now under Yahweh's psychic control, remains adamant and will not allow the Israelites to leave Egypt. Yahweh then proceeds to torment Egypt at great length, first turning the Nile River to blood and then imposing a series of infestations or other afflictions that the anonymous biblical narrator describes in lurid detail: frogs, mosquitoes, horseflies, the sudden death of all livestock, boils, hail, locusts, and darkness. Midway in the plague of locusts,

> Pharaoh sent urgently for Moses and Aaron and said, "I have sinned against Yahweh your God and against you. Now forgive my sin, I implore you, just this once, and entreat Yahweh your God to turn this deadly thing away from me." When Moses left Pharaoh's presence he prayed to Yahweh, and Yahweh changed the wind into a west wind, very strong, which carried the locusts away and swept them into the Sea of Reeds. There was not one locust left in the whole of Egypt. But Yahweh made Pharaoh stubborn, and he did not let the Israelites go. (Exodus 10:16–20)

So it goes after each demonstration of Yahweh's power. Pharaoh may waver or even repent. To choose one example, he says midway in the plague of hail: "This time, I have sinned. Yahweh is in the right; I and my subjects are in the wrong" (9:27). But each time, Yahweh himself forestalls any such conversion and, as the King James Version and derived translations put it, "hardens Pharaoh's heart." Conversion is simply not Yahweh's goal. To underscore the point that He is the God *of the Israelites,* Yahweh sees to it that each plague spares Goshen, where the Israelites live.

In the final plague, Yahweh at last revenges Himself for the slaughter of the Israelite newborn boys by returning the favor to Egypt and redoubling it. As Moses delivers the dire verdict:

> "Yahweh says this, 'At midnight I shall pass through Egypt, and all the first-born in Egypt will die, from the first-born of Pharaoh, heir to his throne, to the first-born of the slave-girl at the mill, and all the first-born of the livestock. And throughout Egypt there will be great wailing, such as never was before, nor will be again. But against the Israelites, whether man or beast, never a dog shall bark, so that you may know that Yahweh distinguishes between Egypt and Israel. Then all these officials of yours will come down to me and, bowing low before me, say: Go away, you and all the people who follow you! After which, I shall go.'" And, hot with anger, he left Pharaoh's presence. (11:4–8)

"Never a dog shall bark": thus does Yahweh demonstrate that He "distinguishes between Egypt and Israel." Converting Egypt is the last thing on his mind. And though Pharaoh's magicians do say to him after the plague of mosquitoes, "This is the finger of God" (8:19), their concession does not bear comparison with the whole-hearted, martyrdom-ready conversion that Allah reports in the Qur'an. In any case, it is not Pharaoh alone whom Yahweh wishes to humiliate. He instructs the Israelites to ask the Egyptians for silver and golden jewelry and for clothing, promising His people that He will render their enemy compliant: "Yahweh made the Egyptians so much impressed with the {Israelite} people that they gave them what they asked. So they despoiled the Egyptians" (12:36).

The plagues leading up to the climactic tenth plague are a vengeful "un-creation" of Egypt's natural wealth and serve, essentially, only to prolong Egypt's agony en route to the final divine atrocity. As an artistic element in the biblical narration, the multiplication of the plagues does undeniably build up suspense and once may have contributed to an actual duel of the deities. It is conceivable that in an earlier version of the myth, Yahweh combatted Satan or an Egyptian god for control over Pharaoh. In such a version, Yahweh would attempt to induce Pharaoh to let Israel go, and it would fall to Satan or the rival deity to "harden Pharaoh's heart." The oddity of what we now read in the Bible, with Yahweh at cross-purposes with himself, could reflect later, radical editing to bring the myth into conformity with Israel's later, stricter monotheism, a monotheism with no room for Satan or any other supernatural power alongside Yahweh Elohim. Be that as it may, the effect of the artistically extended narrative as we now read it upon the characterization of Yahweh is to underscore His vengefulness and His determination to make dramatically visible the distinction that He wants to preserve between the Israelites and the Egyptians.

Allah, as we have already noted, mutes the centrality of Israel in telling the story of Moses. Allah also severely mutes the matter of the Egyptian plagues. He mentions them only once, in the account given in Sura 7, whose continuation carries us to the fabled miraculous crossing of the Red Sea:

> [The House of Pharaoh] said: "Whatever wonder you work to bewitch us, we will not believe in you." So We brought down upon them the flood, locusts, lice, frogs and blood—wonders most evident. But they grew conceited and were a people reprobate.

> When God's torment fell upon them they said: "O Moses, call upon your Lord according to the covenant you have with Him—if you take away this torment from us, we shall have faith in you and send out the Children of Israel with you." But when We relieved them of the torment for a period of time set for them to reach, there they were, breaking their promise. So We took revenge upon them and drowned them in the sea because they called the lie to Our signs and paid them no heed. And to the nation considered weak We gave in inheritance the eastern and western parts of the land which We had blessed. Thus was the good Word of your Lord fulfilled upon the Children of Israel, for they had endured with patience; and We utterly destroyed the works of Pharaoh and his people, together with all the monuments that they had built.

> Then We led the Children of Israel across the sea.... (7:132–138)

So vengeance or at least retribution figures, finally, not only in the story that the biblical narrator tells about Yahweh but also in the one that Allah tells about Himself. Allah includes as well both the liberation of Israel and the fulfillment of His promise to Abraham of a homeland. Like Yahweh, Allah punishes those who defy Him and rewards those who honor Him. But only Yahweh wants so badly to humiliate Pharaoh that He actively prevents the Egyptian ruler from acceding to His wishes. Allah wants Egypt, and even Pharaoh himself, to convert; Yahweh wants nothing of the sort.

In the Bible, it is unclear whether Pharaoh accompanies the army that, after reneging one last time, he has sent to halt the Israelite exodus. In the Qur'an, it is quite clear that Pharaoh does accompany them, but what does the haughty monarch think as the waves of the returning Red Sea began to engulf him? Allah tells us at Sura 10:91:

> Then we led the Children of Israel across the sea, and Pharaoh and his troops pursued them, in their insolence and aggression. When drowning was near, he said: "I believe that there is no god except Him in Whom the children of Israel believe, and I am a Muslim."

So Pharaoh dies a Muslim, and such conversion, all along, has been Allah's agenda. Why beat them when you can persuade them to join you?

Yahweh's focus is far more tightly riveted on victory as such. Yahweh has by no means forgotten His wish to grow Israel into a mighty nation and settle that nation in Canaan, but His desire for a spectacular victory over Pharaoh has acquired a momentum all its own. Yahweh orders the hastily emigrating Israelites to camp on the shore of the Red Sea so as deliberately to lure Pharaoh into pursuing them:

> "You must pitch your camp opposite this place, beside the sea, and then Pharaoh will think, 'The Israelites are wandering to and fro in the countryside; the desert has closed in on them.' I shall then make Pharaoh stubborn and he will set out in pursuit of them; and I shall win glory for myself at the expense

of Pharaoh and his whole army, and then the Egyptians will know that I am Yahweh." And the Israelites did this. (14:2–4)

Pharaoh's army does set out in pursuit. Moses stretches out his hand, as instructed by Yahweh, and Yahweh sends a great wind that drives the water back: "The waters were divided and the Israelites went on dry ground right through the sea, with walls of water to right and left of them" (14:22). The Egyptian army gives chase, but their chariots bog down. The waters begin to return; the Egyptians then cry in panic, "Let us flee from Israel, for Yahweh is fighting on their side" (14:25). But it is too late: the sea swallows them, and—horse and rider together—they all drown. On the far shore, the exultant Israelites sing in triumph:

> Yah is my strength and my song,
> to him I owe my deliverance.
> He is my God and I shall praise him,
> my father's God and I shall extol him.
> Yahweh is a warrior;
> Yahweh is his name. (Exodus 15: 2–3)

Yahweh—in poetry, sometimes "Yah," as in *hallelu-yah,* "praise Yah"—is indeed a warrior and not a missionary. He was out to show them, not tell them, and He has triumphantly done so. Egypt now knows in its broken bones that "I am Yahweh."

And as for His own people, as the climactic tenth plague is approaching, Yahweh provides them with elaborate instructions for an annual future commemoration of His coming victory and their own coming liberation. This commemoration is to be inaugurated in a ritual meal that will take place for the first time during the very slaughter of the Egyptian firstborn. The Israelites are to splash the blood of a sacrificed sheep on their lintels, signaling to Yahweh's Angel of Death that he is to "pass over" these households on his grim errand. The ritual replication of this meal is to become Israel's annual Passover feast. Allah, unsurprisingly, makes no provision for any such commemoration. As already noted, the story that He tells, rather than principally the story of Israel's liberation, is principally the story of Moses's prophetic vocation. Moses looms larger in Allah's telling than do the Children of Israel themselves, Moses's people.

In an earlier chapter, we noted that Allah portrays Abraham as a prophet inveighing against the idolatry of his people, while the anonymous narrator of the Book of Genesis portrays an Abraham who in his migrations never once encounters an idolater. No such idolatry contrast applies when we turn to the two portrayals of Moses in action after the Israelite exodus from Egypt. In both accounts, the Israelites lapse into idolatry, worshipping a golden calf instead of the one true God. In both accounts, Moses reacts as angrily as God does. And yet one key difference does remain between the two portrayals. Yahweh, with Moses as His captain, punishes Israel with ferocious violence, including a slaughter whose scope bears comparison with the drowning of Pharaoh's army. Allah, by contrast, though He angrily condemns the faithless idolaters, forbears to punish them with any comparable severity. In the Qur'an, the Israelite idolaters immediately repent, and Allah never fails to answer repentance with mercy.

In both accounts, the liberated Israelites proceed through the desert and encamp at the foot of a mountain—called Mount Sinai or Mount Horeb in the Bible, called simply "the Mountain" in the Qur'an. Moses ascends to the top of the mountain, remains for forty days and forty nights, and receives in writing a momentous revelation from God. Meanwhile, in Moses's absence, Aaron and the Israelites lapse into idolatry, worshipping a golden calf that they fashion from the gold and silver brought with them as booty from Egypt. Allah and the biblical narrator tell the story of this golden calf with differing, sometimes quite colorfully differing, details: in the Qur'an, the calf lows, for example; in the Bible, it does not. However, it is the aftermath of the scandalous apostasy that reveals most about the anonymous biblical narrator's understanding of Yahweh as compared with Allah's self-understanding in the Qur'an.

We begin with Allah:

> Thirty nights did We appoint for Moses, and thereto added ten, so the period with his Lord was complete in forty nights. Moses said to his brother Aaron: "Be my deputy among my

people; act with righteousness and do not follow the path of the corrupt." When Moses came to Our appointment and his Lord spoke to him, he said: "My Lord, show me Yourself that I may look upon You." He said: "You shall not see Me, but look instead upon that mountain. If it remains firmly in place you shall see Me." When the glory of his Lord appeared upon the mountain, it leveled it to the ground. Moses fell down, unconscious. When he came to, he said: "Glory be to You! I have repented before You and I am the first among believers."

He said: "O Moses, I have preferred you above mankind with My mission and My speech. So receive what I bring you and be thankful." And We inscribed for him on tablets moral precepts regarding all matters, specific in all their details. "So grasp them firmly and command your people to adopt what is best in them. I shall show you the abode of wrongdoers." (Qur'an 7:142–145)

After the miracle of the crumbled mountain, Moses humbly repents of his audacious request to see Allah. Allah, tacitly embracing his prophet's repentance, proceeds to give him tablets upon which Allah has written "moral precepts regarding all matters." The word *Torah* is not used in this passage but occurs often elsewhere in the Qur'an with reference to Allah's great gift to Moses of comprehensive guidance for his people. Muslim commentators debate what is to be understood by "the abode of wrongdoers." *The Study Quran* offers several suggestions, of which the most interesting is that this is a reference to the Land of Canaan, whose iniquitous inhabitants are shortly to be displaced by the conquering Israelites.

The biblical narrator says nothing about a leveled mountain but does tell a related story about Moses asking to see Yahweh:

[Moses] then said, "Please show me your glory." Yahweh said, "I shall make all my goodness pass before you, and before you I shall pronounce the name Yahweh; and I am gracious to those to whom I am gracious and I take pity on those on whom I take pity. But my face," he said, "you cannot see, for no human being can see me and survive." Then Yahweh said,

"Here is a place near me. You will stand on the rock, and when my glory passes by, I shall put you in a cleft of the rock and shield you with my hand until I have gone past. Then I shall take my hand away and you will see my back; but my face will not be seen." (Exodus 33:18–23)

The cleft in the rock where Yahweh hides Moses is the cleft alluded to in a well-known Christian hymn that begins: "Rock of Ages cleft for me, / Let me hide myself in Thee." Both the qur'anic and the biblical story bespeak the awesome and fearsome power of God. Allah implies to Moses that if he were ever to look upon Allah, he would crumble as the mountain crumbled. Yahweh, who regards the very enunciation of His name as a dread manifestation of His power, states quite clearly that if Moses were to gaze upon the glory of His face, he would die. In either case, God wishes to be known yet proclaims that, past a certain limited point, He cannot be known.

Allah continues:

After Moses had departed, his people fashioned from their jewellery a calf, an effigy that lowed. Did they not see that it neither spoke to them nor guided them to any path? Yet they worshipped it and were truly sinful. But when they rued their handiwork and saw that they had strayed in error, they said: "If God does not show us mercy and forgive us we shall surely be lost."

When Moses returned to his people, furious and grieving, he said: "Wretched is the way you acted on my behalf while I was away! Do you wish to hasten the decree of your Lord?" He threw down the tablets and grasped his brother's head, dragging it towards him.

He said: "Son of my mother, the people took me for a weakling and were about to kill me. Do not let my enemies rejoice at my misfortune, and do not count me among those who do wrong."

He said: "O Lord, forgive me and my brother, and admit us into Your mercy, for You are the most merciful of those who show mercy. As for those who worshipped the calf, the anger of their Lord shall blaze forth upon them and disgrace will be their lot in this present life."

This is how We requite those who utter falsehood.

As for those who commit evil deeds and then repent and believe, your Lord thereafter is All-Forgiving, Compassionate to each.

When the anger of Moses was stilled, he took up the tablets, inscribed with guidance and mercy toward those who piously fear their Lord. (7:148–154)

Even before Moses returns from the mountaintop, the people have repented of their sin. Moses is angry nonetheless. He tells them that they have acted like people who want to bring on the Last Judgment ("the decree of your Lord") with all the Lord's righteous wrath. In his fury, Moses throws down the tablets and grabs his brother, Aaron, by the head. Poor Aaron pleads with him, however, alleging his own weakness, and Moses immediately relents, begging Allah's forgiveness on the two of them, "for You are the most merciful of those who show mercy."

The passage concludes with Allah's own commentary on the episode, predicting punishment, to be sure, but only "in this present life"—that is, not forever in hell—for the briefly idolatrous Israelites and presumably promising a fuller pardon for Moses and Aaron. Why? Simply because—as Allah says, characterizing Himself—"your Lord thereafter is All-Forgiving, Compassionate to each." The story resumes as Moses picks up the dropped tablets and, his anger abated, prepares to lead his people on to the Promised Land with the precious tablets for guidance. The mood, as the episode concludes, is one of forgiveness and reconciliation.

The same episode comes to a far more turbulent and violent resolution in the Bible. Descending the mountain, Moses

saw the calf and the groups dancing. Moses blazed with anger. He threw down the tablets he was holding, shattering them at the foot of the mountain. He seized the calf they had made and burned it, grinding it into powder which he scattered on the water, and made the Israelites drink it. (Exodus 32:19–20)

As in the Qur'an, Aaron tries to exonerate himself by blaming the Israelite people. Ignoring him, Moses abruptly takes his stand at the gate of the camp and cries out: "Who is for Yahweh? To me!" (32:26). All the Levites rally around him, Moses himself being of the tribe of Levi. Moses then reveals to his brethren that they are to be the instruments of Yahweh's dire rage:

> He said to them, "Yahweh, God of Israel, says this, 'Buckle on your sword, each of you, and go up and down the camp from gate to gate, every man of you slaughtering brother, friend and neighbour.'" The Levites did as Moses said, and of the people about three thousand men perished that day. "Today," Moses said, "you have consecrated yourselves to Yahweh, one at the cost of his son, another of his brother, and so he bestows a blessing on you today." (32:27–29)

We have seen Allah, in conversation with Noah and later with Abraham, insisting that devotion to Him must take priority over mere friendly affection or family feeling. We see the same severity here in Yahweh. Later in the Bible, the Levites' place in the life of Israel will be that of a landless priestly or semi-priestly caste supported by a tithe on the other Israelites.[1] The biblical narrator explains here that they earned this privilege through their ruthlessness at Mount Sinai.

As in the Qur'an, so in the Bible, Moses eventually begs forgiveness from Yahweh for his people's sin. A day after leading the Levites in their punitive massacre, Moses says to the people:

> "You have committed a great sin. But now I shall go up to Yahweh: perhaps I can secure expiation for your sin." Moses then went back to Yahweh and said, "Oh, this people has committed a great sin by making themselves a god of gold. And yet, if it pleased you to forgive their sin...! If not, please blot me out of the book you have written!" Yahweh said to Moses, "Those

who have sinned against me are the ones I shall blot out of my book. So now go and lead the people to the place I promised to you. My angel will indeed go at your head but, on the day of punishment, I shall punish them for their sin." (32:30–34)

And Yahweh then proceeds to send a plague upon the Israelite camp: the day of punishment turns out to be the very day of Moses's intercession.

In the story that the biblical narrator tells, Yahweh is far more violent with the Israelites than Allah is in the story that He tells. Moses as well is a far angrier, more impetuous figure in the Bible than he is in the Qur'an. In the Qur'an, Moses casts the tablets down but does not break them and later picks them up again. In the Bible, Moses shatters them. Earlier, some of Moses's words to Pharaoh were virtual rants. With regard to the Levite slaughter and the following plague, Yahweh's vengeance may seem warranted inasmuch as, first, the Israelites do not repent in the Bible as they do in the Qur'an, and, second, while Allah punishes both in this life and in the life to come, Yahweh punishes only in this life and so, as it were, must inflict more or less immediately whatever punishment has been merited.

Nonetheless, reading these two accounts side by side, one comes away with the strong impression that Allah is positively eager to forgive, while Yahweh has to be talked into it. At Exodus 33:11, we read, "Yahweh would talk to Moses face to face, as a man talks to his friend." The Old Testament makes this claim of intimacy with Yahweh for no one but Moses. Yet in seeking Yahweh's forgiveness, Moses must put this very friendship into play. Forgive my people, he says in effect, or we can no longer be friends. Yahweh has to be cajoled or almost bribed into mercy. And even then, He must give Israel one last kick, that final plague, for good measure. The Hebrew root *n-g-f* usually means "strike with plague" but can simply mean "strike" or, in my (admittedly loose) translation, "kick."

Both the qur'anic and the biblical accounts end with the Israelites and their divine Lord exiting stage left, bound for Canaan. In our comparative review of the two accounts and their respective characterizations of God, we have not considered every stage in the story. We have not discussed the infancy of Moses, for example, or told of his early murder of an Egyptian. We have not recounted his flight into the desert, where he takes a Midianite wife who mysteriously circumcises him in the middle of the night, shortly before God appears to him. We have not considered the hugely detailed provisions and prescriptions of Torah as the Bible conveys them—or the Books of Leviticus, Numbers, or Deuteronomy, or even the Ten Commandments incised on tablets "by the finger of God." Nor have we considered in their entirety the different accounts of Moses given in the Qur'an, with their often quite specific details and their sometimes complementary morals. We have offered only a harmonized selection from them, just enough for the purposes of comparison.

Within that comparison, the story that the biblical narrator tells, despite the violence of its characterization of Yahweh, has remained with reason an archetypal legend of up-from-slavery liberation. African slaves in the pre–Civil War United States sang,

> Go down, Moses,
> way down in Egypt's land.
> tell ole Pharaoh
> to let my people go!

The legend, its commemoration in the beautiful ritual meal of the Passover seder, the charming, child-centered, early-medieval Hebrew Haggadah—all this has been borrowed and borrowed and borrowed again by other groups than the Jews, and not without textual warrant. Exodus 12:37–38 says that the Israelites departed Egypt as

> about six hundred thousand on the march—men, that is, not counting their families. A mixed crowd of people went with them, and flocks and herds, quantities of livestock.

Taking that "mixed crowd" to be non-Israelites who followed Moses to freedom, there is reason for the Passover seder to have become a kind of universal liturgy of liberation with Yahweh at its center as the divine liberator who "brought us up out of Egypt."

But enough has been shown along the way of this double exposition to make clear a further point of overriding importance for our understanding of Allah. By Allah's own account, no figure in the Qur'an had a vocation more closely paralleling Muhammad's vocation than did Moses. For besides being the Prophet of Islam, Muhammad—in this regard very clearly paralleling Moses—was the unifier and liberator of the Arab people, and Allah was his guide, his support, and his refuge as he fulfilled that vocation. In responding to Allah's call, Muhammad was required to be as determined as Allah Himself to proclaim Allah's unique divinity and to summon first the Arabs and then the world beyond Arabia to worship Him. In so doing, he was required to be as ready as Allah shows Himself ready at all times to be "the most Merciful of those who show mercy" (Qur'an 7:151). A historian would call Muhammad's vocation historic. Unsurprisingly, the Muslims of the world have been content to call it by the nobler term *prophetic*.

8

Jesus and His Mother

Some years ago, I published, on Christmas Eve, an article in *The New York Times Magazine* entitled "Jesus Before He Could Talk." In a psychological or literary reading of the Christmas story, as opposed to a historical or theological one, I wrote,

> The silence of the central character, the infant Himself, deserves particular attention. True, nobody expects the infant Jesus to speak, and the artistic maturity of the canonical Gospels is such that He never abuses His divine power to perform nature-defying tricks of precocity. (Not so the apocryphal gospels: in the "Infancy Gospel of Thomas," to name one example, the 2-year-old Jesus brings a salted fish back to life.)...
>
> The instinct to protect an endangered infant is hard-wired into the human species, a response that begins in the body, not the mind, in held breath and tensed muscles. A writer of fiction or drama who is able to activate this circuitry can achieve vivid emotional effects.... When we, the audience, know something about a character that the character does not know about himself, a powerful dramatic tension results; when the oblivious character is an infant in mounting danger,

this tension engages, in addition, the latent, instinctive parent in every adult.[1]

My remarks, in that article, are obviously all predicated on the assumption that what any writer, even of sacred scripture, should most want to do is build suspense, build tension, go past the argument-following mind to the instinct-driven body. Given this assumption, I gave the canonical Gospels high marks for building suspense by preserving the expected speechlessness of an infant and for the danger that mounts around him and faulted the apocryphal "Infancy Gospel of Thomas" for making Baby Jesus not just a talker but also a precocious little wonder-worker.

But must this assumption always apply? In this book, we have already seen several examples of Allah's determination in the Qur'an to forestall suspense, to deliberately "spoil" or "give away" the story. Clearly, what is normative in the kinds of fiction, drama, and cinema we know best is not normative for Him. It is the moral of any story that makes it worth His telling, worth His calling a given story to Muhammad's attention, and, accordingly, He builds the moral into any story that He tells from the very beginning.

So it is in the story that Allah tells of the infant Jesus and his mother.

And mention in the Book Mary, when she withdrew from her people to an eastern place.

She set up a screen to veil her from them.

And We sent her Our Spirit, which appeared before her as an immaculate human.

She said: "I take refuge in the All-Merciful from you, if you fear God."

He said: "I am but a messenger from your Lord, to bestow upon you a son most pure."

She said: "How can I have a son when no man has ever touched me, nor am I an adulteress?"

He said: "Thus did your Lord speak: 'It is a matter easy for Me. We shall make him a wonder to mankind and a mercy from Us—a decree ordained.'"

So she conceived him and withdrew with him to a distant place. And labor pains came upon her by the trunk of a palm tree.

She said: "I wish I had died before this and become a thing utterly forgotten!"

He called out to her from beneath her: "Do not grieve. Your Lord has made a brook to flow beneath you. So shake towards you the trunk of the palm and it will drop down on you dates soft and ripe. Eat and drink and be of good cheer. And if you happen to see any human being, tell him: 'I have vowed to the All-Merciful a fast, and will not speak a word today to any human being.'"

And she came to her people, carrying him.

They said: "O Mary, you have committed a monstrous act! Sister of Aaron, your father was not an evildoer, nor was your mother an adulteress."

She pointed to him.

They said: "How do we speak to an infant in his cradle?"

He said: "I am the servant of God. He brought me the Book and made me a prophet, and made me blessed wherever I may be. He charged me with prayer and alms-giving as long as I live, and to be dutiful to my mother. And He did not make me arrogant and wicked. Peace be upon me the day I was born, the day I die, and the day I am resurrected, alive!"

This is Jesus, son of Mary: a statement of truth, concerning which they are in doubt.

It is not for God to take a child—Glory to Him! When He determines any matter, He merely says to it: "Be!" and it is.

God is my Lord and your Lord, so worship Him.

This is a straight path." (Qur'an 19:16–36)

Allah quotes Jesus at only a very few points in the Qur'an. The words spoken by the newborn Jesus in this passage loom large within that small complement of quoted words. That Jesus speaks as an infant is only the first of many corrections that Allah makes in the received Christian account of Jesus's origin, character, and mission.

Thus, as Allah tells that story, Mary has no husband, while in three of the four canonical Gospels, Joseph is both her husband and Jesus's legal father. In the Gospels of Matthew and Luke, although both include Jesus's virgin birth, Jesus's genealogy is explicitly reckoned through Joseph. Jesus is a Jew of the tribe of Judah, descended through Judah's son, Perez, and, generations later, through King David down to Joseph and only through him to Jesus. In the Gospel according to John, which includes no account of a virgin birth at all, Jesus is referred to quite routinely at 6:42 as the son of Joseph. By telling the story of Jesus and his mother without Joseph as his guardian and legal father, Allah corrects the received account to mute the centrality in it of Israel and of Jesus as Jewish while sharply underscoring the virginity and holy purity of Mary.

Just as in Allah's telling of Moses's story Israel as a people was less important than was Moses himself, so also here: in Allah's telling of Jesus's story, his identity as a Jew of royal descent plays no part at all. What matters is that Jesus is a Muslim who has received his own "Book" from Allah himself and indeed while still in his cradle.

Within the two Gospels that do include Jesus's virgin birth, Mary's virginity is not celebrated as such, any more than menopause is celebrated in the Genesis account of Isaac's miraculous birth to Sarah and Abraham. Neither Gospel implies that Jesus's virgin birth entailed a vow of virginity for Mary. The Gospel of Luke may imply that Mary married Joseph so soon after conceiving Jesus that no public scandal could be occasioned. She was, after all, betrothed to him at the time when the Angel Gabriel appeared to her, and betrothal was a state nearer to marriage than engagement is in our world. In the Gospel of Matthew, an angel appears to Joseph in a dream, after Mary's pregnancy has first become apparent, and says:

> "Joseph son of David, do not be afraid to take Mary home as your wife, because she has conceived what is in her by the Holy Spirit. She will give birth to a son and you must name

him Jesus, because he is the one who is to save his people from their sins." (Matthew 1:20–21)

The Gospels are written in Greek, and *Iēsous* is the Greek form of the name Joshua, a sentence name in Hebrew meaning "Yahweh is salvation" and the name of Moses's first lieutenant and later, by Yahweh's power, the conqueror of Canaan. In any case, in this account, too, Jesus's birth occasions no scandal because Mary does have a husband and so the world at large assumes that Jesus's birth to the two of them came about in the natural way.

In the Qur'an as in both of the biblical accounts, Mary's conception, like Sarah's, comes about through the power of God, and it is God's power to create life—rather than the women's respective biological conditions—that matters. The Sarah/Mary, menopause/virginity connection is further underscored in the Gospel of Luke when the Angel Gabriel, after delivering his momentous message to Mary, goes on to say:

> "Your cousin Elizabeth also, in her old age, has conceived a son, and she whom people called barren is now in her sixth month, *for nothing is impossible to God.*" (Luke 1:36–37)

(The final phrase, italicized in the *New Jerusalem Bible,* is a loose quotation of Jeremiah 32:27.) That nothing is impossible for God is the point in the Gospel accounts that makes closest contact with the Qur'an, for in the Qur'an, where Mary has no male partner at all, God undoubtedly looms even larger than He does in the Gospels.

Allah looms large in the Qur'an's account of Jesus's conception for another reason—namely, that it is not the Angel Gabriel, as Allah tells the story, who announces to Mary that she is to conceive by the power of Allah but rather "Our Spirit, which appeared before her as an immaculate human." Mary protests to this "immaculate human" that she has had no contact with a man, just as she does to the Angel Gabriel in the Gospel of Luke. In Luke, the angel replies in elevated tones:

> "The Holy Spirit will come upon you, and the power of the
> Most High will cover you with its shadow. And so the child
> will be holy and will be called Son of God." (1:35)

Allah's likeness replies more tersely and peremptorily, quoting Allah:
"Thus did your Lord speak: 'It is a matter easy for Me.'"

And Allah then resumes the narration, underscoring Mary's isola-
tion and her dependence upon Him. Having already withdrawn from
her family to "an eastern place," she now withdraws further to "a distant
place" where, all alone, she goes into labor and groans, "I wish I had
died before this and become a thing utterly forgotten." It is at this point,
before his birth, that Jesus begins to speak from within Mary's womb,
forthrightly instructing his mother to expect the miraculous and comforting intervention of Allah:

> "Do not grieve. Your Lord has made a brook to flow beneath
> you. So shake towards you the trunk of the palm and it will
> drop down on you dates soft and ripe. Eat and drink and be
> of good cheer. And if you happen to see any human being,
> tell him: 'I have vowed to the All-Merciful a fast, and will not
> speak a word today to any human being.'"

A majority of Muslim commentators interpret the voice that calls out
"from beneath her" as the voice of the unborn Jesus. Do dates and water
alleviate the pangs of childbirth? Perhaps they did in this instance.
Allah says nothing about Mary's parturition itself and nothing further
about the behavior of the date palm. We may assume that it performed
as, from the womb, Jesus said it would.

The next stage in the story, as Allah tells it, is Mary's return home.
Having left home before Allah's messenger appears to her, Mary has
retreated very far since her pregnancy began and may now have been
absent from her family for more than nine months. How does her family receive her when she returns with a baby in her arms?

To digress for a moment on her genealogy, Mary—Miriam in
Hebrew, *maryam* in Arabic—has the same name as another Miriam/
maryam in both the Old Testament and the Qur'an, namely, Moses and
Aaron's sister Miriam. As Allah tells the story of Jesus's mother, she, too,

has a brother named Aaron, unmentioned in the Gospels. Their father coincidentally has the name, Imran, that Muslim tradition assigns to the father of Moses, of Aaron, and of their sister Miriam. (His biblical name is Amram.) According to *The Study Quran*, Allah's inclusion of Aaron in His account of Mary's homecoming, correcting the Gospel's omission, may refer to a half-brother or may be intended to suggest somehow that Mary is related to the earlier Aaron and so to the earlier Imran.

In any case, this "sister of Aaron" faces a family dismayed as she returns home an unaccompanied mother. What can she say to them? She is "fasting" from speech at her son's command, so she can only point to him, at which moment he astonishes them by delivering, from the cradle, his already quoted inaugural speech:

> "I am the servant of God. He brought me the Book and made me a prophet, and made me blessed wherever I may be. He charged me with prayer and alms-giving as long as I live, and to be dutiful to my mother. And He did not make me arrogant and wicked. Peace be upon me the day I was born, the day I die, and the day I am resurrected, alive!" (Qur'an 19:30-33)

Rather like Moses in his confrontation with Pharaoh, Jesus begins by identifying himself as a Muslim (a "servant of God") obligated to pray and give alms like any other Muslim. What makes him exceptional is that Allah has made him both a prophet and, as he has been given a "Book," also a messenger. It is because of this that he can pronounce upon himself the traditional honorific blessing "Peace be upon him" (pbuh). But in so doing, Jesus takes care, in Allah's telling, to locate himself securely within the standard human arc of birth-death-resurrection. *Everyone* will rise on "the Day," so when Baby Jesus speaks of being "resurrected, alive!" he is not laying claim here to anything remotely like resurrection in the portentous Christian understanding of the term.

But can even an infant divinely empowered to speak as an adult be entrusted with an entire "Book"? Fortunately, even determined suspension of disbelief does not in this case require that we imagine a chunky bound volume dropped by the power of Allah into Jesus's cradle. "Book," here, like every other element in the set of stories that Allah tells about Muhammad's prophetic predecessors, must be understood to conform to what "Book" means in the prophetic work of Muhammad himself—namely, Allah's unchanging message. As entrusted to Baby Jesus, it would not be the written Gospels as Christians know them.

In this connection, we should recall that not one of the canonical Gospels nor even any of the various apocryphal gospels claims to be the work of Jesus as the scribal, quill-on-papyrus author. The canonical Gospels—the four that are a part of the Bible—all narrate the death of Jesus and so are understood to be the work of others writing about him afterward. We speak commonly of the (plural) Gospels of Matthew, Mark, Luke, and John. But more traditionally, the four have been referred to in Christianity as the (single) Gospel *according to* Matthew, Mark, etc. The point of the word *according* is that the Gospel itself—the "Good News" of Christian revelation—was brought by Jesus himself through his life, death, and resurrection. The Good News was thus *his* Good News in the first instance. The traditional Four Evangelists then merely delivered their versions of what they understood to be his message. In the qur'anic episode, what was entrusted to Jesus might be seen as this single Gospel, not yet corrupted by Christian hands.

As I've said, Muhammad is known and, in fact, celebrated in Islam as an illiterate prophet. His followers recorded what he recited as dictation from Allah through the Angel Gabriel during the final twenty-two years of his life, collated what they had recorded after his death, and Caliph Uthman finally promulgated the written Qur'an as we now know it. Unlike Muhammad, Jesus was literate, according to the Gospels. In Luke 4:16–22, he reads in the Nazareth synagogue from the scroll of the prophet Isaiah, concluding dramatically: "This text is being fulfilled today even while you are listening." In John 8:6, he writes in the dust with his finger. But had Jesus been as illiterate as Muhammad, he could still have preached the same Gospel and stood in the same relation to the later written Gospels.

The larger correction of the Gospels that Allah delivers through the Qur'an is the implicit assertion that Allah entrusted the Gospel to Jesus as he entrusts the Qur'an to Muhammad or, in other words, that Jesus's relation to the Gospel parallels Muhammad's to the Qur'an. A Gospel or Gospels that read that way would, clearly enough, not read like the

Gospels that Christians honor as scripture, so Allah delivers, in effect, a major challenge to the trustworthiness of the Gospels as Christians know them.

Baby Jesus's cradle speech, though it addresses all these larger confessional issues, actually does not address the Imran family's concern that Mary may have disgraced her worthy parents and them as well. We may perhaps assume that they were so stunned and humbled by her son's words from the cradle that they refrained from further indignation toward her.

It is a striking fact that Mary is the only woman named in the Qur'an and that she is named there more than seventy times, many more times than she is mentioned in any of the Gospels. A great many of these references to her, however, come simply by their inclusion in many iterations of the phrase "Jesus, son of Mary," and many of these, in turn, are pointed assertions that Jesus is indeed the son of this woman rather than the Son of God.

Interestingly, the designation "Son of God" is actually rare in the Gospels and does not necessarily confer divinity on a man so designated. Thus, tracing Jesus's genealogy back through Joseph to Adam, the Gospel of Luke concludes: "son of Enos, son of Seth, son of Adam, son of God" (Luke 3:38). Adam, never considered as divine, is nonetheless a true son of God. When Jesus teaches the hallowed "Lord's Prayer," he makes all his hearers children of God by urging them to begin their prayer, "Our Father who art in heaven...." It is true, however, that the Gospels—at least the Gospel of John—claim a unique and exceptional filial status for Jesus. John 3:16 reads:

> For this is how God loved the world:
> he gave his only Son,
> so that everyone who believes in him may not perish
> but may have eternal life.

It is this claim of a relationship tantamount to divinity itself that Allah's repeated designation of Jesus as "son of Mary" is intended to correct. And yet in other ways Allah dwells with greater insistence on the holiness of Mary herself than any of the Gospel writers do.

Nothing that Allah says about Mary will more sharply startle Christian or Jewish readers than something he reports Himself asking about Mary in a question to Jesus:

> Remember when God said to Jesus son of Mary: "Did you really say to people: 'Take me and my mother as two gods, instead of God?'"
> He said: "Glory be to You! What right have I to assert what does not in truth belong to me?
> If I had said it, You would have known it;
> You know what is in my soul and I know not what is in Your soul, For it is You Who are the All-Knower of the Unseen.
> I said nothing to them except what You commanded me:
> 'Worship God, my Lord and your Lord.'
> I was a witness to them while I lived among them,
> But when you caused me to die, it was You Who kept watch over them.
> You are a witness over all things.
> If You torment them, they are Your servants,
> And if You forgive them, it is You Who are Almighty, All-Wise." (Qur'an 5:116–118)

The context for the closing statement just above is Allah's evocation for Muhammad of the "Day when God gathers all the messengers together, and He will ask: 'What was the response to you?'" (5:109). The context, in other words, is the Last Judgment, when all Allah's prophets or messengers will be on hand to testify regarding their acceptance or rejection by the respective peoples to whom Allah sent them. With this statement, Allah clarifies for Muhammad what Jesus's message truly was to the Jewish people, including, of course, those Jews who founded Christianity. Jesus's message to all of them was identical to the message that Muhammad is delivering to the people of Mecca and Medina, and on that "Day" Christians will merit severe punishment if they have wantonly distorted Jesus's true message by divinizing him.

That Allah should wish to make this point to Muhammad is no surprise. What is surprising is that a claim of divinity should need to be repudiated for Mary as well. Why should a claim need to be repudiated,

Christian readers will ask, when Christians have never made one in the first place? To answer speculatively and, for a change, historically, that claim might have to be repudiated because of the character of what was in the seventh century the grandest building in the known world, certainly the grandest in Europe or the Middle East.

This was the magnificent Basilica of Holy Wisdom (in Greek, *Hagia Sophia*) in Constantinople, the capital of the Roman Empire. Any outsider visiting that awesome edifice and observing the stunning prominence afforded Mary—as *Theotokos* or "God-bearer"—in its glittering mosaics might well imagine that just as Jesus was adored as *Christos Pantocrator*, "Christ the Ruler of All," in its dome, so also was she adored who had borne him.[2] Centuries later, Protestantism would find fault with the early church for "Mariolatry"—namely, treating Mary as a virtual goddess. We may well recognize a kind of Muslim proto-Protestant radicalism in Allah's care to deny divinity to the mother when denying it to the son.

And yet while denying the divinity of Mary, Allah lingers more over her holiness than the biblical Gospels do. Upon conceiving her, Mary's mother dedicates her to God with the words:

> "My Lord, I pledge to You what is in my womb. It shall be dedicated to Your service. Accept this from me for it is You— You Who are All-Hearing, All-Knowing." (Qur'an 3:35)

This passage continues as, after giving birth, she says:

> "My Lord, I have given birth and it is a female"—and God knew best what she had given birth to—"and a male is not like a female. I have called her Mary. I seek refuge in You for her and her progeny from Satan, ever deserving to be stoned."
>
> God accepted her offering graciously and caused her to grow up admirably, and entrusted Zachariah with her upbringing. Whenever Zachariah entered in upon her in the sanctuary he found food by her side.
>
> He said: "Mary, from where do you have this?"
>
> She said: "It is from God. God provides for whomever He wills, without reckoning." (Qur'an 3:36–37)

Mary is not like the angels who visited Abraham and did not eat because they were spiritual beings who required no food. Mary requires food, but Allah provides for her directly. And a bit later the angels say to her:

> "O Mary, God has chosen you, made you pure and chosen you above all the women of the world. O Mary, pray constantly to your Lord, and bow down in worship, and kneel alongside those who kneel." (Qur'an 3:42–43)

Of God's direct provision of food to Mary, there is not a word in the Gospels, and this angelic paean to Mary has no Gospel parallel either. There is an exchange in the Gospel of Luke, however, including a poem spoken by Mary about herself that might be a relevant parallel to these qur'anic celebrations of Jesus's mother.

Mary has just arrived at the home of Elizabeth, her six-months-pregnant cousin, to help her through the final three months of her pregnancy.

> Now it happened that as soon as Elizabeth heard Mary's greeting, the child leapt in her womb and Elizabeth was filled with the Holy Spirit. She gave a loud cry and said, "Of all women you are the most blessed, and blessed is the fruit of your womb. Why should I be honored with a visit from the mother of my Lord?" (Luke 1:41–43)

Mary's reply is a poem with repeated allusions to the Old Testament prophets, all italicized in the *New Jerusalem Bible* translation:

> My soul proclaims the greatness of the Lord
> And my spirit *rejoices in God my Saviour;*
> because *he has looked upon the humiliation of his servant.*
> Yes, from now onwards all generations will call me blessed,
> for the Almighty has done great things for me.
> *Holy is his name,*
> and *his faithful love extends age after age to those who fear him.*
> He has used the power of his arm,
> he has routed the arrogant of heart.

He has pulled down princes from their thrones *and raised high the
lowly.*

He has filled the starving with good things, sent the rich away
empty.

*He has come to the help of Israel his servant, mindful of his faithful
love*

—according to the promise he made to our ancestors—

of his mercy to Abraham and to his descendants for ever.

(Luke 1:46–55)

We may concede that between them Elizabeth and Mary celebrate
Mary in their words nearly as much as Allah celebrates her by His
actions from the moment of her conception down to the messages He
sends to her through His angels, but it is one thing for women to celebrate Mary in God's name and quite another for God to celebrate her
Himself.

As we have seen before, it is Allah's way to be involved step-by-step
in any significant action involving one of His prophets. This could
scarcely be clearer than it is in Jesus's summary-in-advance of the miracles that He will perform in his public life. Speaking in the manner of
a prophet to His people, he says:

"I bring you a sign from your Lord. I will fashion for you from
clay the likeness of a bird, and I shall breathe upon it and it
will become a bird, by God's leave. I shall cure the blind and
the leper and revive the dead by God's leave. I shall reveal to
you what you eat and what you store in your homes. In this
assuredly is a sign for you, if you are true believers. I confirm
what lies before me of the Torah and to make licit for you
some of what had been made illicit. I come to you with a sign
from your Lord. So fear God and obey me. God is my Lord
and your Lord; so worship Him, for here lies a path that is
straight." (3:49–51)

Christians in Muhammad's day read some of the apocryphal (extra-
biblical) gospels as widely as they read the canonical (biblical) Gospels;
and so when correcting Christians' received beliefs about Jesus, Allah

sometimes corrects an apocryphal gospel. As it happens, the Infancy Gospel of Thomas 2:2–4 contains an episode in which the child Jesus creates a dozen clay birds and then makes them fly away with a clap and a shout. Inasmuch as the passage above is spoken before even the miracle of the clay bird has been performed, we must hear it as spoken by Jesus either as a baby or as a small boy. As quoted by Allah, Jesus corrects the Infancy Gospel of Thomas regarding the number of clay birds brought to life.

Much more important, little Jesus stresses that any miracles he will seem to perform will have been performed by Allah's leave. He stresses, in other words, that he will have no godlike powers of his own. Though Jesus's hearers are to obey him as the messenger of Allah when, for example, he relaxes one or another stricture of Jewish religious practice, it is Allah alone—"my Lord and your Lord"—whom they are to worship, "for here lies a path that is straight."

The phrase "straight path" being always a synonym for Islam, the fact that so significant a summary should be proclaimed by Jesus as a baby or, at most, a small child only underscores that Jesus will do nothing except as an instrument of Allah.

In discussing how Allah corrects the canonical Gospels' accounts of Jesus by denying his divinity, we have spoken so far about Christians and Christian scriptures. But is Allah also correcting Jews in this regard? The answer is clearly no. Israelite monotheism became so absolute around the time of the Babylonian Exile as to rule out any role even for Satan. Later, probably under Persian influence, Satan did emerge as a powerful being, though ultimately subordinate to Yahweh. During the final pre-Christian centuries, Jewish speculation began to make further room for a different, benign ancillary or auxiliary power alongside the unmediated power of God. After the rise of Christianity, however, with its celebration of a divine messiah, Rabbinic Judaism decisively repudiated belief in any supernatural power alongside the power of God, with Satan as a limited exception developing gradually over several centuries' time. The core Rabbinic belief came to be summarized and rhetorically signaled by the phrase "no two powers in heaven." The Jewish condemnation expressed by this phrase, almost a kind of mantra, is virtually indistinguishable from the Muslim condemnation expressed in a term we encountered previously, *shirk*, "association" in Arabic—namely, the association of any second god or godlike being with God himself. The sin of unrepentant *shirk* is the one sin, according to the Qur'an, that cannot be forgiven.[3]

Could the Jews of Arabia then have accepted Muhammad as the latest of their prophets more easily than could the Christians? Edward Gibbon wrote in *The Decline and Fall of the Roman Empire* that it would have served the Jews' temporal happiness to do so:

> The choice of Jerusalem for the first kebla of prayer discovers the early propensity of Mahomet in favor of the Jews; and happy would it have been for their temporal interest, had they recognized, in the Arabian prophet, the hope of Israel and the promised Messiah. Their obstinacy converted his friendship into implacable hatred, with which he pursued that unfortunate people to the last moment of his life; and in the double character of an apostle and a conqueror, his persecution was extended to both worlds.[4]

Gibbons in his arch, *de haut en bas* manner condescends insufferably to the Jews and almost equally so the Muslims, Muhammad in particular. But his "enlightened" condescension aside, the Jews of Arabia would have had no difficulty denying divinity to Jesus of Nazareth, as they had long since done, and asserting—as in effect Muslims before Muhammad that there is no god but God. It was accepting Muhammad—as the last of God's prophets that presented an obstacle, for that acceptance entailed accepting the Qur'an as a scripture superseding their own much larger set of scriptures and pleading guilty to the Qur'an's charge that they had failed by negligence or malice to preserve their own scriptures. This they declined to do, and in retrospect one may doubt that their long-term "temporal interest" would have been served had they taken Gibbon's advice.

Two matters need to be dealt with before we conclude this chapter on Jesus in the Qur'an as against Jesus in the Bible and on the implications of that difference for our understanding of God in the Qur'an. The first matter, which can be addressed with some brevity, is the teachings of

Jesus. The second, much more tangled and charged matter is his death (if ever) and his resurrection (and if so, when).

These two matters command nearly the entirety of the four biblical gospels. By contrast, the story of Mary's virginal conception and parturition and of Jesus's childhood are no more than a relatively brief prologue, and at that in only two of the four. Christian tradition has referred to Jesus's childhood as his "hidden life" because the Bible has so very little to say about it. The overwhelming bulk of the biblical gospels falls, in each case, into two divisions:

First, the miracle working of Jesus and, even more, his teaching during what is classically called his "public life." He was commonly addressed as "rabbi" or "teacher" by his disciples, and much of his teaching and storytelling was imparted in the course of conversations either with his Jewish disciples or with his various Jewish opponents. His miracles, too, typically have a clear didactic purpose. Through Jesus's teaching and these "signs," his disciples gradually come to recognize his identity not just as the long-awaited Jewish Messiah but also as something breathtakingly more than that.

Second, the story of his condemnation, torture, and death by crucifixion (called, together, his "passion"), followed by his miraculous return to life and mysterious appearances to his disciples (called, together, his "resurrection"). Jesus's condemnation and execution seemed at the time completely incompatible with all traditional expectations for the Jewish Messiah, much less with any identity even more exalted than that one. In the Gospels, Jesus's disciples are understandably troubled and confused about who he really is. Their slowly dawning awareness of once unthinkable possibilities creates much of the suspense that the Gospels clearly aim to create.

Jesus touches on a great many concrete aspects of human life in the course of his teaching: agriculture, business, banking, war and peace, marriage and divorce, motherhood and fatherhood, many aspects of religious practice, and finally death, burial, and the afterlife. Among the salient emphases in his teaching are

—his recurrent focus on the poor and the ethnically or socially marginalized and despised in society
—his related (and repeated) attention to children and to women

—his confidence that God, frequently referred to as his Father, is about to establish His sovereignty (His "kingdom")—a transformation that does not eliminate the next world of heaven or hell but begins in this world as great tribulation precedes anticipated triumph and exaltation. He instructs his followers to pray to their heavenly Father that this kingdom may come "on earth as it is in heaven"

—his constant exhortation to forgive harm done by one to another not just once or twice but "seventy times seven"

—his celebration of sincerity and humility and his condemnation of hypocrisy and pride, especially where religion is concerned

—his embrace of his own identity as a Jew coupled with his transcendence of ethnicity and even family by his praise of virtuous men and women from outside Jewry and even from among the Jews' oppressors or enemies

—his call for trust in God as opposed to the anxious pursuit of security through wealth or power

In the following passage from the Qur'an, Allah acknowledges Jesus as an example but stresses first, that he is *only* an example; second, that he is not the only example that Allah could have provided; and third, and most important, that he is principally an example by being a good Muslim:

> He is but a servant on whom We conferred Our grace, and We made him a model for the Children of Israel.
>
> Had We willed We could have created you as angels, to take your place on earth.
> Jesus is a portent of the Hour, so be in no doubt regarding it, and follow Me, for this is a straight path.
> Let not Satan bar your way: to you he is a manifest enemy.
>
> When Jesus came with evident signs, he said: "I come to you with wisdom, and to make clear to you some of what you differ about. Be pious before God and obey me. God is my

Lord and your Lord, so worship Him, for this is the straight path." (43:59–64)

Jesus, as Allah characterizes him, has the right to say, "Worship God *and obey me,*" a sentence already quoted once from Qur'an 3:50. Jesus teaches with a divine grant of authority, in other words, more or less as he does in the Gospels. But as for the distinctive themes enumerated above (in an incomplete list), Allah never touches on them with any specific reference to Jesus. He cites rather the extensive doctrinal factionalism that had arisen among Christians by Muhammad's day.

At this point, however, a genre issue becomes relevant. If attention is directed to Christianity's way of taking Jesus as a moral model (as in "What would Jesus do?"), a more relevant comparison than that of Jesus in the Gospels to Jesus in the Qur'an is Jesus in the Gospels to Muhammad in the Hadith.

Hadith is the term for Islam's painstakingly assembled body of tradition about what Muhammad said and how he acted in an immense variety of human situations. Taken to be the perfect or complete man, Muhammad constitutes a model for all human behavior and the starting point for Islamic jurisprudence. In the Qur'an, by contrast, Muhammad is only very rarely mentioned by name. To be sure, he is omnipresent in the Qur'an as the Prophet to whom Allah addresses all that He says. But to the extent that moral guidance structurally parallel to that which Christianity derives from Jesus is to be sought in Islam, it will be found in the hallowed Hadith rather than in the holy Qur'an. A Jesus/ Muhammad, Gospel/Hadith comparison would be a worthy subject but would call for another entire book.

From the list of Jesus's teachings just above, I have postponed to this moment the two that are most definitive, for these are the two that bear most directly on the last subject of this chapter—namely, the Bible's and the Qur'an's sharply different accounts and interpretations of Jesus's death, destiny, and religious significance. The two omitted biblical teachings are as follows:

First, Jesus's belief in (and enactment of his belief in) the merit of vicarious suffering—that is, suffering that one man or woman accepts in place of another or others.

Second, his signature, scandalous teaching that if slapped on one cheek, one should "offer him the other as well" (Matthew 5:39)—that is, one should return violence with nonviolence. This, again, is a teaching that Jesus both preaches and, by enduring his crucifixion without protest or resistance, enacts.

Expiation or atonement is action undertaken to avert deserved punishment by some kind of substitution for it. The Old Testament, particularly in the Book of Leviticus, makes elaborate provision for the expiation of sin by animal sacrifice. In Leviticus 5, for example, various offenses are listed for which Yahweh requires the expiatory sacrifice of a female sheep or goat. But what if a given sinner cannot afford to sacrifice an animal?

> "If he cannot afford an animal from the flock as a sacrifice of reparation for the sin he has committed, he will bring Yahweh two turtledoves or two young pigeons—one as a sacrifice for sin and the other as a burnt offering. He will bring them to the priest who will first offer the one intended for the sacrifice for sin. The priest will wring its neck but not remove the head. He will sprinkle the side of the altar with the victim's blood, and then squeeze out the rest of the blood at the foot of the altar. This is a sacrifice for sin. He will then offer the other bird as a burnt offering according to the ritual. This is how the priest must perform the rite of expiation for the person for the sin he has committed, and he will be forgiven." (Leviticus 5:7–10)

This minor sacrifice, just a pair of birds, suffices for the listed minor offenses against ritual purity. For many graver offenses, no expiatory sacrifice is allowed, and the penalty for guilt is often death—in effect, the sacrifice of the perpetrator.

Yet expiation even for the taking of a human life remains conceivable, and with it the notion of expiatory human sacrifice. This is the notion darkly hinted at in a set of poems in the Book of Isaiah. One of them speaks of "a man of sorrows, familiar with suffering,"

> one from whom, as it were, we averted our gaze,
> despised, for whom we had no regard.
> Yet ours were the sufferings he was bearing,
> ours the sorrows he was carrying,
> while we thought of him as someone being punished
> and struck with affliction by God;
> whereas he was being wounded for our rebellions,
> crushed because of our guilt;
> the punishment reconciling us fell on him,
> and we have been healed by his bruises. (Isaiah 53:3–5)

Carrying this line of thought a large step further, if one man can atone by his suffering or death for the sins of many, who if anyone can atone for the sins of all mankind for all time? No one, it might seem, except God Himself, who made the world and placed Adam and Eve and all their myriad descendants within it. This is the traditional expiatory logic of the cross. Yahweh becomes a Jew, accepts undeserved suffering and death by crucifixion, and thereby wins forgiveness for the sins of all men and women for all time. They need not be punished, for He has been punished in their place.

But does the sacrifice of a pair of pigeons really take away the guilt of the sinner who brings the pigeons to the officiating priest? Since the sin was against Yahweh, the sacrifice erases the guilt only if Yahweh chooses to regard it as erased. And, accordingly, the sinner will bring the pigeons to the altar only if he trusts that Yahweh will indeed erase the guilt once the sacrifice has taken place. Atonement thus requires faith and consent on either side.

To be sure, there are kinds of sin for which reparation can be simply and materially made. A thief may restore what was stolen or even, in expiation, reimburse the victim twice what the stolen item was worth. And yet obviously not all crimes are susceptible to such reversal. Rape and murder are irreversible in their effect, and in such cases can punishment inflicted on a third party actually accomplish anything at all to either atone to the victim for the grievous wrong inflicted or somehow take away the guilt of the perpetrator?

One major school of Christian thought has always answered yes, believing that the character of God is such that he does indeed accept vicarious suffering as expiatory and redemptive and does regard guilt as truly expunged by forgiveness. The suffering of Christ on the cross is the supreme redemptive sacrifice—"ransoming sinners," to use a classic phrase, from the otherwise deserved punishment of hell. But redemptive as well is the suffering of any Christian who accepts Jesus's challenge:

> "If anyone wants to be a follower of mine, let him renounce himself and take up his cross and follow me. Anyone who wants to save his life will lose it; but anyone who loses his life for my sake will find it." (Matthew 16:24–25)

In countless ways, this soteriology, or theology of redemption, has become an ideal of nobility penetrating Western culture far beyond conscious Christianity. The story of a scorned outsider, abandoned by all, who seems to lose everything but then gains everything in the end and for the good of everyone is the master plot of a thousand Hollywood movies. The sacrifice of life itself out of love, as in the closing moments of the 1997 film *Titanic*, carries forward the same secularized ideal of vicarious suffering that thrills in the final words of Charles Dickens's *A Tale of Two Cities*. In that novel, Sydney Carton loves Lucie Manette, who is married to Charles Darnay. Charles has been wrongfully sentenced to death in the Paris of the French Revolution. But Sydney, who bears a remarkable, entirely coincidental resemblance to Charles, has himself smuggled into the prison as Charles is smuggled out. Christlike, Sydney dies to save Charles, and the novel ends with his last words: "It is a far, far better thing that I do, than I have ever done; it is a far, far better rest that I go to, than I have ever known."[5] Sydney Carton, one of the countless Christ-figures of Western literature, owes his romantic appeal, if we take the long view, to centuries of Christian literary conditioning. He appeals, in the end, because the West has believed in a God who wanted and celebrated redemptive self-sacrifice. Why does God want this? At the end of the reckoning, simply because this is what God is like.

And yet, in the Qur'an, Allah makes clear that God is not like that at all. Again and again, He makes clear that on "the Day" of His judgment each man and each woman will be rewarded for what he or she has done to merit heaven and punished for what he or she has done to merit hell and for that alone. No one will be either punished or rewarded for what someone else has done. However nobly tricked out, two wrongs do not make a right. Allah is just not like that. And, accordingly, there is no room in Allah's correction of Christian scripture for Jesus's redemptive death on the cross or even, as it turns out, for Jesus's physical death in the first place. Just as ruling out any husband for Mary makes her virginity and Allah's unique role in the conception of Prophet Jesus unmistakable, so here: by denying altogether that Jesus actually died on the cross, Allah rules out any possibility of Jesus's death being anything other than ordinary, inevitable human death, thus any possibility of its being redemptive in the Christian sense of that word.

What then did happen on that day when—at least as it appeared to all witnesses—Jesus died? As Allah explains, the Romans played no part; they are never mentioned. Responsibility lay entirely with the Jews, but their rejection of and plotting against Jesus, whom Allah does refer to elsewhere as the Messiah, was just the latest of their rejections of Allah's prophets, and in the end Allah foiled their plot:

> The People of the Book ask you to bring down upon them a book from heaven. But surely they asked Moses a thing even more outrageous than this. They said to him: "Show us God face to face," and were struck by lightning for their sin. Then they took up the worship of the calf even after clear signs had come to them. But We forgave that sin and granted Moses manifest authority. And We raised above them the Mountain in accordance with their covenant and We said to them: "Enter the gate in prostration," and We said to them: "Do not transgress the Sabbath"; and We took from them a most solemn covenant.

> Therefore, by renouncing their covenant, by blaspheming against the revelations of God, by killing prophets unjustly and claiming: "Our hearts are sealed"—rather, it is God Who sealed them with their blasphemy—they believe not, except a few. So also by their blasphemy and their terrible words of slander against Mary, and their saying: "It is we who killed

the Christ Jesus son of Mary, the messenger of God"—they killed him not, nor did they crucify him, but so it was made to appear to them. Those who disputed concerning him are in doubt over the matter; they have no knowledge thereof but only follow conjecture. Assuredly they killed him not, but God raised him up to Him, and God is Almighty, All-Wise. Among the People of the Book none there are but shall believe in him before his death, and on the Day of Resurrection he shall be a witness against them.

Thus, through the wrongdoing of the Jews, We forbade them certain delectable foods which had been made licit to them; by reason, too, of their obstructing the path to God, repeatedly; their taking usury, though forbidden to do so; and their devouring the wealth of people dishonestly—to the unbelievers among them We have readied a painful torment.

But those steeped in knowledge, as also the believers among them, believe in what has been revealed to you and what was revealed before you. And those who perform the prayer, who pay their alms, who believe in God and the Last Day—upon these we shall bestow a glorious recompense. (Qur'an 4:153–162)

Allah's rejection of Christian claims of divinity for Jesus coincides exactly, as we have already noted, with Rabbinical Judaism's rejection of the same claims. But since, according to Allah, Jesus, while making no such claims himself, was both the Messiah and a prophet of Allah, the Jews of his day had every reason to accept him. That they not only rejected him but sought to kill him as, according to Allah, they had killed earlier prophets, was the latest of their sins. Jewish dietary laws themselves are part of Allah's punishment for this latest sin. But Jesus's vindication will come on the "Day of Resurrection" when the Jews will all believe in him as he becomes "a witness against them." Allah, we might say, is anti-Christian but fiercely pro-Christ.

Is He also anti-Jewish? It may be passages like this one, with its condemnation of the Jews for usury and financial predation, a charge with so long and brutal a history in Europe, that Edward Gibbon had in mind in the delicately anti-Semitic passage quoted above. And yet, in the end, the same "straight path" lies open to Jews that lies open to all, with on the last day the prospect of a "glorious recompense."

If Jesus did not actually die on the cross, how was it made to appear to the witnessing Jews that he did? Was someone else crucified in his place? Muslim commentators have speculated about this possibility for centuries, and various candidates have been proposed. Was he crucified but then taken down from the cross alive after all the witnesses had departed? Further speculation has occurred about variations on that possibility as well. Since that dark day, has Jesus lived on in heaven with Allah? Or has he died in some other way and, if so, when? Allah leaves no doubt that Jesus is but a mortal man, a point that He stresses repeatedly, and so Jesus must die as all mortals do. But, again, at what point? Within the Qur'an itself, Allah leaves all these questions unanswered, and we must do so as well.

Our point is that the effect of Allah's foiling the Jews' plot, as He describes it, radically undercuts the Christian celebration of Jesus as the sacrificial "Lamb of God," dying that others may have eternal life. Such was not the assignment that Allah gave to Jesus as his second-to-last prophet. Jesus's calling—begun with his holy mother's calling—was to witness that there is no god but God, to pray and pay alms, and to summon his people, the Jews, to do the same: all of that, and nothing more than that. Like all the Muslim prophets before him, he was sent to a people who had not heard or were not properly responding to Allah's "signs." The Jews' obligation was to respect and not slander Jesus's mother and to receive Jesus's message dutifully as a message from Allah Himself, just as the Jews' obligation in Muhammad's day was to receive His message, the Qur'an, and His messenger, Muhammad, in the same spirit.

Such is the message—the invitation and the linked ultimatum—that Allah has placed before all mankind from the earliest generations:

> Remember when your Lord took away from Adam's children the seeds from their loins, and made them witness upon themselves: "Am I not your Lord?" They answered: "Yes, we witness"—lest you should claim on the Day of Resurrection: "We were unaware of this." Or else you might claim: "But our ancestors too were once guilty of polytheism, and we are

merely their later seed. Will You therefore destroy us because of the works of falsifiers?" Thus do We clarify Our revelations; perhaps they will turn back. (7:172–174)

Allah punishes no one for anyone else's failure to submit. And no one, from the beginning, has lacked the opportunity to submit. Before Allah sent prophets to deliver reminders and warnings, Allah himself served the first universal notice and delivered the first universal warning. Everyone has had a fair chance. Any who have missed their chance have only themselves to blame.

Given that Allah's message in the Qur'an is true and given that Allah does not change, it can only be that Allah's message to all His previous messengers has been the same as His message to Muhammad. It is a simple message, a clear message, a reasonable message, even a natural message. How can it ever have been lost if not through malice or culpable neglect? But Allah is, above all else, Compassionate and Merciful, and his Compassion and Mercy are manifest to perfection in His having at last consigned His original and unchanging message in one pure, final, crowning formulation to his ultimate prophet, Muhammad, the perfect Messenger of His perfect Mercy. This is what God in the Qur'an is like.

Afterword

On the Qur'an as the Word of God

Is the Qur'an the Word of God? Wilfred Cantwell Smith, a Christian scholar who devoted much of his career as a scholar of religion to the study of Islam, made that question the final chapter of his book *On Understanding Islam*.[1] I open this afterword with his question because the moment is at hand to stop talking about Yahweh and Allah and start talking about God.

Both the Bible and the Qur'an claim to be the Word of God; and whatever else that Word is about, it is necessarily and unavoidably about God Himself. Each scripture, in other words, claims to be a kind of guide to God. But which guide should be trusted, and who has the authority to answer questions about them? The statement just above, "Both the Bible and the Qur'an claim to be the Word of God," is effectively metaphorical, for both scriptures are silent until someone reads them—silently or aloud, alone or in company—and *honors* them as the Word of God.

Lofty claims are easily made, after all, and have been made by countless claimants far beyond not just these two originally West Asian scriptures but far beyond even all the great historic scriptures of the world's religions put together. Thousands have made such grand claims, and almost none have had their claims honored for long or by many. Why is this? We have every reason to wonder why. What did the few have that the many lacked?

In Act 3, scene 1 of Shakespeare's *Henry IV, Part 1,* when Glendower boasts "I can call spirits from the vasty deep," Hotspur shoots back:

> Why, so can I, or so can any man,
> But will they come when you do call for them?

I may call for the whole world to honor a given text as the Word of God, but will the world come when I do call upon it? The question is entirely serious, for when the answer to such a question is massively yes and millions come forward in response, the consequences can be titanic.

In *The Kingdom,* Emmanuel Carrère's semi-confessional, semi-historical, semi-polemical *jeu d'esprit* of a book, a French television director compares Christianity to the bizarre imaginings of the neo-gnostic, science-fiction fantast Philip K. Dick and then, struck by his own comparison, goes on:

> He says it's strange, when you think about it, that normal, intelligent people can believe something as unreasonable as the Christian religion, something exactly like Greek mythology or fairy tales. In ancient times, okay: people were gullible, science didn't exist. But today! Nowadays if a guy believed stories about gods turning into swans to seduce mortals, or princesses kissing frogs that become Prince Charmings, everyone would say he's nuts. But tons of people believe in something just as outrageous and no one thinks they're nuts. Even if you don't share their faith, you take them seriously. They play a social role, less important than in the past, but one that's respected and rather positive on the whole. Their pie-in-the-sky ideas coexist alongside perfectly level-headed activities. Presidents pay deferential visits to their leader. Really it's kind of strange, isn't it?[2]

Is Fabrice Gobert, director of the French TV series *Les Revenants* (later, in English, *The Returned*), right to assume that "In ancient times, okay: people were gullible, science didn't exist"? Science in its latest forms did not exist, of course, but were people really any more gullible then than they are now? We have the very word *skeptic* from the Greek *skeptikos*; skepticism constituted an entire recognized school of philosophical thought in late classical antiquity. When Saint Paul expounded Christianity before the Council of Athens (the Areopagus), his more skeptical hearers walked out on him.

And yet there was skepticism within Christianity itself. Read Saint Augustine in the *Confessions* arguing

> that astrology is not a science through which one can foresee the future, but that men's reading its signs has the same power as casting lots. As these astrologers say so much, some of what they say is bound to come to pass, not because they know something, but because by constantly talking they stumble upon the truth.[3]

Augustine believed many things that Fabrice Gobert would find strange, some of them more Platonic than Christian, but in this passage the Christian saint is entirely modern in his determination to be skeptical rather than gullible where astrology is concerned.

Earlier, the prophet Isaiah was scathing in his sarcasm about idolatry. He evokes the picture of a wood-carver preparing to make an idol—ah, but not before a fireside dinner!

> Half of [the wood] he burns on the fire, over this half he roasts meat, eats it and is replete; at the same time he warms himself and says, "Ah, how warm I am, watching the flames!" With the remainder he makes a god, his idol, bows down before it, worships it and prays to it. "Save me," he says, "for you are my god." (Isaiah 44:16–17)

Isaiah believed in God, but intellectually, psychologically, and aesthetically he was as capable as Gobert of standing back from idolatry and remarking, "How strange!" and even "How ridiculous!" The Jews and Christians of the Roman Empire were atheists vis-à-vis all gods but their own, and don't suppose that the Romans failed to notice!

The deeper questions then are why people like Gobert himself do indeed take seriously strange beliefs that they themselves do not accept and how in the world such strange beliefs can end up playing a social role "that's respected and rather positive on the whole." Why is such an outcome *ever* possible, even remotely, even just occasionally? Why did the Jews and Christians, so skeptical about all other religions, make an exception for their own beliefs? And, by the same token, why does Gobert make a comparable exception for modernity and science? Is the world that science and modernity have made really doing all that well?

Carrère himself does not think so. "We're heading straight for the wall," he writes:

> if not for the end of the world, then at least for a major historic catastrophe that will entail the disappearance of a significant part of humanity. Those who hold this belief [Carrère includes himself] have no idea how it will happen or what it will lead to, but they think that if not they themselves, then at least their children will be in the front row.[4]

And yet these secular apocalyptics do continue to have children, perhaps out of blind faith that modernity and science, against all the accumulating evidence, will somehow save their children or that, even if that faith is misplaced, it is the only alternative. But is it? Is there truly no alternative?

Is, for example, Philip K. Dick an alternative? If there is no difference in strangeness between Christianity and Philip K. Dick, why not give Philip K. Dick a try? Might one not imagine building a movement around Dick's fictions, calling it Dickianity or some such name, and seeing whether it would prove to play a social role that's as "respected and rather positive on the whole" as the role played by Christianity? To that question, the answer comes quick, loud, and easy: of course, you can *imagine* such a thing. Such concoctions are only too easy to imagine. The novelist Robert Coover imagined the founding of a new religion in his satirical *The Origin of the Brunists,* and other novelists and screenwriters have dreamed up other cults, all well within the rules of realist fiction. This much is easy. What is incomparably harder is actually *doing* such a thing, actually founding a new religion and sustaining it not just for a few years or decades but even for centuries or millennia.

Individuals have sometimes taken works of fiction as guiding revelations for their lives. The journalist Rebecca Mead reports such an attempt in her 2014 book *My Life in Middlemarch*, about the existential importance to her of George Eliot's novel by that title. Joyce Carol Oates, reviewing this "bibliomemoir," as she called it, for *The New York Times Book Review*, listed an impressive assortment of earlier such efforts. So fictions can to a point serve as guides to life, and a fiction like Coover's—a fiction about a community organized around a fiction—need not be dismissed as strange or laughed off as mere farce but may well be honored as serious fiction. "Serious fiction," we say, as the literary awards are presented, implicitly distinguishing it from "trivial fiction" and granting that the serious variant plays some role in real life that is denied to the trivial, even though both are made up, and neither is true. What the serious variant is—we say, rather revealingly—is "believable."

In sum, even in the realm of strange fictions, certain tests do seem to be available. A given fiction may "work" at least at the level of an individual life. It may be consulted, recalled to mind at critical moments, consulted as private scripture, "believed in," if you will. It may be the one book that you must have with you on the proverbial desert island. It may even carry some sort of message for an entire society, in which case it may approach the status of the Word of God. But for the Word of God offered as such, there are, as we shall see, certain other tests available.

Let me now pause to tell you a story, a simple story originating perhaps in the late Middle Ages but perhaps much earlier and surviving in several forms. Maybe you have heard it already, but no matter: it has survived many retellings. Here is how I would tell it:

> A kind and wealthy father had three sons whom he loved very much. All three longed to inherit their father's golden ring, an ancient ring, handed down from generation to generation, a ring that—they knew, for he had told them—conferred upon the wearer the power to be beloved by God and by all God's creatures.
>
> As the father's life lengthened and as death, all knew, could not be far off, each of the three sons begged that it might be he to whom the wondrous ring would pass.

Poor father! He loved each of his sons so much that he could not deny any one of them this treasure, yet to give it to any one of them would so grieve the others! What to do?

Secretly, the father sought out a highly skilled goldsmith and, entrusting him with the golden ring, commissioned him to make two identical copies. Now, with three rings in hand, the father gave one to each son, each son believing that he had inherited the one and only ring and thus that he and only he would soon be beloved by God and by all God's creatures.

Before long, the kindly old man breathed his last, with his three sons at his bedside, and after laying him to rest, each son stepped forward to claim his role as his father's successor, each offering the golden ring in proof of his claim, each stoutly maintaining—as was indeed true!—that he had received it from his father's own hand. On one thing the brothers all agreed—namely, that only one ring could be the true ring, but which ring was it?

The matter could only be resolved in court, and the presiding judge first ordered that goldsmiths and other experts examine the three rings for signs of forgery. After extended examination and the application of all available tests, the experts returned their verdict: the three rings were identical in every regard; there was no slightest difference among them.

The three sons, nonetheless, demanded that the judge resolve their dispute, declaring one ring authentic and the other two fake. Patiently, the judge pointed out that there was no fair and equitable way to do this, but the three sons were adamant. Finally, growing indignant, the judge delivered his verdict.

Undoubtedly, one ring was authentic, he said, but determining which one it was could only be done retrospectively. Let the three sons, then, each wear his ring and years later, as their lives lengthened and, like their father's, were nearing the end, let them then return to the court, doubtless to a different judge. At that point, looking back on their respective lifetimes, that future judge could determine which son had been beloved by God and (for this at least would be measurable) by all God's

creatures. Such would be the test, the best test, and the only
test available.

Where was this story first told? No one really knows. The oldest
extant version of it appears in an anonymous Latin compilation of tales,
the *Gesta Romanorum,* dating from the late 1200s. That title means "The
Deeds of the Romans," but the tales often bear little or no connection
with Rome and may come from much earlier times; some of them, perhaps, from distant Arab, Persian, or Indian locales. In the *Gesta Romanorum* version, the tale of the miraculous ring is a parable, the judge is
God, and the three sons are Judaism, Christianity, and Islam. Expert
testing, in this version, proves that the Christian son has the real ring.

Decades later, Giovanni Boccaccio in his *Decameron* revised the tale
to make the precious ring a precious gem, the teller of the tale a Jew,
and his hearer a famous Muslim sultan. In this version, in effect, the Jew
comes out subtly on top. Four centuries later, the German playwright
Gotthold Ephraim Lessing, in his drama *Nathan the Wise,* retained the
Jew as the tale-teller and the Muslim sultan as his hearer but gave the
tale the form in which I have just retold it—a form in which there is no
immediate winner, yet there is an answer to the key question. There
is an answer because there is a relevant and reasonably empirical test,
however long it may take to conduct that test.

Bearing this kind of life-test in mind and bearing in mind as well
the background question of why and how any seeming fiction, however
strange, comes to be honored as "serious fiction" or as a guide not just
to life but even to God, let us now return to Wilfred Cantwell Smith's
question, "Is the Qur'an the Word of God?"

Smith begins by noting that the question has been answered "yes" by
millions and "no" by as many millions more and that, either way, the
answer has had consequences not just at the level of private lives led one
way or another but at the level of entire civilizations shaped one way
or another:

> It is no small band of eccentrics that holds [the Qur'an] to be
> God's word; nor is the idea a passing fashion among some vol-
> atile crowd.... Civilizations are not easy to construct, or to
> sustain; yet great civilizations have been raised on the basis

of this conviction. Major cultures have sprung from it, winning the allegiance and inspiring the loyalty and shaping the dreams and eliciting the poetry of ages proud to bow before its manifest grandeur and, to them, limpid truth....

Equally impressive, however, have been those who have said "no." They, too, are not negligible. They, too, are to be numbered in the hundreds or thousands of millions. They, too, have constructed great civilizations, have made great cultures dynamic. The outsider [to Islam] distorts his world if he fails to recognize what has been accomplished on earth by those inspired by the positive response. The Muslim distorts *his*, if he fails to appreciate the possibilities evidently open and beckoning to those who say "no."[5]

Had Egypt remained as Christian as it was in the sixth century, it would be culturally as much a part of Europe today as Greece or Germany. Had Spain remained as Muslim as it was in the ninth century, it would be culturally as much a part of North Africa as Morocco or Tunisia. In either case, the lives of Egyptians or of Spaniards would be profoundly different.

Historically, the baton of leadership has passed back and forth between these two. From the time of Napoleon's invasion of Egypt at the end of the eighteenth century through Britain's overthrow of the Mughal Empire in India and Russia's colonial expansion through Muslim Central Asia to the Pacific in the nineteenth, the civilization that said "yes" to Smith's question has felt the painful and humiliating encroachment of the civilization that said "no." Now, in the twenty-first, the civilization that said "no" is feeling the encroachment of the civilization that said "yes." Michel Houellebecq's recent novel *Submission,* in which a Muslim political party becomes the governing party in France, probably captures France's preoccupation with religion, such as it is, better than Emmanuel Carrère's *The Kingdom* does with its novelistic speculations about the early Christian Church.

Smith notes, astutely, that once the Qur'an question has been answered in the affirmative at the civilizational level, it is typically no longer even asked at the individual or even cultural level. "Muslims do not read the Qur'ān and conclude that it is divine," he writes.

Rather, they believe it to be divine, and then they read it. This makes a great deal of difference, and I urge upon Christian or secular students of the Qur'ān that if they wish to understand it as a religious document, they must approach it in this spirit.[6]

I have urged a semblance of this spirit upon the non-Muslim readers of this book by introducing, early in its foreword, the notion of "suspension of disbelief."

What is true at the civilizational level of the affirmative answer is equally true, of course, of the negative answer. Historically, Jews and Christians have not read the Bible to determine whether it was merely human. They have believed that it was somehow much more than merely human and read it for that reason. And just as Muslims generally ignore the Bible, so Jews and Christians have ignored the Qur'an for the obvious and analogous reason. In either case, whether or not there has been prejudice in any invidious or interpersonal sense of that word, there has clearly been a prejudgment.

In making this claim, I have in mind lay readers rather than scholars, but I would go beyond Smith in claiming that Western historical critics of all sacred scripture—that is, not just of the Qur'an—never read these texts as the Word of God, abstaining from any such engagement for methodological reasons that Smith ultimately respects. Of such academic criticism of the Qur'an, he writes:

> The Western academic scholar, too, has not studied the Qur'ān, asking himself whether this be divine or human. He has presumed before he started that it was human, and he has studied it in that light.[7]

Such scholars, he writes, look for the source of the Qur'an

> in the psychology of Muhammad, in the environment in which he lived, in the historical tradition that he inherited, in the socio-economic-cultural milieu of his hearers. They look for it, and they find it. They find it, because quite evidently it is there....
>
> Those who hold the Qur'ān to be the word of God, have

found that this conviction leads them to a knowledge of God. Those who hold it to be the word of Muhammad, have found that this conviction leads them to a knowledge of Muhammad. Each regards the other as blind. From what I have said, you will perhaps discern that in this matter I feel that in fact each is right.[8]

As a Bible scholar, I readily agree with Smith: one may write vast and penetrating analyses of the views of Israelites and Nazarenes in antiquity, all the while remaining entirely noncommittal on the question of whether the Bible is the Word of God. The latter question, as one that scholarship cannot resolve anyway, is one that scholarship need not ever address.

In effect, then, scholarship about either the Qur'an or the Bible is like the expert testimony of goldsmiths in the Parable of the Ring. Competent as such scholarship may be on its own terms, it is beside the point of a question like "Is the Bible the Word of God?" or "Is the Qur'an the Word of God?" Meanwhile the enormous and, yes, sometimes clashing civilizations that have been so differently shaped by different answers to these questions remain significantly different and, much to the point, are mingling as never before. Once, they could and did ignore one another to a very considerable extent. Now, this is no longer possible, and meanwhile both regularly encounter the secular alternative that preemptively answers all "Word of God" questions in the negative. William Cantwell Smith, as a pioneering scholar of comparative religion, was early in insisting that bilateral relations among religions would prove less fateful in the long run than the relations that each would establish or fail to establish with such operationally secular forces as the market and the media.

So, at the end of a book whose title begins with the word *God* and nearing the end of an afterword in which I said that it was at last time to talk about Him using that dread word, where are we? I promise: we *will* talk again about God before this book ends, but first I need to deliver a little exhortation in favor of the imagination. If you are irreligious, can you imagine yourself religious? I urge that you try doing so. If you are religious, can you imagine yourself irreligious? My advice to you is the same. If you are not a Jew, can you imagine yourself Jewish? If you are Jewish, can you imagine yourself a Muslim? If you are Muslim, can you imagine yourself a Jew or perhaps a Hindu?

Why bother? Because even if you have no intention of changing your views or your habits, the very experience of imagining yourself thinking and living in another way will foster in you, out of transferred self-love, a measure of sympathy. It will foster a sense of the reasonability and human possibility of views and ways of life different from your own. Imagine yourself as other than you are, and you begin imagining others as no less human, no less sincere, no less levelheaded, no less likable than you are yourself.

James Boswell, in his famous *Life of Samuel Johnson,* reports himself asking the great doctor, "Pray, Sir, do you not suppose that there are fifty women in the world, with any one of whom a man may be as happy, as with any one woman in particular?" To which Johnson answered, "Ay, Sir, fifty thousand." Leaving one woman for another is, in a way, like conversion to another religion;[9] and though marital infidelity is common enough, so is marital fidelity, in which a man or a woman imagines intimacy with another partner, even imagines decades of life together, and yet remains faithful to his/her spouse. Absent such imaginings, to be sure, divorce would never happen, but perhaps marriage itself would never happen either. In itself, the act of imagining instructs, enriches, and deepens any man or woman's engagement with his or her own life.

In the mid-1960s, I was a philosophy student at the Pontifical Gregorian University in Rome, where at the time textbooks, lectures, and examinations were all in Latin. (Nowadays, they are mostly in English or Italian.) My ethics professor was a French Jesuit, Père Joseph de Finance, S.J. Dutifully, Père de Finance lectured in Latin, but whenever something amusing occurred to him, as did happen from time to time, he would lapse into French. This he did once as he spoke of a French girl expressing gratitude that she had been born French, for the poor thing would have been oh *so* unhappy if she were English. After quoting the girl (his niece, I bet) in French and with what struck me as an affectionate chuckle, Père de Finance went on in Latin to explain that, of course, if she had been born English, she would have thanked God for her good fortune.

What was his point? Honestly, I can't remember. What I do remember is that I left that lecture thinking a bit admiringly, *What if I had been born French? Would I be like Père de Finance?* I liked de Finance; he was close to my favorite teacher—gentle, subtle, persuasive rather than ever dogmatic, like the clerk in *The Canterbury Tales*: "gladly wolde he lerne and gladly teche." In a word, he seemed wise. If I had been born French, would I have been more like him? Would I have been wise?

Voluntary expatriation is another form of conversion. I have met a good many willing and happy expatriates over the years, yet I know from repeated experience that one can go ever so far in that direction and still head for home in the end. So it can be with religions, as the once relatively isolated and insulated civilizations that have been shaped by those religions begin now to shape themselves into a hybrid, pluriform civilization in which all exert power but none rules. It is an altogether salutary exercise at such a juncture to imagine yourself as other than you are even if, most of the time, you are well advised to take the exercise as just that: an exercise, an excursion, but not your destined home.

Smith, once rigorous honesty about his challenging question has brought him to a virtual impasse, begins casting about for a still-to-be-disclosed middle course between "yes" and "no." He sets aside, to begin with, mass conversion—above all, mass conversion under any kind of duress. Once common enough, this alternative is now beyond reach even if some power were again to seriously attempt it. All the religions of the world, if one truly reckons with the whole world, are now minority religions, and none is ever going to become the ruling majority. Religious domination, even religious tyranny, will remain locally possible, but globally uniformity in this domain is beyond reach, for religion has proven that it defies full state control, even in a highly controlled society like China. Secularists, too, are a minority. And even if, by their own lights, they have all the right answers and the most humane way of life, they, too, will remain a minority. No one of these life-alternatives will ever become the hegemonic host for all the others as its managed guests, however benign the management may promise to be.

We are, in short, really and truly stuck with each other here in the darkness. How to light a candle? Smith sees both Christians and Muslims "in search of an answer to our question more subtle, more realistic, more historical, more complex than the traditional 'yes or no.'" And he offers as an aside what may stand, finally, as the modest rationale for this book:

> Significant in this new situation, where both traditional groups are setting out in search of a larger answer, is the fantastically potential novelty that, in the process, both groups are beginning to deliberate on each other's books.[10]

So now, in cautious hope, deliberating on the Qur'an and more specifically on God in the Qur'an, I address myself to my non-Muslim readers. Recalling all that has filled the earlier chapters of this book, let me invite you to imagine yourself worshipping God as we have seen Him presented in the Qur'an. You don't have to become a Muslim to imagine this. You can be like the little French girl imagining what it would be like to be English, or (probably better) like an American in his green twenties, sitting in a Roman lecture hall imagining what it would be like to be a wise, subtle, and mature French philosopher. You can even be like a married man or a married woman imagining—but only imagining—intimacy with a new partner. This is just an exercise, just a mental experiment.

Agreed? Step into the mosque of your imagination, and as you bow down and touch your forehead to the floor saying, "God is greater," or as you hear others saying those words in Arabic, you remember...

> *that when God placed Adam and Eve in the Garden of Paradise, He warned them that Satan would tempt them.* (In the Bible, no such warning is given.)
>
> *that when they succumbed to temptation but then quickly repented, He forgave them and explained that after a lifetime on Earth, bearing only the trials and tribulations that ordinary human life entails, they could return to Paradise.* (No such forgiveness or distant hope is proffered in the Bible.)
>
> *that when one of Adam's sons slew the other, God condemned the murderer but coached him toward compassion by sending a raven whose scratching in the ground prompted the remorseful killer to bury his dead brother.* (No such solicitous counsel is offered in the Bible.)

that when God sent a destructive flood, he warned those in its path beforehand and provided an ark on which, had they accepted Prophet Noah's warning, they could all have floated to safety. (No such warning is given in the Bible.)

that when God chose Abraham as his prophet, he instructed him in monotheism before sending him against Abraham's idolatrous father and his tribe. (In the Bible, God's command to Abraham is peremptory and linked to fertility rather than to monotheism.)

that when God sent Moses to Pharaoh with the same prophetic message that He later conveyed to Muhammad, Pharaoh initially scoffed but in the end converted and accepted God as the only god. (In the Bible, God takes control of Pharaoh's mind and bars the gate against any such conversion.)

that when God sent Jesus as a prophet to the Jews and they sought to kill him, God rescued him and took him to Himself. (In the Bible, Jesus dies saying, "My God, my God, why have You forsaken me?")

Far be it for me to bash the Bible. The Bible is my scripture. The Qur'an is theirs. In writing this little italicized meditation, I hope only that by exercising your imagination just this much, you may find it a little easier to trust the Muslim next door, thinking of him as someone whose religion, after all, may not be so wildly unreasonable that someone holding to it could not be a trusted friend. Taking a further hopeful step, you might imagine that very Muslim neighbor returning the favor and imagining his way into your mind, your guiding texts, and your religious or irreligious life as you have imagined your way into his.

As general editor of *The Norton Anthology of World Religions*, I chose to begin my introduction to that ample exercise in comparative religion with a simple poem, "It Is Enough to Enter," by Todd Boss. Boss ends his poem with these lines:

It is enough
to have come just so far.
You need
not be opened any more
than does
a door, standing ajar.[11]

The suspension of disbelief, as we have practiced it in this book, is one way to open the door, and I will consider it a major accomplishment if the door remains standing ajar for a while. But at the same time, is there not something finally unsatisfactory about this? I certainly think so, but then, too, one need not leave a door permanently ajar to leave it open for a very long time. Such is the wisdom of the Parable of the Rings, and I find antecedents for such ultra-long-term forbearance in all three of the religions that have figured in this book.

In the Qur'an, this is the patience that God counsels in Sura 5:48:

> For every community We decreed a law and a way of life. Had God willed, He could have made you a single community— but in order to test you in what He revealed to you. So vie with one another in virtue. To God is your homecoming, all of you, and He will then acquaint you with that over which you differed.

The homecoming God alludes to here is the Last Judgment, and so the postponement in question is a postponement to the end of time.

In Judaism, the end of time and the coming of the Messiah are heralded by the return to earth of the prophet Elijah, the prophet who was taken to heaven in a fiery chariot and so never died. But Elijah, at his coming, will also resolve all questions that the rabbis (and everybody else) have been unable to resolve. The Hebrew word *teiko,* meaning "tie" as in "a tie game," is originally a Rabbinic acronym for "Tishbi will resolve all difficulties and problems." (Elijah, who apparently came from a town called something like Tishbah, is called Tishbi or the Tishbite in Rabbinic tradition.) Once again, then, we are counseled to accept with patience the indefinite postponement of answers to the questions and disputes that we ourselves cannot now resolve.

In Christianity, the Last Judgment, as evoked in the Gospel of Matthew, makes the very knowledge of Christ strikingly irrelevant. Those who feed the hungry, shelter the homeless, clothe the naked, and visit the imprisoned will on the Last Day be credited with performing these services for Christ whether they have known Him or not and whether (or so I take it) they have ever even heard of Him. The transparent moral exhortation here is very close to the Qur'an's "So vie with one another in virtue" (5:48), while you wait patiently for the justice to be accomplished that is now beyond all human doing.

Is the Qur'an the Word of God? Ultimately, if that question must be asked, then we must wait for God to answer it. Structurally, the question has a little something in common with the question, as between Jews and Christians, "Is Jesus the Messiah?" Jews believe that the Messiah has not yet come. Christians believe that he has come but will come again. So, rather than fight about it, they may wait for the Messiah to come and then ask him if this is his first visit or his second.[12]

I am being a bit light-hearted about a serious question, but about the wisdom of postponement, I am completely serious. We may die without knowing the answers to certain crucial questions, but we need not surrender them for that reason. Is one lifetime not long enough? So be it, but let the question linger anyway. Let it hang in the air.

> What is a human being, what purpose does he serve?
>> What is good and what is bad for him?
> The length of his life: a hundred years at most.
> Like a drop of water from the sea, or a grain of sand,
>> such are these few years compared with eternity.
> This is why the Lord is patient with them
>> and pours out his mercy on them.
> He sees and recognizes how wretched their end is,
>> and so he makes his forgiveness the greater.
>
> (Ecclesiasticus 18:8–12)

When the Bible and the Qur'an give different versions of the same episode, which is to be judged the correct version and thus the Word of God? This dispute shines through in the Qur'an itself as we saw earlier where Allah counsels Muhammad how he is to respond to the charge that what he recites is a fabrication:

> Or do they say: "He fabricated it"? Say: "If I fabricated it, upon me falls my sinful act, and I am quit of your sinning." (11:35)

Or, as I have paraphrased this line, "If I made all this up, so much the worse for me. But if not, so much the worse for you." Such challenges to Muhammad sometimes came from the Jews of Medina, who recognized that what they heard from Muhammad contradicted what they knew from their scripture.[13] His reply—and his countercharge—could have been a recitation of Qur'an 2:79:

> Wretched too are those who write Scripture with their own
>   hands and then claim it to be from God, that they may sell
>   it for a small price!
> Woe to them for what their hands have written!
> Woe to them for the profit they made!

But while we wait patiently for Elijah or Allah or Jesus or whoever to arrive and adjudicate all such disputes, we don't want to be perpetually on guard that the guy next door may kill us if we don't kill him first, and we don't want him to be perpetually on guard against us out of the same ugly fear. So, let's instead get to know him well enough to live with him in peace; and if that means getting to know his scriptures and his God, let's take the time to do that too.

I do not minimize the obstacles here. As a Christian and a seventy-five-year-old choirboy, I am deeply attached to the American folk hymn "What wondrous love is this?"—a hymn that does not just assert but exultantly sings out what Islam denies—namely, the divinity of Christ, the Lamb of God who *is* God:

> To God and to the Lamb I will sing, I will sing;
> To God and to the Lamb I will sing;
> To God and to the Lamb
> Who is the great I AM
> While millions join the theme, I will sing, I will sing,
> While millions join the theme,
> I will sing.

And if I were a Jew—I, who have imagined being Jewish much more often and much more vigorously than ever I imagined being French—I would mournfully thrill (I do thrill, anyway) to *HaTikvah* ("The Hope"), the national anthem of Israel, and to Deuteronomy 7:7–8:

It is not because you are the most numerous of peoples that the LORD set his heart on you and chose you—indeed, you are the smallest of peoples; but it was because the LORD favored you and kept the oath He made to your fathers that the LORD freed you with a mighty hand and rescued you from the house of bondage, from the power of Pharaoh king of Egypt.[14]

The Lord loved us, and here we are, I would think, *millennia later, not numbering in the hundreds of millions, like the Muslims and Christians, still small, but eternally indestructible because He will never desert us.* I would feel special, ennobled, set apart by just what Islam denies, namely, the special status of Israel as a chosen people and a light unto the nations.

Yet I recognize a brilliant symmetry in how Islam combined Judaism's criticism of Christianity with Christianity's criticism of Judaism. Christianity insisted, against Jewish tradition, on universalizing God's covenant with Israel to include, in potential, all of mankind, dissolving Israel's privilege in the process. Islam accepted this critique: the Muslim *'ummah* is as universal in aspiration as the Christian church. Judaism insisted, against emergent Christianity, that as God alone was divine, there could be "no two powers in heaven": Jesus was not the Lord; only the Lord, *haqadosh baruch hu'*, was the Lord. Islam accepted this critique: there is no room in its theology for a divine Christ or any other power associated with the one and only God.

From each, by a kind of radical simplification, Islam took what was most precious and most defining and yet at the same time eliminated from each what was most problematic. From Christianity, it stripped off the doctrine that had produced, by the time of Muhammad, endless controversy and multiplying sectarian division, while from Judaism— or from the Jews as a people—it stripped off the sense of privilege as the one and only Chosen People of the one and only God.

The Qur'an in translation, I readily admit, has little initial literary appeal for those whose literary sensibility has been shaped outside Islamicate culture, and it certainly never offers any journalistically tidy summary of the sort that I have just risked. Many, perhaps most, first-time readers find it confusing, and yet deliberately willed, aesthetically contrived confusion is part and parcel of a great many masterpieces of modern art, and the easy clarity that we do not demand of them we have no call to demand of ancient art, including ancient literary art—and including the Qur'an.

Forty years ago, I wrote a little essay entitled "Radical Editing: *Redaktionsgeschichte* and the Aesthetic of Willed Confusion" for inclusion in a volume not of Qur'an criticism but of Bible criticism.[15] The Bible is often at its most confusing where successive hands have engaged in the wholesale editing—commonly called redaction—that invites modern scholars to try to tease out the history of the redactions (the *Redaktionsgeschichte,* in German, and German scholars led the way in this effort). The goal, always, has been to recover the original work hiding behind all the later alterations.

Yet who is to say that earlier was better than later? The alterations may have been made to brilliant effect even if they overtook a different effect intended by an earlier author. Some regard the narrative that frames the long poems of lamentation that fill the Book of Job as the addition of a redactor and regret the effect that this later narrative, sometimes disparaged as a happy "folk tale," has on the bleak, despairing grandeur of the poetry alone. Others, however, see the redactor as a genius who by that addition endowed a set of turgid poems—ones that otherwise would have sunk under their own weight—with suspense, drama, and literary immortality.

What Bible readers need to remember when confronting the Qur'an is that redaction need not be a matter of the written revision of written texts alone. Oral redaction is equally possible and can be equally brilliant. In an oral culture, a durable oral redaction can acquire the same sense of unimpeachable truth and authority that the last written redaction of scripture has traditionally enjoyed in Judaism and Christianity.

Historically speaking, there is little doubt that a process of oral redaction of traditions about Adam, Noah, Moses, and others had taken place in Arabia before Muhammad received the revelations of the Qur'an. The Qur'an does not claim to impart these traditions for the first time. Rather it repeatedly reminds Muhammad, and Muslims through him, of the traditions' acknowledged truth. Honored already as the Word of God, they may be amended in detail but are primarily reinforced as they are incorporated into the Qur'an as God's final revelation to Muhammad himself. Thereafter, in perfect parallel to the Bible, the status of the Qur'an as the Word of God is validated by the community that accepts it as such.

As for those outside that community, a little effort in exploring the Qur'an can pay large long-term dividends at the broad civilizational level where the answer to questions like "Is the Qur'an the Word of God?" and "Is the Bible the Word of God?" (not to speak of "Is there a god?") determine entire ways of life. And if you are among the many whose default position on such questions is to regard anything produced in human language as a human creation, another question is worth asking at this point.

Can any truly great literature be entirely secular?

George Steiner addresses this question in his book *Real Presences,* a kind of philosophy of literature:

> The limits of our language are not, *pace* Wittgenstein, those of our world (and as a man immersed in music, he knew that). The arts are most wonderfully rooted in substance, in the human body, in stone, in pigment, in the twanging of gut or the weight of wind on reeds. All good art and literature begin in immanence. But they do not stop there. Which is to say, very plainly, that it is the enterprise and privilege of the aesthetic to quicken into lit presence the continuum between temporality and eternity, between matter and spirit, between man and "the other." It is in this common and exact sense that *poiesis* opens on to, is underwritten by, the religious and the metaphysical. The questions: "What is poetry, music, art?" "How can they not be?" "How do they act upon us and how do we interpret their action?" are, ultimately, theological questions.[16]

If Steiner is right, then taking the time that you have now taken to acquaint yourself with just a small sampling of Islam's scripture and through it with just one approach to God as Islam knows Him, you have been engaged in theology even if you are an atheist. But fear not: it may be that in the process you have helped in a small way to give the emergent hybrid civilization we so badly need a chance to take its first breath and let loose the first cry of a blessed and welcome new life.

Appendix

Of Satan and the Afterlife in the Bible and the Qur'an

In the opening chapters of this book, I repeatedly noted two theographical differences between the anonymous biblical narrator's presentation of Yahweh Elohim in the Book of Genesis and Allah's self-presentation in the Qur'an. In so doing, I unavoidably implied that these differences apply to the entire Bible. In historical fact, they do not.

The two differences are: first, the prominent presence in the Qur'an of references to the Devil (Satan or Iblis) versus the absence of such references in the Bible; and second, the prominent presence in the Qur'an of references to the afterlife versus the absence of such references in the Bible.

These two differences do matter to the characterization of God because God is, after all, differently characterized if He is understood to be opposed by or unopposed by a hostile and powerful being like Satan. Similarly, He is differently characterized if He is understood to grant reward or inflict punishment only in this life and in this world or to do also or even primarily in the afterlife and in a world to come.

So long as we confine our attention to just the Books of Genesis and Exodus, on the one hand, as against the Qur'an, on the other, these differences are undeniably there. Historically, however, it matters that Genesis is one of the earlier books in the biblical canon, though all but certainly not the first. Were we to look at the latest books in the canon, especially the Alexandrian canon[1] that became the canon of the Christian Old Testament, we would find Satan and the afterlife playing a gradually larger role.

A closer look may bring this historical observation into better focus.

SATAN IN AND AFTER THE BOOK OF GENESIS

Is it true that the God of the Bible is unopposed by any opposing power such as Satan? A historian would answer with careful circumspection: *It is true that the God of Genesis, as originally composed and even as later edited, is unopposed by any Satan, but as for the rest of the Bible, the answer to your question depends on what book you are asking about. The Bible as a whole shows a historical evolution of beliefs about Satan.*

The Book of Genesis, a relatively early book of the Bible, understands God in one way. Other, later books of the Bible understand Him in somewhat different ways, and we need to remember that the Bible contains about four dozen different books of greatly varying length. Historically, belief in Satan, though absent at the start, did *develop* over time among the Israelites—later living on as the Jews. By the first century CE, Jews were clearly identifying the Serpent that opposes Yahweh in the Garden of Eden with Satan as a supernatural being in conflict with Yahweh, though these evidently were not the Jews who would found Rabbinic Judaism. In any case, the Satan-idea had by then been in a period of gradual growth for several centuries, beginning probably in the late sixth century BCE when Judaea became part of the Persian Empire.

Persian Zoroastrianism (named for Zoroaster, its great prophet) was not strictly speaking dualistic or ditheistic; it did not recognize two equal gods or two matched primal principles, one standing for good, the other for evil. But alongside Ahura Mazda, its supreme deity, it did recognize a powerful, Satan-like figure called Angra Mainyu. This understanding of a supreme being facing, however, significant and pervasive opposition does seem to have influenced the evolving thought of Jews under Persian rule. The Book of Job—in which Satan makes a bold early appearance, tempting and temporarily confounding Yahweh

Elohim and then brutally tormenting the title character—may reflect a stage in this Persian influence. Or consider this scene from the prophet Zechariah, also writing under Persian rule:

> He [Yahweh] then showed me the high priest Joshua, standing before the angel of Yahweh, with Satan standing on his right to accuse him. The angel of Yahweh said to Satan, "May Yahweh rebuke you, Satan! May Yahweh rebuke you, since he has made Jerusalem his choice. Is not this man [the high priest] a brand snatched from the fire?" (Zechariah 3:1–2)

One cannot infer from this brief scene the presence of an evil power comparable to what Satan would be later in, for example, the Book of Revelation. Satan is present in this scene "to accuse"; this makes him a kind of heavenly prosecutor but not necessarily anything more than that. Nonetheless, the scene represents an early moment in an evolution with an enormous future, not excluding an incipient association of Satan with fire and hellish punishment. Satan is ready to take Joshua into custody, but Yahweh, with his good angel at his side, has snatched his high priest from Satan's clutches like a brand snatched from the fire.

Many historians are prepared to see the striking presence of Satan in later Israelite and early Jewish religion as well as in Christianity and Islam as the continuing assimilation and progressive transformation of Zoroastrian influence. Certainly, the felt presence of Satan was already powerfully alive among the Jews to whom Jesus preached in the first century CE. In the Gospels, this belief surfaces dramatically whenever Jesus expels devils from the demonically possessed. Moreover, in one of the most protracted and cunningly constructed dialogues in the Gospel, Satan tempts Jesus himself for forty days in the Judaean desert.

In short, if you take the Bible, including both Old Testament and New Testament, as a historically developing collection and ask about the prominence of Satan in it at a point late enough in its development, you find Satan quite prominent indeed, and his prominence then becomes a point of similarity rather than a point of difference as between the Bible and the Qur'an.

THE AFTERLIFE IN AND AFTER THE BOOK OF GENESIS

What is true about Satan in the two scriptures is similarly true about the afterlife. If we ask whether in the Bible God rewards or punishes exclusively in this life, our imagined, circumspect historian might answer much as he did when asked about Satan: *It is true that in the Book of Genesis, as originally composed and even as later edited, God promises no one any reward or punishment in an afterlife, but in later books of the Bible, such promises become steadily more prominent.*

Some of the earlier books of the Old Testament show clear evidence of belief in a faint, ghostly afterlife in Sheol, a realm of neither reward nor punishment. Within these earlier books, significant reward comes always and only *within* normal human lifetimes. God's favor takes the form of longevity, security from enemies, and fertility in its various forms: abundant offspring, bounteous fields, and burgeoning livestock. Punishment comes, correspondingly, either as early death or as personal, agricultural, or pastoral sterility or blight. Most often, however, and most spectacularly, punishment comes as actual or threatened defeat by Israel's enemies acting, however unwittingly, as agents of Israel's God.

Such an agent is Babylon, the "distant nation," in the passage from the prophet Isaiah that follows. Yahweh rages against Israel "for having rejected the law of Yahweh Sabaoth, for having despised the word of the Holy One of Israel":

> This is why Yahweh's anger has blazed out against his people;
> and he has raised his hand against them to strike them;
> why the mountains have shuddered
> and why corpses are lying like dung in the streets.
> After all this, his anger is not spent.
> No, his hand is still raised!
> He hoists a signal for a distant nation,
> he whistles them up from the ends of the earth;
> and see how swift, how fleet they come!
> . . . .

Their arrows are sharpened,
their bows are strung,
their horses' hoofs you would think were flint
and their wheels, a whirlwind!
Their roar is like that of a lioness,
like fierce young lions they roar,
growling they seize their prey
and carry it off, with no one to prevent it,
growling at it, that day,
like the growling of the sea.
Only look at the country: darkness and distress,
and the light turned to darkness by the clouds.
  (Isaiah 5:25–26, 28–30)

Though sent to summon sinful Israel to repent, Isaiah proclaims Yahweh's threatened punishment with obvious gusto. In the earlier books of the Old Testament, Yahweh and Yahweh's people never lose. The case of unmerited suffering, bad things happening to good people, simply does not arise.

Later parts of the Old Testament, however, begin to lament that Yahweh is savagely abusing Israel despite her constant obedience and fidelity. This is the sorrowful sentiment heard in Psalm 44:

You hand us over like sheep for slaughter,
you scatter us among the nations,
you sell your people for a trifle
and make no profit on the sale.
You make us the butt of our neighbours,
the mockery and scorn of those around us,
you make us a by-word among nations,
other peoples shake their heads over us.
All day long I brood on my disgrace,
the shame written clear on my face,
from the sound of insult and abuse,
from the sight of hatred and vengefulness.
All this has befallen us though we had not forgotten you,

nor been disloyal to your covenant,
our hearts never turning away,
our feet never straying from your path.
(44:11–18, emphasis added)

Over time, steadfast faith in Yahweh amid continuing foreign oppression—"tears their food, threefold tears their drink," as Psalm 80:5 puts it—gave rise to the thought that perhaps He who had created the heavens and the earth and even time itself did not mete out reward and punishment in this life alone. Perhaps the arena of victory and defeat was larger than human beings could know this side of the grave. And just as the enlargement of the role of Satan in the Old Testament seems to owe much to the influence of Persia, so belief in the existence of an immortal soul, surviving after the death of the body, owes much to the later-arriving influence of Greek rule and Greek influence in the Eastern Mediterranean and well beyond.

A Greek-speaking Jew writing in Alexandria, Egypt, in the first century BCE wrote in the biblical Book of Wisdom that the godless:

do not know the hidden things of God,
they do not hope for the reward of holiness,
they do not believe in a reward for blameless souls.
For God created human beings to be immortal,
he made them as an image of his own nature;
Death came into the world only through the Devil's envy,
as those who belong to him find to their cost.
But the souls of the upright are in the hands of God,
and no torment can touch them.
To the unenlightened, they appeared to die,
their departure was regarded as disaster,
their leaving us like annihilation;
but they are at peace.
If, as it seemed to us, they suffered punishment,
their hope was rich with immortality;
slight was their correction, great will their blessings be.
(2:22–3:5)

The Book of Wisdom, included in the Alexandrian canon of the Jewish Bible, does not use the word *heaven,* at least not in this passage, but obviously it does assert the existence of an afterlife of reward and punishment. Note, too, that the passage quoted reflects the later-developing belief that the Serpent that seduced Adam and Eve into sin was indeed the Devil and that only then did death enter the world. The consoling message of the Book of Wisdom—against the lament of Psalm 44—is that God has the power to reverse the curse of death that he pronounced on his disobedient first human creatures and to bestow a blessed immortality upon those who serve him courageously to the end.

A century or less after the Book of Wisdom, Jesus mentions both heaven and hell in a short speech that he speaks to comfort and reassure those of his disciples who fear lethal persecution at the hands of the Messiah's enemies:

> "Do not be afraid of those who kill the body but cannot kill the soul; fear him rather who can destroy both body and soul in hell. Can you not buy two sparrows for a penny? And yet not one falls to the ground without your Father knowing. Why, every hair on your head has been counted. So there is no need to be afraid; you are worth more than many sparrows.
>
> "So if anyone declares himself for me in the presence of human beings, I will declare myself for him in the presence of my Father in heaven. But the one who disowns me in the presence of human beings, I will disown in the presence of my Father in heaven." (Matthew 10:28–33)

Implied in this passage is not just that forthright, public support for Jesus will be rewarded in the afterlife, but that reward and punishment alike will be meted out at a heavenly judgment scene where Jesus will testify before the judge, God the Father, on behalf of his followers.

For centuries, Israel had dreamed in poetically inflamed language of a great and final Judgment Day—the "Day of Yahweh," often enough referred to simply as "That Day." For centuries, too, the assumption had been that this Day would inaugurate the imposition of God's rule *on earth*, His sovereignty, and a blessed peace within which the wolf would lie down with the lamb. The inauguration Day itself, however, would be one of enormous violence. Thus, in the seventh century BCE, the prophet Zephaniah wrote:

> The great Day of Yahweh is near,
> near, and coming with great speed.
> How bitter the sound of the Day of Yahweh,
> the Day when the warrior shouts his cry of war.
> That Day is a day of retribution,
> a day of distress and tribulation,
> a day of ruin and devastation,
> a day of darkness and gloom,
> a day of cloud and thick fog,
> a day of trumpet blast and battle cry
> against fortified town
> and high corner-tower.
> I shall bring such distress on humanity
> that they will grope their way like the blind
> for having sinned against Yahweh.
> Their blood will be poured out like mud,
> yes, their corpses like dung;
> nor will their silver or gold
> be able to save them.
> On the Day of Yahweh's anger,
> by the fire of his jealousy,
> the whole earth will be consumed.
> For he will destroy, yes, annihilate
> everyone living on earth. (1:14–18)

The Day of Yahweh was the day when Yahweh, tarrying no longer, would at last reveal himself in all his explosive and definitive power. We call passages like the one just quoted "apocalyptic" because *apocalypsis* in Greek means "revelation," and such passages "reveal" what the great and terrible Day will be like.

The more grandiose such visions of Yahweh's triumph became, however, the more they seemed to entail the absolute end of the world as we know it. A further, distinctive feature of apocalyptic writing came to be its coded revelation of *when* the both dreaded and hoped for Day would come. But as predictions came and went, as hopes for a transformation of this world arose and were repeatedly shattered, the infinite postponement of God's definitive intervention was displaced spatially to a place beyond time altogether. God's intervention came then to coincide with the onset of a new creation or heavenly afterlife bringing permanent—in effect, eternal—gratification for the long-suffering just and, of course, eternal confinement and punishment for the once cruel, once proud, but now humbled unjust.

This cosmic vision, firmly in place in the latest books of the Bible, coincides very closely with the cosmic vision of the Qur'an. We might say, speaking loosely, that the Qur'an was there already, while the Bible had to get there. But in the foreword to this book, I made a historical observation that bears repeating at this point:

> The Bible, five times longer than the Qur'an, is a vast anthology, the work of many different authors, who wrote over one thousand years' time between about 900 BCE and about 100 CE. The Qur'an as historians know it came into being during an intense twenty years' time, late in the life of just one man: the prophet Muhammad, who received it in the early seventh century CE as a revelation from Allah.

For the writing of the thousand-year history of belief in the God of the Bible, well-attested historical methods come readily enough to hand. In broad or schematic terms, the matter is one of

1) rearranging and contextualizing the Bible's component books into some hypothesized chronological order,

2) considering how God appears in each successive book or period,

3) noting continuities and discontinuities from one book to the next as well as revisions, revivals, and so forth, then

4) attributing all these presentations of God to those who successively wrote the respective books, and

5) at last assembling a chronologically arranged account of their evolving beliefs.

When this is done, the evolution within so long a history is quite considerable. But within the twenty-year history of the Qur'an's composition, no comparable evolution takes place at all. Learned exegetes (interpreters) do distinguish the earlier Mecca period from the later Medina period in the reception of the Qur'an. The year 622 divides the two periods—the year of the *hijra* when Muhammad and a group of his earlier followers fled from Mecca, his birthplace, to Medina, a town slightly to the north of Mecca. The Meccan and the Medinan suras have somewhat different emphases, but in all essential regards Allah's message—and certainly the character of Allah Himself—does not change from the earlier period to the later.

As for the congruence of the mythic cosmologies and chronologies of the later Bible and the Qur'an, this is rather what historians would expect since Jews and Christians had been well established in Muhammad's native region for centuries by the time he received the Qur'an and since his claim was that the Qur'an was no more than a purified version of the Book earlier given to them.

But having strayed thus far into history, let me now pull back and stress, in conclusion, that this historical interlude is *only* an interlude. For our purposes in this book, and for all those who would seek an aesthetically rewarding encounter with sacred scripture, history can occasionally make a wonderful servant but is on the whole a very bad master. We have by no means taken either the Bible or the Qur'an as raw material for a mere history of Jewish, Christian, or Muslim beliefs about God. Our method has been, as I promised in the foreword that it would be, theographical rather than historical, using the descriptive, sometimes quasi-biographical tools of literary analysis rather than those of history. It is this approach that has enabled us to suspend disbelief in either Yahweh or Allah and do just as we so readily do when reading a novel or watching an art film. It has enabled us to engage Yahweh and Allah directly as a single real character operating under two different names in two different scriptures.

Acknowledgments

God in the Qur'an is a book I wrote only after repeatedly telling inquiring readers, colleagues, and sundry friends and associates that, no, I would not, could not, dare an assignment for which I was so poorly prepared. Meanwhile, however, for professional, political, and personal reasons, I was reading about Islam and its scripture more all the time. Finally, I began to think that, after all, I might follow the example of C. S. Lewis who once said that he wrote only books that he wanted to read and that no one had yet written for him.

I was still hesitant, however, about whether my voice would be welcome on this subject—particularly, of course, among Muslims—and so I asked around. I am grateful now in retrospect to several people who provided the credible early encouragement that made the difference. Among these are the late Maher Hathout, founder of the Muslim Public Affairs Council of Los Angeles, and his successor at the head of MPAC, Salam al-Marayati; Reza Aslan, from the moment our friendship began with the publication of his breakthrough book *No god but God*; Amir Hussain, professor of theological studies at Loyola Marymount University, who recognizes as too few do the pivotal importance of the Muslim community of North America and who models its future in his own work; Reuven Firestone, professor of Medieval Jewish and Islamic Studies at Hebrew Union College, whose penetrating and courageous little book *Who Are the Real Chosen People? The Meaning of Chosenness in*

Judaism, Christianity, and Islam taught me that the best path forward in interfaith relations leads through rather than around the toughest questions and whose conversations have taught me much more; Fr. Patrick J. Ryan, S. J., who as my fellow Harvard graduate student induced me to read the Qur'an for the first time; and finally Jane Dammen McAuliffe, editor of the five-volume *Encyclopaedia of the Qur'an* and associate editor for Islam in *The Norton Anthology of World Religions:* I knew that if there was no point in even starting, Jane could be counted on to say so, but she said start, and so start I did.

I started, yes, but thanks to many interruptions, it has taken me years to finish, and I am grateful to Jonathan Segal, my good friend and loyal editor at Alfred A. Knopf, who could have given up several times along the way but did not, and to Georges Borchardt, my agent (with Anne and Valerie Borchardt), friends and counselors for a generation, for sticking with me. I am grateful to my colleagues at the University of California, Irvine, and to UCI's devoted and competent staff, especially in Langson Library and in Computer Services. I am grateful to Sam Aber, for astute assistance with permissions, and to Helen Maggie Carr and Victoria Pearson for able assistance in preparing the manuscript for publication. Last of all and most of all, I am grateful to my wife, Catherine Miles, to whom this book is dedicated, for making this last stage in my life the happiest of all.

Notes

The epigraph is from *Rumi, Poet and Mystic (1207-1275), Selections from His Writings, Translated from the Persian, with Introduction and Notes by the late Reynold A. Nicholson* (London: George Allen and Unwin, 1950), p. 36.

FOREWORD: OF GOD, RELIGION, AND THE VIOLENCE
OF SACRED SCRIPTURE

1. The Tanakh and the Old Testament overlap massively but do not entirely coincide. Briefly, two ancient Jewish communities—one centered on Jerusalem, the other on Alexandria—determined two overlapping but not entirely coinciding canons or "tables of contents" for the Jewish Bible. It was the Alexandrian canon, a translation of the earlier Hebrew scriptures into Greek with significant additions, that became, first, the Bible for the Jewish Diaspora in Alexandria; later, the Bible for the newborn and substantially Grecophone Christian church; and, still later, once the maturing church had begun to write new scriptures for itself, the "Old Testament" for the emergent, two-testament Christian Bible. Thus did Christianity partly inherit and partly create its Bible.

Meanwhile, the Jerusalem canon lived on to become the Tanakh, Judaism's Bible to this day. The Tanakh and the Old Testament differ not just by the slightly longer canon of the latter but, more important, by the latter's sharply different eventual ordering of the constituent books. In the Christian Old Testament, the excitement and agitation of the biblical Prophets is moved to the end, just before the appearance of the Messiah in the Gospels, which open the New Testament. In the Jewish Tanakh, the Prophets are located in the middle, with other writings trailing behind, so that the order of appearance is Torah-Prophets-Writings. The initial letters of those three words in Hebrew—T + N + K—stand behind *Tanakh* as a pronounced acronym.

In *God: A Biography* (Alfred A. Knopf, 1995), I wrote about God as the protagonist of the Tanakh. When writing about the Qur'an, I find it preferable to use the term *Old Testament* or, more often, simply *Bible* when referring to the older scriptures. The reason is that although in the Qur'an Allah refers to "Torah" (rather than to either Old Testament or Tanakh) and to "Gospel" (rather than to New Testament) and although He clearly understands Jews and Christians to belong to different groups, He also often refers to "the Book" as a singular object and to Jews and Christians together as "People of the Book." In the process, He rather fuses their earlier scriptures as jointly superseded by His Qur'an. The "Book" of the "People of the Book" thus appears most plausibly to be the two-testament Christian Bible; and in this book, when I use the term *Bible,* I will use it in this sense. The term *Tanakh* is best used, I believe, when the New Testament is entirely out of the interpretive picture and the Hebrew scriptures are engaged either alone or in tandem with their true complement in later Jewish literature—namely, Talmud and Midrash.

    A final note: in the sixteenth century, Protestantism deleted from the canon of what would become its Old Testament all books, or parts of books, that were not included in the Tanakh. However, the Protestants retained the *order* of the earlier Christian Old Testament as well as its practice of translating Hebrew *yhwh,* the divine proper name, as Greek *Kyrios* or Latin *Dominus,* yielding LORD in English. The hybrid result is the Old Testament that is familiar to readers of the King James Version and its many descendants in English.

2. On this repugnance, see Omar Saif Ghobash, "Advice for Young Muslims: How to Survive in an Age of Extremism and Islamophobia," *Foreign Affairs,* January/February 2017, adapted from his book *Letters to a Young Muslim* (Picador, 2017).

3. "'A New Amalek Is Appearing,' Netanyahu warns at Auschwitz. 'Never again will we allow the hand of evil to sever the life of our people,' says PM, in veiled reference to Iranian threat," *Jerusalem Post,* January 10, 2010.

4. Let me mention a few:

    Carol Bakhos, *The Family of Abraham: Jewish, Christian, and Muslim Interpretations* (Harvard University Press, 2014).

    Reuven Firestone, *Journeys in Holy Lands: The Evolution of the Abraham-Ishmael Legends in Islamic Exegesis* (State University of New York Press, 1990).

    Robert C. Gregg, *Shared Stories, Rival Tellings: Early Encounters of Jews, Christians, and Muslims* (Oxford University Press, 2015).

    John Kaltner, *Ishmael Instructs Isaac: An Introduction to the Qur'an for Bible Readers* (The Liturgical Press, 1999).

    Michael Lodahl, *Claiming Abraham: Reading the Bible and the Qur'an Side by Side* (Brazos Press, 2010).

    Jane Dammen McAuliffe, editor, *The Cambridge Companion to the Qur'ān* (Cambridge University Press, 2006).

    Geoffrey Parrinder, *Jesus in the Qur'an* (Oneworld Publications, 2013).

    F. E. Peters, *A Reader on Classical Islam* (Princeton University Press, 1994).

    Gabriel Said Reynolds, *The Qur'ān and Its Biblical Subtext* (Routledge, 2010). I regret that Reynolds's *The Qur'an and the Bible: Text and Commentary* (Yale University Press, 2018) appeared too late for me to consult.

    Zeki Saritoprak, *Islam's Jesus* (University Press of Florida, 2014).

    Roberto Tottoli, *Biblical Prophets in the Qur'an and Muslim Literature* (Curzon, 2001).

5. Muslim tradition understands the Qur'an to have existed from all time as the "Preserved Tablet." Jewish tradition similarly understands Torah to have existed from all time. Similarly, again, Christian tradition understands Jesus to have existed from all time as the *Logos*—the Word or the Mind—of God.

In all three cases, the pre-existent entity precedes the creation of the world. Historical understanding, by contrast with all three, is time-bound. For more on the strength and limitation of historical understanding of the Qur'an, see the afterword, pp. 192–211.

6. Seyyed Hossein Nasr, editor-in-chief, *The Study Quran: A New Translation and Commentary*, (New York: HarperOne, 2015), p. xxxi.

7. *The Qur'an, A New Translation,* trans. Tarif Khalidi (New York: Penguin Books/ Penguin Classics, 2009), p. xxi. Like nearly all Qur'an translations into English, the Penguin Classics *Qur'an* occasionally finds it necessary to insert an English word in [square brackets] to clarify the Arabic. On a few occasions, when I find it helpful to insert a further word, I do so in {bow brackets}. On a few occasions, I do this as well with the *New Jerusalem Bible*.

8. Cf. Bruce B. Lawrence, *The Koran in English, A Biography* (Princeton, NJ: Princeton University Press, 2017), especially chapters 2 and 6.

9. While I do not know Arabic, I do know three related Semitic languages, a general linguistic familiarity that has eased my occasional consultation of *A Concordance of the Qur'an* by Hanna E. Kassis (Oakland, Calif.: University of California Press, 1983; foreword by Fazlur Rahman). This concordance tracks the English of A. J. Arberry's *The Koran Interpreted* (London: Allen and Unwin, 1955) through the underlying Arabic roots to the morphologically derived forms and then onward to the locations of these in the affected passages of the Qur'an. The process is intricate but can significantly enrich a reader's grasp of nuance when and where nuance matters most. The reader may also use its index of proper names to visit every reference to a biblical figure who is also named in the Qur'an.

10. Edward Gibbon, *The Decline and Fall of the Roman Empire* (Washington Square Press, 1962), abridgment by D. M. Low, p. 825.

"While the state [the Roman Empire in the East] was exhausted by the Persian war, and the church was distracted by the Nestorian and Monophysite sects, Mahomet, with the sword in one hand and the Koran in the other, erected his throne on the ruins of Christianity and of Rome."

I ADAM AND HIS WIFE

1. On a few occasions, this being one, the two Hebrew names appear in sequence. *The Jerusalem Bible* translates "Yahweh God."

2. https://www.dartmouth.edu/~milton/reading_room/.

3. Blake produced a series of twenty pen-and-watercolor illustrations of scenes from John Milton's *Paradise Lost*. Five of these, including this one, were exhibited at the Huntington Gallery as part of an exhibition entitled *Drawn to Paradise: Picturing the Bible from the 16th to the 19th Centuries* (San Marino, California, July 1 to October 23, 2017).

4. Dr. Piero Ferrucci explains that the *ig-* prefixed to *nudo* is not the *in-* of negation or privation but is rather *d'appoggio,* "of support"—of support, that is, to the smooth flow of pronunciation that Italian ever favors. He offers as a comparable example the Italian word for *history,* which may take the form either of *storia* or of *istoria,* depending on its phonetic environs. Over time, a nuance of difference does seem to have accrued to *ignudo,* but it is not a nuance of humiliation or reprobation (as in ignoble and ignominious) but only of deprivation. A rough English equivalent in this sense might be *bare* or *meager*—that is, lacking in some regard.

5. https://www.dartmouth.edu/~milton/reading_room/.

6. Ibid.

7. John Milton, *Paradise Regained, the Minor Poems, and Samson Agonistes,* ed. Merritt Y. Hughes (The Odyssey Press, 1937), p. 504.

8. James H. Charlesworth, ed., *The Old Testament Pseudepigrapha,* vol. 2 (New York: Doubleday, 1985), p. 262. The translation of *Life of Adam and Eve* is edited and translated by M. D. Johnson. His commentary includes a discussion of the likely Hebrew original for the *Life.* In the passage quoted, Johnson italicizes *breath of life* and the first occurrence only of *image of God.* The other italicizations are my addition.

   Christianity—founded by Jews—preserved a number of Jewish texts that Rabbinic Judaism, developing alongside it, discarded. The *Life of Adam and Eve* is one such text and reflects the fact that belief in Satan as the personification of all that opposes God took hold more quickly and more solidly in early Christian tradition than in Rabbinic tradition of the same period. Later Talmudic and post-Talmudic tradition, however, would also recognize Satan as the dark master of the *sitra 'ahra* or "other side." See the appendix.

9. Dan O'Brien, *Scarsdale, Poems* (Evansville, Ind.: Measure Press, 2015), p. 8. Who is the "God's brother" addressed in this poem? It could be the speaker, who in arrogating to himself a judicial power proper to God, is implicitly claiming to be at least God's brother. Or it could be the older boy, older than the speaker "by ages," who, claiming only to be related to God, rebukes the younger boy for claiming to be God Himself. Is the Islamic sin of *shirk* committed whenever one mere human being presumes to judge another?

10. At Genesis 3:4–5, the serpent tells Eve that, contrary to what Yahweh has said, Adam and she will not die if they eat the forbidden fruit:

    No! You will not die! God knows in fact that the day you eat it your eyes will be opened and you will be like gods, knowing good from evil.

    But against this *New Jerusalem Bible* translation, I prefer the Jewish Publication Society *Tanakh* version, which reads:

    You are not going to die, but God knows that as soon as you eat of it your eyes will be open and you will be like divine beings who know good and bad.

    At issue for me is the difference between "good from evil" and "good and bad." The former is the knowledge of a distinction; the latter may be something more like the knowledge of a giant inventory. It may be that the Hebrew *tov vara'*— literally "good and bad"—is an instance of the rhetorical device called hendiadys or "one through two." In other words, it may be an expression like "soup to nuts" or "A to Z" signaling completeness. If so, then the Serpent in Genesis promises Eve that Adam and she will become divine by knowing everything. And in that case, we have a point of sharp contrast between Genesis, where the first couple is punished for aspiring to know everything, and the Qur'an, where Adam (notably, not Eve) is actually taught everything, at least if "the names" is properly taken to stand for "everything" in Qur'an 2:31.

11. *The Study Quran,* p. 1114.

12. Eric Auerbach, *Mimesis: The Representation of Reality in Western Literature,* 15th anniversary edition, trans. Willard R. Trask, with a new introduction by Edward W. Said (Princeton, NJ: Princeton University Press, 1953, 2003), p. 157.

13. Ibid., p. 158.
14. Ibid., p. 156.

2 ADAM'S SON AND HIS BROTHER

1. "The man" in Hebrew is *ha'adam*. The article, "the," is *ha;* the noun, "man," is *'adam*. This personage, *ha'adam*, will not lose the *ha* and become simply *'adam*, "Adam," until Genesis 4:25: "Adam had intercourse with his wife, and she gave birth to a son [their third] whom she named Seth." By this point, it seems that Eve, who has named all three boys, may have coined a name for her husband, their father, as well—not an especially original name, but a real one. But, again, the usage here is really that of the mysterious narrator.
2. To gloss briefly:
   —*unhousel'd:* having not received the sacrament of Holy Communion;
   —*disappointed:* unprepared, as by repentance and confession;
   —*unanel'd:* "un-oiled," not having received the final sacramental anointing with oil.
3. Michael Lodahl, *Claiming Abraham: Reading the Bible and the Qur'an Side by Side* (Grand Rapids, Mich.: Brazos Press, 2010), p. 109.

3 NOAH

1. As part of the Skirball Cultural Center in Los Angeles: www.skirball.org /noahs-ark.
2. Cf. Genesis 12:7: "Yahweh appeared to Abram and said, 'I shall give this country to your progeny.'"
3. For the original text, part of the Chester Cycle of mystery plays, visit www .chestermysteryplays.com/history/history/texts_iframe.html.
   The eminent twentieth-century British composer Benjamin Britten produced a musical adaptation of the play, which he entitled *Noye's Fludde*, suitable for performance by children. A summer performance of *Noye's Fludde* in a church on a wooded island off the coast of New England is the setting for the 2012 film *Moonrise Kingdom*.

4 ABRAHAM AND HIS FATHER

1. James H. Charlesworth, ed., *The Old Testament Pseudepigrapha* (New York: Doubleday, 1983), p. 693.
2. Confusingly, the place Haran and the man Haran share the same name, though this does not seem to be in any way a meaningful coincidence. Cf. Jacob Neusner, *Confronting Creation: How Judaism Reads Genesis: An Anthology of Genesis Rabbah* (Columbia: University of South Carolina Press, 1991).

5 ABRAHAM AND HIS SONS

1. On this shift through its many phases, see Jon D. Levenson, *The Death and Resurrection of the Beloved Son: The Transformation of Child Sacrifice in Judaism and Christianity* (New Haven, Conn.: Yale University Press, 1995).
2. Pirkê de Rabbi Eliezer *(The Chapters of Rabbi Eliezer the Great) According to the Text*

of the Manuscript Belonging to Abraham Epstein of Vienna, trans. and annotated with an introduction and indices by Gerald Friedlander (Hermon Press, 2009), p. 227.

3. Ibid., p. 224.

6 JOSEPH

1. Ghazal (Ode) no. 1827, translated by William C. Chittick in his book *Sufism: A Beginner's Guide* (Oxford, UK: Oneworld, e-book edition 2011), pp. 89–90. I am indebted to my friend and colleague Amir Hussain for drawing this beautiful poem to my attention.

2. Quoted in Bruce B. Lawrence, *The Koran in English, A Biography* (Princeton, NJ: Princeton University Press, 2017), p. 69. Lawrence notes that shortly before making this statement, Asad has quoted Sura 102 in his own translation, but back at the time of the conversion, which occurred in Berlin, Asad (then still Leopold Weiss) had not yet learned Arabic and so must have been reading a translation—probably, Lawrence astutely infers, a German translation of the earlier twentieth-century translation by Muhammad Ali.

7 MOSES

1. For a cogent and original account of the Levites' role in the Exodus and the later life of Israel, see Richard Elliott Friedman, *The Exodus* (San Francisco: HarperOne/HarperCollins, 2017).

8 JESUS AND HIS MOTHER

1. *The New York Times,* December 24, 1995.

2. As a shrine to "Holy Wisdom," the basilica is most probably to be understood as a shrine to Christ as the *Logos* or Word of God. Cf. the opening words of the Gospel of John: "In the beginning was the Word, the Word was with God, and the Word was God." Divine Wisdom and the Divine Word, either phrase a metonymy for Divine Thought, were easily interchangeable, at least partly because in the Old Testament Book of Proverbs, Wisdom, personified as feminine, states that she too has been with God from the very beginning. This very association, however, can also suggest either that Mary, identified with this feminine principle, was also somehow with God from the beginning or, as in contemporary feminist theology, that God can be imagined no less readily as feminine than as masculine.

3. Gordon D. Newby, *A Concise Encyclopedia of Islam* (Oxford, UK: Oneworld Publications, 2002), p. 195, on *shirk:* "This is the sin of associating another deity with ALLÂH, the most severe sins mentioned in the QUR'ÂN. Polytheism is the one sin that cannot be forgiven, according to the Qur'an." On "no two powers in heaven," see Alan F. Segal, *Two Powers in Heaven: Early Rabbinic Reports About Christianity and Gnosticism* (repr., Waco, Tex.: Baylor University Press, 2012).

4. *The Decline and Fall of the Roman Empire* (Washington Square Press, 1962), abridgment by D. M. Low, p. 866.

5. *A Tale of Two Cities* (New York: Grosset and Dunlap, 1948), p. 416.

AFTERWORD: ON THE QUR'AN AS THE WORD OF GOD

1. Wilfred Cantwell Smith, *On Understanding Islam, Selected Studies* (The Hague, Netherlands: Mouton, 1981).
2. Emmanuel Carrère, *The Kingdom* (New York: Farrar, Straus and Giroux, 2014), p. 5.
3. *Confessions: A New Translation,* trans. Peter Constantine, with foreword by Jack Miles (New York: Liveright, 2018), p. 121.
4. Carrère, *The Kingdom,* pp. 103–4.
5. Smith, *On Understanding Islam,* p. 285.
6. Ibid., p. 291.
7. Ibid.
8. Ibid., pp. 292–3.
9. I wish to acknowledge my indebtedness to the prophets Yirmiyahu, Yehezkel, and Hosea for first drawing this analogy to my attention.
10. *On Understanding Islam,* p. 298.
11. Todd Boss, "It Is Enough to Enter" in *Pitch, Poems* (New York: W.W. Norton, 2012), p. 15.
12. The founders of Christianity, all of them Jews, believed that the Second Coming of Christ was imminent. When that hoped-for event failed to happen as soon as expected, Saint Paul, the most important of them, concluded in his Letter to the Romans that Christ would return only after all the nations of the world *except* the Jews had become Christian. Christ would return after that universal conversion, and only *then* would the Jews come around at last. Centuries of persecution might have been averted had Christians taken chapters 9 through 11 of Saint Paul's Letter to the Romans to heart, for Paul, rather than merely resigned to an indefinite postponement of the conversion of the Jews, saw this very postponement as a part of God's grand plan. After sharing his vision of the End Times, he cries out joyously:

    > How rich and deep are the wisdom and the knowledge of God! We cannot reach to the root of his decisions or his ways. *Who has ever known the mind of the Lord? Who has ever been his adviser? Who has given anything to him, so that his presents come only as a debt returned?* Everything there is comes from him and is caused by him and exists for him. To him be glory for ever! Amen. (Romans 11:33–36; the italicized sentences are quotes from elsewhere in scripture.)

13. Cf. Reuven Firestone, *Journeys in Holy Lands, The Evolution of the Abraham-Ishmael Legends in Islamic Exegesis* (Albany: State University of New York Press, 1990), p. 157:

    > When the Jews of Medina criticize Muhammad for reciting legends which they considered inaccurate, they call our attention to the probability that by virtue of their oral nature, the legends Muhammad faithfully retold had evolved to the point that they no longer corresponded well to the written version known to educated Rabbinite Jews in the Bible and the Midrash. For his part, Muhammad sincerely believed that he knew the legends correctly.... In the context of his relations with the Jews of Medina, Muhammad's attitude can hardly be construed as anything but genuine anger and even shock at what he considered the complete Jewish disregard for the true story. The Qur'an portrays the tension resulting

from two different versions of parallel scriptural tales. Each version is claimed by separate parties as being the unchangeable word of God. The standard against which the Medinan Jews judged the legends and sermons recited by Muhammad would have been their Hebrew Bible and Midrash, although they were undoubtedly familiar with the versions to which Muhammad referred as well. Muhammad's was a version known in oral form in Mecca and Medina and common to Jews and Christians as well as his followers and Arab pagans. Muhammad's anger at their rejection was not merely a reaction to personal insult, but rather a natural response to the rejection of what he believed was authentic scripture, which indeed it was, although not identical to the scripture that the Jews considered authentic.

14. Quoted from *JPS Hebrew-English Tanakh* (Philadelphia: The Jewish Publication Society, 1985). If I were Jewish, the *New Jerusalem Bible,* a Catholic Bible, would not be my translation of choice.

15. "Radical Editing: *Redaktionsgeschichte* and the Aesthetic of Willed Confusion" in *The Creation of Sacred Literature,* ed. Richard Elliott Friedman (Oakland: University of California Press, 1981).

16. George Steiner, *Real Presences* (Chicago: University of Chicago Press, 1989), p. 227.

APPENDIX: OF SATAN AND THE AFTERLIFE
IN THE BIBLE AND THE QUR'AN

1. On the Alexandrian canon and its connection to the original Christian Bible, see note 1 to the Foreword.

Index

INDEX OF QUR'ANIC CITATIONS

INDEX OF BIBLICAL CITATIONS